THE ENGLISH COMPOSITION READER

Coordinating Editors

Jennifer Alberico
Shirley X. Glines
Shawn Kerivan
Janice Mitchell-Love
Marianne Shaughnessy

Community College of Vermont

Copley Custom Textbooks

An imprint of XanEdu Custom Publishing

Printed in the United States of America

ISBN 13: 978-1-58152-873-2
ISBN 10: 1-58152-873-6

Cover Image:© Can Stock Photo, Inc./Stokkete

Acknowledgments:

p.5: From *Collected Poems of Langston Hughes* by Langston Hughes, edited by Arnold Rampersad with David Roessel, Associate Editor. Copyright © 1994 by the Estate of Langston Hughes. Reprinted by permission Alfred A. Knopf, a division of Random House, Inc. Electronic rights © The Estate of Langston Hughes via Harold Ober Associates, Inc.

pp. 6–8: From *Dust Tracks on a Road* by Zora Neale Hurston. Copyright © 1942 by Zora Neale Hurston. Copyright renewed 1970 by John C. Hurston. Published by HarperCollins Publishers in 1991.

pp. 9–22: As appeared in the *New Yorker*, February 13, 2006. Copyright © 2006 by Condé Nast Publications, Inc. Reprinted by permission of the publisher via the Copyright Clearance Center.

pp. 23–33: From *The Woman Warrior* by Maxine Hong Kingston. Copyright © 1975, 1976 by Maxine Hong Kingston. Published by Alfred A. Knopf, a division of Random House, Inc.

pp. 34–37: Originally appeared in the *New York Times*, March 27, 1964. Copyright © 1964.

pp. 38–44: From *Mary* by Mary Mebane. Copyright © 1981 by Mary Elizabeth Mebane. Used by permission of Viking Penguin, a division of Penguin Group (USA) Inc. Electronic rights © by Barry Malzberg. Used by permission.

pp: 45–48: From *Zami: A New Spelling of My Name* by Audre Lorde. Copyright © 1981 by Audre Lorde. Reprinted by permission of the Charlotte Sheedy Agency.

pp. 53–68: From *The Omnivore's Dilemma* by Michael Pollan. Copyright © 2006 by Michael Pollan. Used by permission of The Penguin Press, a division of Penguin Group (USA) Inc.

pp. 69–75: From *Take the Cannoli: Stories from the New World* by Sarah Vowell. Copyright © 2000 by Sarah Vowell. Reprinted by permission of Simon & Schuster, Inc. All rights reserved. Electronic rights © Sarah Vowell via The Wendy Weil Agency.

pp. 76–77: From *When You Are Engulfed in Flames* by David Sedaris. Copyright © 2008 by David Sedaris. Published by Hachette Book Group USA.

pp. 78–82: Copyright © 2003 by Bradley Manning.

pp. 83–85: As appeared in the *Saturday Evening Post*. Copyright © 1965 by the Saturday Evening Post. Reprinted by permission of the publisher via the Copyright Clearance Center.
pp. 86–91: From *The Way to Rainy Mountain* by N. Scott Momaday. Copyright © 1976 by the University of New Mexico Press. Reprinted by permission of the publisher via the Copyright Clearance Center.
pp. 92–95: From *Teaching a Stone to Talk* by Annie Dillard. Copyright © 1982 by Annie Dillard. Published by HarperCollins Publishers.
pp. 96–102: From *Desert Solitaire* by Edward Abbey. Copyright © 1968. Published by Don Congdon Associates, Inc.
pp. 103–107: From *Living by the Word: Selected Writings 1973–1987* by Alice Walker. Copyright © 1986 by Alice Walker. Reprinted by permission of Houghton Mifflin Harcourt Publishing Company. All rights reserved. Electronic rights © Alice Walker via The Wendy Weil Agency.
pp. 114–120: From *On Writing Well*, seventh (Thirtieth Anniversary) edition, by William Zinsser. Copyright © 1976, 1980, 1985, 1988, 1990, 1994, 1988, 2001, 2006 by William Zinsser. Reprinted by permission of the author.
pp. 121–124: As appeared in *Ms.*, September, 1986. Copyright © 1986 by Ms. Reprinted by permission of Liberty Media for Women, L.L.C./Ms. Magazine via the Copyright Clearance Center.
pp. 125–127: As appeared in the *New York Times Magazine*. Copyright © 1998 by David Birnbaum.
pp. 128–134: As appeared in the *New York Times*, January 1, 2005. Copyright © 2005.
pp. 135–137: As appeared in the *International Herald Tribune*. Copyright © 2008.
pp. 138–140: From *Living Out Loud* by Anna Quindlen. Copyright © 1987. Published by Random House, Inc.
pp. 144–150: From *Doublespeak: From Revenue Enhancement to Terminal Living* by William Lutz. Copyright © 1989. Published by Harpercollins Publishers.
pp. 151–153: As appeared in *Time*, February 8, 2004. Copyright © 2004 by Time, Inc. Reprinted by permission of the publisher via the Copyright Clearance Center.
pp. 154–156: As appeared in the *New York Times*, February 20, 1986. Copyright © 1986.
pp. 157–161: From *America's Other Children: Public Schools Outside Suburbia* by Jo Goodwin Parker. Copyright © 1971 by the University of Oklahoma Press. Reprinted by permission of the publisher via the Copyright Clearance Center.
pp. 162–164: As appeared in *Ms*. Copyright © 1972 by Judy Brady. Reprinted by permission of the author.
pp. 168–179: From *Travels with Lizbeth* by Lars Eighner. Copyright © 1994. Published by Bedford/St. Martin's Press.
pp. 180–183: From *The Autobiography of Malcolm X* by Malcolm X and Alex Haley. Copyright © 1964 by Alex Haley and Malcolm X. Copyright © 1965 by Alex Haley and Betty Shabazz. Published by Random House, Inc.
pp. 184–187: From *A Writer's Companion* by Richard Marius. Copyright © 1985 by McGraw-Hill, Inc.
pp. 188–195: From *The American Way of Death Revisited* by Jessica Mitford. Copyright © 1963, 1978 by Jessica Mitford. Copyright © 1998 by the Estate of Jessica Mitford. Reprinted by permission of the Estate of Jessica Mitford. All rights reserved.
pp. 200–202: As appeared in the *New York Times*, July 10, 2004. Copyright © 2004.

Copley Custom Textbooks
An imprint of XanEdu Publishing, Inc.
530 Great Road
Acton, MA 01720
800-562-2147

Contents

Writing at CCV

It's likely that no matter what you're teaching at CCV, you will be asking students, at one time or another, to write a paper. That's because CCV knows effective communication skills—writing and speaking—are critical both in the classroom and in the workplace. However, if your students have been away from college for a long time or this is their first college experience, they may be unsure of how to write a paper, especially a research paper.

Rest assured that CCV has support for you! Ask an academic coordinator about writing or learning labs, which are free to all students. Ask also about special workshops on topics like research paper writing. A wide range of library services is available to students and instructors, including classroom and individual instruction in research techniques. Don't be afraid to talk to a coordinator about your students' learning needs; he or she can be a valuable resource for you.

There are also some simple things you can do when assigning writing at CCV. You can talk with students about the guidelines for the assignment and provide this information in a written format along with sample papers or an evaluation rubric. Encourage your students to ask for clarification. By asking questions, they'll not only help others to think about the assignment more carefully, but they may help you to see possible obstacles or confusion surrounding an assignment *before* it's completed. Below are just a few questions you might consider whenever you're assigning a piece of writing:

- What are the requirements for the paper?
- When is it due? What are the consequences if it is late?
- What kind of documentation style should students use (MLA, APA, etc)?
- How many sources and what kinds of sources would be ideal for this assignment?
- How will you evaluate the paper? What elements would the paper need in order to be successful, from your perspective?

Plagiarism

Whenever you're assigning a paper, especially a paper that involves using sources to support ideas, it's important to think about issues of plagiarism. *Plagiarism, as defined by CCV, is the presentation of the language, ideas, or thoughts of another person as one's own work in the preparation of a paper, laboratory report, oral presentation, or any other type of presentation.* Of course, many students understand that buying a paper or purposely using someone else's ideas or language as one's own is academic dishonesty. However, it's also important for students to understand that plagiarism can result from carelessness or misunderstanding the rules.

To help students understand this issue, we have outlined some general tips for appropriately crediting sources in a paper. These are specifically written for students, so feel free to share them with your class. If you do encounter an incidence of plagiarism in your course, please contact an academic coordinator. For more information on this topic, see the *Instructor Handbook: Teaching for Development* (pages 63–69).

Tips for Avoiding Plagiarism

1. Keep track of all sources. Whenever you are consulting a source that you may or may not use in your final paper, be sure to copy down the bibliographic information about the source. This varies depending on the type of source it is, but, in general, you need the author(s), title, publisher, and date. If it is a web source, you will also need the address and the date of access.

2. Take careful notes. You must be very careful when writing notes from your source. Make sure you include the page number and indicate, with quotation marks, whether or not the passage is a direct quote. If you are paraphrasing a passage from the source, be sure that you are really putting it in your own words and that you are also changing the way the words are arranged. Perhaps you want to highlight the words that appear in both the original passage and in your notes. If there are too many of the same words in both, you're probably in danger of plagiarizing the passage.

In addition, it's a good idea to keep copies of your work. You will want to double-check your notes once the paper is completed. It's easy for mistakes to happen and a source to get omitted from your final draft, resulting in plagiarism. If you photocopy pages from a book or print Web pages from your source, be sure to keep them also.

3. Avoid "cutting and pasting" from an Internet source into your paper. Though it may save you time in retyping quoted material, the potential consequences outweigh any gain. First, there's the problem of overusing direct quotes, especially long or extended quotes. It's so easy to cut and paste from the Internet that many student writers over-rely on this kind of material, which leads to papers that are choppy, confusing and disjointed. Secondly, and more importantly, it's easy to forget—in the revising process—which is the borrowed material and which is your own, often resulting in plagiarism. Since instructors readily use the Internet to check the writing in papers, carelessness here can result a failed assignment and/or a failed class, which is too high a price to pay for the ease of cutting and pasting.

4. Understand the system of documentation that's appropriate for your paper. Most CCV instructors require students to use MLA or APA style of documentation. MLA is often used for papers in English, humanities, and history courses. APA is often used for papers in the social sciences or education. You can easily find information about these documentation styles at a CCV site and online.

An important thing to know here is that both of these styles use *parenthetical citations.* In other words, footnotes or endnotes are not needed. A parenthetical citation is when you include a brief reference to the source right in the text of your paper—every time you use a direct quote, paraphrase, or idea. A Works Cited or Reference page is added at the end, which lists your sources in full detail.

5. Understand when and how to appropriately cite sources in your paper. What you include in a parenthetical citation depends on which style (MLA or APA) you're following. In general, when using MLA style, you include the author's last name and the page number. When using APA style, you include the author's last name, the publication date, and the page number (if it is a direct quote). Again, information on MLA and APA styles of documentation is readily available at CCV and online.

Whatever style of documentation you use, it is probably most important to know *when* you must cite a source, and this is the same for all styles. You must cite the following types of material from a source:

Direct Quotes

This is when you use quoted material in your paper. The quote should include the exact words of the author or source framed within quotation marks and then include the source citation at the end of the sentence. For example, if you were to use a direct quote from George J. Demko's book, *Why in the World: Adventures in Geography,* it would look like:

> "It's hard to think of any place that is untouched by human contact, even the cruelest, most hostile environments, such as the glaciers of Antarctica and the broiling, waterless Sahara. All places bear the imprimatur of human visits and habitations, or the vestiges of such connections" (Demko 13).

Or you might preface the quote, connecting it to the point you were making in your paper:

> George Demko, former director of the United States Office of the Geographer, might agree that humans have impacted, sometimes significantly, the areas we have come to see as wilderness. After all, he writes, "It's hard to think of any place that is untouched by human contact, even the cruelest, most hostile environments, such as the glaciers of Antarctica and the broiling, waterless Sahara"(13).

Note that the second example is more effective than the first because it gives a context for the quote. It lets the reader know a little more about the author of your source, which can be helpful to establish his or her credibility. Even more importantly, however, is the way the second example reinforces the paper's thesis or main point. Many writers forget to make these connections, thinking that a quote speaks for itself. Only rarely is this true. It is very important in a paper to provide more than facts or quotes; most instructors are looking to you, as the writer of the paper, to interpret or analyze the information you're including. How does a particular fact or figure support your point?

Also, this quote demonstrates why students should use direct quotes sparingly in their papers. For a paper to be most effective, it's important to get a sense of the writer's voice. When direct quotes from different sources are used frequently in a paper, it's difficult to keep that sense of the one writer's voice.

Paraphrasing

This is when you use the basic meaning of an author's statement but change the words and structure of the sentence. For example, using Demko's quote above, you might paraphrase it in the following way:

> Humans leave their mark wherever they go, even those places we have come to see as inhospitable or extreme (Demko 13).

Or you might write:

> According to George Demko, former director of the United States Office of the Geographer, humans leave their mark wherever they go, even those places we have come to see as inhospitable or extreme (13).

Notice that you can't just change a few words or shuffle words around and still call it a paraphrase. If you do, it's considered plagiarism—even when you have a citation right next to it! In addition, many student writers assume that it is acceptable to paraphrase an entire paragraph as long as a citation is included at the end of the paragraph. However, this is *not* acceptable and can also be perceived as plagiarism. After all, how would a reader know which ideas in the paragraph were those of the author and which were those of the student writer? Remember that all documentation styles aim for clarity and appropriate ownership of words and ideas.

Ideas

This is when you take the idea or information that the author provides but *completely change* the wording and structure of the sentence(s).

> Although the conditions of a place vary widely, they do share one thing in common. It's rare to find a place that is not impacted in some way by humans (Demko 13).

Here you give credit for the information that is derived from your source, but you are really only summarizing that information rather than paraphrasing it. You might wonder why it is important to cite Demko's idea; after all, Demko's statement seems like good common sense. However, this is Demko's idea, one derived from experience in this field. Citing him is a way of properly crediting him for his work and insights. Citing him also contributes to your paper's credibility and persuasion. Finally, while the statement may seem to be one of general common sense, a careful reader could challenge you. Without extensive geographical knowledge of the world, how could one make such a statement without generalizing? Giving proper credit not only acknowledges the experts in a particular field, but it illustrates your understanding of their contributions.

6. Include a Reference or Works Cited Page. A Reference or Works Cited page lists the sources that you have cited in your paper. Only sources that show up in the body of the paper should be listed on this page. (If you don't use and cite a source in the body of your paper, it can't be listed in the Works Cited).

Conversely, all the sources that you use in the body of your paper must be listed here. (You can't cite a source in the paper then forget to include it on the Works Cited page). Because you are only giving a small amount of information about each source within the paper (like last name of author and page number), the Works Cited or Reference page is where the reader can find the full bibliographic information about each source. Remember that there are plenty of reference guides to help you with this. To illustrate how a source might be listed, according to MLA style, here's the source used in the examples above:

Demko, George J. with Jerome Agel and Eugene Boe. *Why in the World: Adventures in Geography.* NY: Doubleday, 1992.

7. It's important to understand what plagiarism is and how to avoid it. Academic dishonesty is taken very seriously at CCV. It can result in failed assignments or courses and even suspension or dismissal for more than one incident. However, plagiarism doesn't have to happen. By asking questions and paying attention to the "rules" associated with citing sources, anyone can avoid making a costly mistake.

VSC Graduation Standards

Students must successfully demonstrate mastery of four specific skill areas prior to, and as a requirement for, graduation. Students who have achieved proficiency in these areas are better able to work effectively with others, live as informed and involved community members, and think critically in order to solve problems and make decisions.

Information Literacy

Upon graduation, students will be able to:

- define a research topic and the information needed;
- collect and organize information, utilizing a variety of traditional and electronic resources;
- evaluate the information and its sources critically;
- acknowledge and document the sources needed.

Skills focused in:

- First Semester Seminar

Skills strengthened in:

- Research & Writing Intensive course
- Courses that integrate information literacy
- Seminar in Educational Inquiry

Graduation standard demonstrated by:

- Final research paper requirement in Seminar in Educational Inquiry

Oral Communication

Upon graduation, students will be able to:

- determine the nature and purpose of a presentation;
- prepare a well-organized presentation utilizing appropriate supporting evidence;

- communicate in a manner that engages and holds the attention of the audience;
- use language and syntax appropriate for the audience and purpose.

Skills focused in:

- Communication course

Skills strengthened in:

- First Semester Seminar course
- Courses that integrate oral communication
- Seminar in Educational Inquiry

Graduation standard demonstrated by:

- Oral presentation component of Communication course

Quantitative Reasoning

Upon graduation, students will be able to:

- select and perform appropriate procedures to solve mathematical problems arising in various disciplines;
- interpret quantitative information accurately;
- present quantitative information effectively;
- evaluate the reasonableness of quantitative conclusions.

Skills focused in:

- Mathematics course

Skills strengthened in:

- Technological Literacy course
- Scientific Method course
- Human Behavior course

Graduation standard demonstrated by:

- Quantitative Reasoning Assessment

Writing

Upon graduation, students will be able to:

- demonstrate in their written work an awareness of the relationships among writer, subject, audience, and purpose;
- focus written work around an explicit or an implied central thesis;
- develop this central thesis systematically using specific details and supporting evidence;
- organize subject matter of written work using appropriate sentence structure and paragraphing;
- use correct grammar, syntax, punctuation, and spelling;
- follow standard practices in quotation, summary, paraphrase and citation of textual material.

Skills focused in:

- English Composition
- Research & Writing Intensive course

Skills strengthened in:

- Courses that integrate writing
- Seminar in Educational Inquiry

Graduation standard demonstrated by:

- Final research paper requirement in Seminar in Educational Inquiry

Link to the Hartness Research Paper Writing Process

http://hartness.vsc.edu/guidesccv/rbccv

Narration

Narration

Narration is often one of the first rhetorical methods composition students are assigned because the narrative form is the one we are most comfortable with. Storytelling is a natural tendency. Telling stories is something we do all the time. Think about how often you have come home or gone to work and said to family or friends, "You'll never guess what I saw . . . or heard" or "You'll never guess what happened to me."

Even as children, we instinctively told stories, sometimes real or sometimes imagined, for communicating or for fun. Telling stories not only has its roots in our childhood but also in antiquity. Since the dawn of language, people have told stories to try to make sense of their lives and their world. Among ancient people, the stories recorded the tribe's or culture's history, glorified their great feats, preserved the old legends, and upheld their religious beliefs. Just like the ancient people, we tell stories, or narratives, today in the hope that others will understand the common and uncommon truth of our lives and in the telling be able to make sense of it ourselves.

The Process

Purpose

What might be different from the stories we tell and the academic form of narrative essays is that our essays must have a purpose, a reason for our writing them. You don't want someone to come to the end of your essay and say, "And your point is?" For example, a narrative about a time when you made a fool of yourself might have the purpose of portraying how we often take ourselves too seriously and how allowing ourselves to be vulnerable can be liberating instead of humiliating. When writing a narrative essay, the larger purpose of the story—whether it is your story or someone else's—must always be in mind.

Thesis

One of the debates about narratives is over whether or not narratives need to have thesis statements. While many narratives do not have formal thesis statements located at the end of the first or second paragraph, that does not mean that the story lacks a thesis or main point that guides the narrative and gives it a sense of purpose.

Organization

While telling a story may be instinctive, writing a story requires thought and planning. Narration recounts an event or a sequence of events as they took place over time. The narrative form can be used to inform, to entertainment, or share an aspect of the human condition. How you plan the organization of your story will depend on your purpose and what you want to do to the audience. Do you want to make the audience laugh, cry, or make connections? Do you want to create suspense in the opening or build to a dramatic ending? Whatever the answers to these questions are, you want to craft your story in a way that grabs the reader's attention and holds it throughout. You can organize your story in a number of ways:

- Chronologically with the events in the order they occurred and the ending being the most dramatic
- Dramatically, with the climax or conclusion at the beginning and the explanation following
- With flashbacks, where the narrator or the central character shifts back in time to mentally replay a previous event

Whatever form you choose, it is important to include enough detail to make sure you present your reader the whole story. A good story should have all the elements—the ones journalists refer to as "the five Ws and the H":

- What happened
- Who are there
- When it happened
- Where it happened

- Why this situation took place
- How it happened, or under what circumstances

Other aspects to keep in mind when writing your narrative are:

- Maintain a consistent point of view. Don't shift back and forth between first or third person, for example, or shift between participant and observer.
- Maintain consistent verb tense throughout.
- Use strong, active verbs.
- Select or emphasize events that are particularly significant to your purpose.
- Use vivid details in a scene that you want well-drawn; use summary for parts of the story that might be less significant.
- Use dialogue correctly and appropriately when it serves a clear purpose.
- Use transitions to keep the order of the story clear.

A Dream Deferred

Langston Hughes

What happens to a dream deferred?

Does it dry up
like a raisin in the sun?
Or fester like a sore—
And then run?
Does it stink like rotten meat?
Or crust and sugar over—
like a syrupy sweet?

Maybe it just sags
like a heavy load.

Or does it explode?

from Dust Tracks on a Road

Zora Neale Hurston

We lived on a big piece of ground with two big chinaberry trees shading the front gate and Cape jasmine bushes with hundreds of blooms on either side of the walks. I loved the fleshy, white, fragrant blooms as a child but did not make too much of them. They were too common in my neighborhood. When I got to New York and found out that the people called them gardenias, and that the flowers cost a dollar each, I was impressed. The home folks laughed when I went back down there and told them. Some of the folks did not want to believe me. A dollar for a Cape jasmine bloom! Folks up north there must be crazy.

There were plenty of orange, grapefruit, tangerine, guavas and other fruits in our yard. We had a five-acre garden with things to eat growing in it, and so we were never hungry. We had chicken on the table often; home-cured meat, and all the eggs we wanted. It was a common thing for us smaller children to fill the iron tea-kettle full of eggs and boil them, and lay around in the yard and eat them until we were full. Any left-over boiled eggs could always be used for missiles. There was plenty of fish in the lakes around the town, and so we had all that we wanted. But beef stew was something rare. We were all very happy whenever Papa went to Orlando and brought back something delicious like stew-beef. Chicken and fish were too common with us. In the same way, we treasured an apple. We had oranges, tangerines and grapefruit to use as hand-grenades on the neighbors' children. But apples were something rare. They came from way up north.

Our house had eight rooms, and we called it a two-story house; but later on I learned it was really one story and a jump. The big boys all slept up there, and it was a good place to hide and shirk from sweeping off the front porch or raking up the back yard.

Downstairs in the dining-room there was an old "safe," a punched design in its tin doors. Glasses of guava jelly, quart jars of pear, peach and other kinds of preserves. The left-over cooked foods were on the lower shelves.

There were eight children in the family, and our house was noisy from the time school turned out until bedtime. After supper we gathered in Mama's room, and everybody had to get their lessons for the next day. Mama carried us all past long division in arithmetic, and parsing sentences in grammar, by diagrams on the blackboard. That was as far as she had gone. Then the younger ones were turned over to my oldest brother, Bob, and Mama sat and saw to it that we paid attention. You had to keep on going over things until you did know. How I hated the multiplication tables—especially the sevens!

We had a big barn, and a stretch of ground well covered with Bermuda grass. So on moonlight nights, two-thirds of the village children from seven to eighteen would be playing hide and whoop, chick-mah-chick, hide and seek, and other boisterous games in our yard. Once or twice a year we might get permission to go and play at some other house. But that was most unusual. Mama contended that we had plenty of space to play in; plenty of things to play with; and, furthermore, plenty of us to keep each other's company. If she had her way, she meant to raise her children to stay at home. She said that there was no need for us to live like no-count Negroes and poor-white trash—too poor to sit in the house—had to come outdoors for any pleasure, or hang around somebody else's house. Any of her children who had any tendencies like that must have got it from the Hurston side. It certainly did not come from the Pottses. Things like that gave me my first glimmering of the universal female gospel that all good traits and leanings come from the mother's side.

Mama exhorted her children at every opportunity to "jump at de sun." We might not land on the sun, but at least we would get off the ground. Papa did not feel so hopeful. Let well enough alone. It did not do for Negroes to have too much spirit. He was always threatening to break mine or kill me in the attempt. My mother was always standing between us. She conceded that I was impudent and given to talking back, but she didn't want to "squinch my spirit" too much for fear that I would turn out to be a mealy-mouthed rag doll by the time I got grown. Papa always flew hot when Mama said that. I do not know whether he feared for my future, with the tendency I had to stand and give battle, or that he felt a personal reference in Mama's observation. He predicted dire things for me. The white folks were not going to stand for it. I was going to be hung before I got grown. Somebody was going to blow me down for my sassy tongue. Mama was going to suck sorrow for not beating my temper out of me before it was too late. Posses with ropes and guns were going to drag me out sooner or later on account of that stiff neck I toted. I was going to tote a hungry belly by reason of my forward ways. My older sister was meek and mild. She would always get along. Why couldn't I be like her? Mama would keep right on with whatever she was doing and remark, "Zora is my young'un, and Sarah is yours. I'll be bound mine will come out more than conquer. You leave her alone. I'll tend to her when I figger she needs it." She meant by that that Sarah had a disposition like Papa's, while mine was like hers.

Behind Mama's rocking-chair was a good place to be in times like that. Papa was not going to hit Mama. He was two hundred pounds of bone and muscle and Mama weighed somewhere in the nineties. When people teased him about Mama being the boss, he would say he could break her of her headstrong ways if he wanted to, but she was so little that he couldn't find any place to hit her. My Uncle Jim, Mama's brother, used to always take exception to that. He maintained that if a woman had anything big enough to sit on, she had something big enough to hit on. That was his firm conviction, and he meant to hold on to it as long as the bottom end of his backbone pointed towards the ground—don't care who the woman was or what she looked like, or where she came from. Men like Papa who held to any other notion were just beating around the bush, dodging the issue, and otherwise looking like a fool at a funeral.

Papa used to shake his head at this and say, "What's de use of me taking my fist to a poor weakly thing like a woman? Anyhow, you got to submit yourself to 'em, so there ain't no use in beating on 'em and then have to go back and beg 'em pardon." . . .

Million-Dollar Murray

Why problems like homelessness may be easier to solve than to manage.

Malcolm Gladwell

1.

Murray Barr was a bear of a man, an ex-marine, six feet tall and heavyset, and when he fell down—which he did nearly every day—it could take two or three grown men to pick him up. He had straight black hair and olive skin. On the street, they called him Smokey. He was missing most of his teeth. He had a wonderful smile. People loved Murray.

His chosen drink was vodka. Beer he called "horse piss." On the streets of downtown Reno, where he lived, he could buy a two-hundred-and-fifty-millilitre bottle of cheap vodka for a dollar-fifty. If he was flush, he could go for the seven-hundred-and-fifty-millilitre bottle, and if he was broke he could always do what many of the other homeless people of Reno did, which is to walk through the casinos and finish off the half-empty glasses of liquor left at the gaming tables.

"If he was on a runner, we could pick him up several times a day," Patrick O'Bryan, who is a bicycle cop in downtown Reno, said. "And he's gone on some amazing runners. He would get picked up, get detoxed, then get back out a couple of hours later and start up again. A lot of the guys on the streets who've been drinking, they get so angry. They are so incredibly abrasive, so violent, so abusive. Murray was such a character and had such a great sense of humor that we somehow got past that. Even when he was abusive, we'd say, 'Murray, you know you love us,' and he'd say, 'I know'—and go back to swearing at us."

"I've been a police officer for fifteen years," O'Bryan's partner, Steve Johns, said. "I picked up Murray my whole career. Literally."

Johns and O'Bryan pleaded with Murray to quit drinking. A few years ago, he was assigned to a treatment program in which he was under the equivalent of house arrest, and he thrived. He got a job and worked hard. But then the program ended. "Once he graduated out, he had no one to report to, and he needed that," O'Bryan said. "I don't know whether it was his military background. I suspect that it was. He was a good cook. One time, he accumulated savings of over six thousand dollars. Showed up for work religiously. Did everything he was supposed to do. They said, 'Congratulations,' and put him back on the street. He spent that six thousand in a week or so."

Often, he was too intoxicated for the drunk tank at the jail, and he'd get sent to the emergency room at either Saint Mary's or Washoe Medical Center. Marla Johns, who was a social worker in the emergency room at Saint Mary's, saw him several times a week. "The ambulance would bring him in. We would sober him up, so he would be sober enough to go to jail. And we would call the police to pick him up. In fact, that's how I met my husband." Marla Johns is married to Steve Johns.

"He was like the one constant in an environment that was ever changing," she went on. "In he would come. He would grin that half-toothless grin. He called me 'my angel.' I would walk in the room, and he would smile and say, 'Oh, my angel, I'm so happy to see you.' We would joke back and forth, and I would beg him to quit drinking and he would laugh it off. And when time went by and he didn't come in I would get worried and call the coroner's office. When he was sober, we would find out, oh, he's working someplace, and my husband and I would go and have dinner where he was working. When my husband and I were dating, and we were going to get married, he said, 'Can I come to the wedding?' And I almost felt like he should. My joke was 'If you are sober you can come, because I can't afford your bar bill.' When we started a family, he would lay a hand on my pregnant belly and bless the child. He really was this kind of light."

In the fall of 2003, the Reno Police Department started an initiative designed to limit panhandling in the downtown core. There were articles in the newspapers, and the police department came under harsh criticism on local talk radio. The crackdown on panhandling amounted to harassment, the critics said. The homeless weren't an imposition on the city; they were just trying to get by. "One morning, I'm listening to one of the talk shows, and they're just trashing the police department and going on about how unfair it is," O'Bryan said. "And I thought, Wow, I've never seen any of these critics in one of the alleyways in the middle of the winter looking for bodies." O'Bryan was angry. In downtown Reno, food for the homeless was plentiful: there was a Gospel kitchen and Catholic Services, and even the local McDonald's fed the hungry. The panhandling was for liquor, and the liquor was anything but harmless. He and Johns spent at least half their time dealing with people like Murray; they were as much caseworkers as police officers. And they knew they weren't the only ones involved. When someone passed out on the street, there was a "One down" call to the paramedics. There were four people in an ambulance, and the patient sometimes stayed at the hospital for days, because living on the streets in a state of almost constant intoxication was a reliable way of getting sick. None of that, surely, could be cheap.

O'Bryan and Johns called someone they knew at an ambulance service and then contacted the local hospitals. "We came up with three names that were some of our chronic inebriates in the downtown area, that got arrested the most often," O'Bryan said. "We tracked those three individuals through just one of our two hospitals. One of the guys had been in jail previously, so he'd only been on the streets for six months. In those six months, he had accumulated a bill of a hundred thousand dollars—and that's at the smaller of the two hospitals near downtown Reno. It's pretty reasonable to assume that the other hospital had an even larger bill. Another individual came from Portland and had been in Reno for three months. In those three months, he had accumulated a bill for sixty-five thousand dollars. The third individual actually had some periods of being sober, and had accumulated a bill of fifty thousand."

The first of those people was Murray Barr, and Johns and O'Bryan realized that if you totted up all his hospital bills for the ten years that he had been on the streets—as well as substance-abuse-treatment costs, doctors' fees, and other expenses—Murray Barr probably ran up a medical bill as large as anyone in the state of Nevada.

"It cost us one million dollars not to do something about Murray," O'Bryan said.

2.

Fifteen years ago, after the Rodney King beating, the Los Angeles Police Department was in crisis. It was accused of racial insensitivity and ill discipline and violence, and the assumption was that those problems had spread broadly throughout the rank and file. In the language of statisticians, it was thought that L.A.P.D.'s troubles had a "normal" distribution—that if you

It turns out, furthermore, that this group costs the health-care and social-services systems far more than anyone had ever anticipated. Culhane estimates that in New York at least sixty-two million dollars was being spent annually to shelter just those twenty-five hundred hard core homeless. "It costs twenty-four thousand dollars a year for one of these shelter beds," Culhane said. "We're talking about a cot eighteen inches away from the next cot." Boston Health Care for the Homeless Program, a leading service group for the homeless in Boston, recently tracked the medical expenses of a hundred and nineteen chronically homeless people. In the course of five years, thirty-three people died and seven more were sent to nursing homes, and the group still accounted for 18,834 emergency-room visits—at a minimum cost of a thousand dollars a visit. The University of California, San Diego Medical Center followed fifteen chronically homeless inebriates and found that over eighteen months those fifteen people were treated at the hospital's emergency room four hundred and seventeen times, and ran up bills that averaged a hundred thousand dollars each. One person—San Diego's counterpart to Murray Barr—came to the emergency room eighty-seven times.

"If it's a medical admission, it's likely to be the guys with the really complex pneumonia," James Dunford, the city of San Diego's emergency medical director and the author of the observational study, said. "They are drunk and they aspirate and get vomit in their lungs and develop a lung abscess, and they get hypothermia on top of that, because they're out in the rain. They end up in the intensive-care unit with these very complicated medical infections. These are the guys who typically get hit by cars and buses and trucks. They often have a neurosurgical catastrophe as well. So they are very prone to just falling down and cracking their head and getting a subdural hematoma, which, if not drained, could kill them, and it's the guy who falls down and hits his head who ends up costing you at least fifty thousand dollars. Meanwhile, they are going through alcoholic withdrawal and have devastating liver disease that only adds to their inability to fight infections. There is no end to the issues. We do this huge drill. We run up big lab fees, and the nurses want to quit, because they see the same guys come in over and over, and all we're doing is making them capable of walking down the block."

The homelessness problem is like the L.A.P.D.'s bad-cop problem. It's a matter of a few hard cases, and that's good news, because when a problem is that concentrated you can wrap your arms around it and think about solving it. The bad news is that those few hard cases are hard. They are falling-down drunks with liver disease and complex infections and mental illness. They need time and attention and lots of money. But enormous sums of money are already being spent on the chronically homeless, and Culhane saw that the kind of money it would take to solve the homeless problem could well be less than the kind of money it took to ignore it. Murray Barr used more health-care dollars, after all, than almost anyone in the state of Nevada. It would probably have been cheaper to give him a full-time nurse and his own apartment.

The leading exponent for the power-law theory of homelessness is Philip Mangano, who, since he was appointed by President Bush in 2002, has been the executive director of the U.S. Interagency Council on Homelessness, a group that oversees the programs of twenty federal agencies. Mangano is a slender man, with a mane of white hair and a magnetic presence, who got his start as an advocate for the homeless in Massachusetts. In the past two years, he has crisscrossed the United States, educating local mayors and city councils about the real shape of the homelessness curve. Simply running soup kitchens and shelters, he argues, allows the chronically homeless to remain chronically homeless. You build a shelter and a soup kitchen if you think that homelessness is a problem with a broad and unmanageable middle. But if it's a problem at the fringe it can be solved. So far, Mangano has convinced more than two hundred cities to radically reevaluate their policy for dealing with the homeless.

"I was in St. Louis recently," Mangano said, back in June, when he dropped by New York on his way to Boise, Idaho. "I spoke with people doing services there. They had a very difficult group of people they couldn't reach no matter what they offered. So I said, Take some of your money and rent some apartments and go out to those people, and literally go out there with the key and say to them, 'This is the key to an apartment. If you come with me right now I am going to give it to you, and you are going to have that apartment.' And so they did. And one by one those people were coming in. Our intent is to take homeless policy from the old idea of funding programs that serve homeless people endlessly and invest in results that actually end homelessness."

Mangano is a history buff, a man who sometimes falls asleep listening to old Malcolm X speeches, and who peppers his remarks with references to the civil-rights movement and the Berlin Wall and, most of all, the fight against slavery. "I am an abolitionist," he says. "My office in Boston was opposite the monument to the 54th Regiment on the Boston Common, up the street from the Park Street Church, where William Lloyd Garrison called for immediate abolition, and around the corner from where Frederick Douglass gave that famous speech at the Tremont

Temple. It is very much ingrained in me that you do not manage a social wrong. You should be ending it."

3.

The old Y.M.C.A. in downtown Denver is on Sixteenth Street, just east of the central business district. The main building is a handsome six-story stone structure that was erected in 1906, and next door is an annex that was added in the nineteen-fifties. On the ground floor there is a gym and exercise rooms. On the upper floors there are several hundred apartments—brightly painted one-bedrooms, efficiencies, and S.R.O.-style rooms with microwaves and refrigerators and central airconditioning—and for the past several years those apartments have been owned and managed by the Colorado Coalition for the Homeless.

Even by big-city standards, Denver has a serious homelessness problem. The winters are relatively mild, and the summers aren't nearly as hot as those of neighboring New Mexico or Utah, which has made the city a magnet for the indigent. By the city's estimates, it has roughly a thousand chronically homeless people, of whom three hundred spend their time downtown, along the central Sixteenth Street shopping corridor or in nearby Civic Center Park. Many of the merchants downtown worry that the presence of the homeless is scaring away customers. A few blocks north, near the hospital, a modest, low-slung detox center handles twenty-eight thousand admissions a year, many of them homeless people who have passed out on the streets, either from liquor or—as is increasingly the case—from mouthwash. "Dr. Tichenor's—Dr. Tich, they call it—is the brand of mouthwash they use," says Roxane White, the manager of the city's social services. "You can imagine what that does to your gut."

Eighteen months ago, the city signed up with Mangano. With a mixture of federal and local funds, the C.C.H. inaugurated a new program that has so far enrolled a hundred and six people. It is aimed at the Murray Barrs of Denver, the people costing the system the most. C.C.H. went after the people who had been on the streets the longest, who had a criminal record, who had a problem with substance abuse or mental illness. "We have one individual in her early sixties, but looking at her you'd think she's eighty," Rachel Post, the director of substance treatment at the C.C.H., said. (Post changed some details about her clients in order to protect their identity.) "She's a chronic alcoholic. A typical day for her is she gets up and tries to find whatever she's going to drink that day. She falls down a lot. There's another person who came in during the first week. He was on methadone maintenance. He'd had psychiatric treatment. He was incarcerated for eleven years, and lived on the streets for three years after that, and, if that's not enough, he had a hole in his heart."

The recruitment strategy was as simple as the one that Mangano had laid out in St. Louis: Would you like a free apartment? The enrollees got either an efficiency at the Y.M.C.A. or an apartment rented for them in a building somewhere else in the city, provided they agreed to work within the rules of the program. In the basement of the Y, where the racquetball courts used to be, the coalition built a command center, staffed with ten caseworkers. Five days a week, between eight-thirty and ten in the morning, the caseworkers meet and painstakingly review the status of everyone in the program. On the wall around the conference table are several large white boards, with lists of doctor's appointments and court dates and medication schedules. "We need a staffing ratio of one to ten to make it work," Post said, you go out there and you find people and assess how they're doing in their residence. Sometimes we're in contact with someone every day. Ideally, we want to be in contact every couple of days. We've got about fifteen people we're really worried about now."

The cost of services comes to about ten thousand dollars per homeless client per year. An efficiency apartment in Denver averages $376 a month, or just over forty-five hundred a year, which means that you can house and care for a chronically homeless person for at most fifteen thousand dollars, or about a third of what he or she would cost on the street. The idea is that once the people in the program get stabilized they will find jobs, and start to pick up more and more of their own rent, which would bring someone's annual cost to the program closer to six thousand dollars. As of today, seventy-five supportive housing slots have already been added, and the city's homeless plan calls for eight hundred more over the next ten years.

The reality, of course, is hardly that neat and tidy. The idea that the very sickest and most troubled of the homeless can be stabilized and eventually employed is only a hope. Some of them plainly won't be able to get there: these are, after all, hard cases. "We've got one man, he's in his twenties," Post said. "Already, he has cirrhosis of the liver. One time he blew a blood alcohol of .49, which is enough to kill most people. The first place we had he brought over all his friends, and they partied and trashed the place and broke a window. Then we gave him another apartment, and he did the same thing."

Post said that the man had been sober for several months. But he could relapse at some point and perhaps trash another apartment, and they'd have to figure out what to do with him next. Post had just been on a conference call with some people in New York City who run a similar program, and they talked about whether giving clients so many chances simply encourages them to behave irresponsibly. For some people, it probably does. But what was the alternative? If this young man was put back on the streets, he would cost the system even more money. The current philosophy of welfare holds that government assistance should be temporary and conditional, to avoid creating dependency. But someone who blows .49 on a Breathalyzer and has cirrhosis of the liver at the age of twenty-seven doesn't respond to incentives and sanctions in the usual way. "The most complicated people to work with are those who have been homeless for so long that going back to the streets just isn't scary to them," Post said. "The summer comes along and they say, 'I don't need to follow your rules.'" Power-law homelessness policy has to do the opposite of normal-distribution social policy. It should create dependency: you want people who have been outside the system to come inside and rebuild their lives under the supervision of those ten caseworkers in the basement of the Y.M.C.A.

That is what is so perplexing about power-law homeless policy. From an economic perspective the approach makes perfect sense. But from a moral perspective it doesn't seem fair. Thousands of people in the Denver area no doubt live day to day, work two or three jobs, and are eminently deserving of a helping hand—and no one offers them the key to a new apartment. Yet that's just what the guy screaming obscenities and swigging Dr. Tich gets. When the welfare mom's time on public assistance runs out, we cut her off. Yet when the homeless man trashes his apartment we give him another. Social benefits are supposed to have some kind of moral justification. We give them to widows and disabled veterans and poor mothers with small children. Giving the homeless guy passed out on the sidewalk an apartment has a different rationale. It's simply about efficiency.

We also believe that the distribution of social benefits should not be arbitrary. We don't give only to some poor mothers, or to a random handful of disabled veterans. We give to everyone who meets a formal criterion, and the moral credibility of government assistance derives, in part, from this universality. But the Denver homelessness program doesn't help every chronically homeless person in Denver. There is a waiting list of six hundred for the supportive-housing program; it will be years before all those people get apartments, and some may never get one. There isn't enough money to go around, and to try to help everyone a little bit—to observe the principle of universality—isn't as cost-effective as helping a few people a lot. Being fair, in this case, means providing shelters and soup kitchens, and shelters and soup kitchens don't solve the problem of homelessness. Our usual moral intuitions are little use, then, when it comes to a few hard cases. Power-law problems leave us with an unpleasant choice. We can be true to our principles or we can fix the problem. We cannot do both.

4.

A few miles northwest of the old Y.M.C.A. in downtown Denver, on the Speer Boulevard off-ramp from I-25, there is a big electronic sign by the side of the road, connected to a device that remotely measures the emissions of the vehicles driving past. When a car with properly functioning pollution-control equipment passes, the sign flashes "Good." When a car passes that is well over the acceptable limits, the sign flashes "Poor." If you stand at the Speer Boulevard exit and watch the sign for any length of time, you'll find that virtually every car scores "Good." An Audi A4—"Good." A Buick Century—"Good." A Toyota Corolla—"Good." A Ford Taurus—"Good." A Saab 9-5—"Good," and on and on, until after twenty minutes or so, some beat-up old Ford Escort or tricked-out Porsche drives by and the sign flashes "Poor." The picture of the smog problem you get from watching the Speer Boulevard sign and the picture of the homelessness problem you get from listening in on the morning staff meetings at the Y.M.C.A. are pretty much the same. Auto emissions follow a power-law distribution, and the air-pollution example offers another look at why we struggle so much with problems centered on a few hard cases.

Most cars, especially new ones, are extraordinarily clean. A 2004 Subaru in good working order has an exhaust stream that's just .06 per cent carbon monoxide, which is negligible. But on almost any highway, for whatever reason—age, ill repair, deliberate tampering by the owner—a small number of cars can have carbon-monoxide levels in excess of ten per cent, which is almost two hundred times higher. In Denver, five per cent of the vehicles on the road produce fifty-five per cent of the automobile pollution.

"Let's say a car is fifteen years old," Donald Stedman says. Stedman is a chemist and automobile-emissions specialist at the University of Denver. His laboratory put up the sign on Speer Avenue. "Obviously, the older a car is the more likely it is to become broken. It's the same as human beings. And by broken we mean any number of mechanical malfunctions—the computer's not working anymore, fuel injection is stuck open, the catalyst died. It's not unusual that these failure modes result in high emissions. We have at least one car in our database which was emitting seventy grams of hydrocarbon per mile, which means that you could almost drive a Honda Civic on the exhaust fumes from that car. It's not just old cars. It's new cars with high mileage, like taxis. One of the most successful and least publicized control measures was done by a district attorney in L.A. back in the nineties. He went to LAX and discovered that all of the Bell Cabs were gross emitters. One of those cabs emitted more than its own weight of pollution every year."

In Stedman's view, the current system of smog checks makes little sense. A million motorists in Denver have to go to an emissions center every year—take time from work, wait in line, pay fifteen or twenty-five dollars—for a test that more than ninety per cent of them don't need. "Not everybody gets tested for breast cancer," Stedman says. "Not everybody takes an AIDS test." On-site smog checks, furthermore, do a pretty bad job of finding and fixing the few outliers. Car enthusiasts—with high-powered, high-polluting sports cars—have been known to drop a clean engine into their car on the day they get it tested. Others register their car in a faraway town without emissions testing or arrive at the test site "hot"—having just come off hard driving on the freeway—which is a good way to make a dirty engine appear to be clean. Still others randomly pass the test when they shouldn't, because dirty engines are highly variable and sometimes burn cleanly for short durations. There is little evidence, Stedman says, that the city's regime of inspections makes any difference in air quality.

He proposes mobile testing instead. Twenty years ago, he invented a device the size of a suitcase that uses infrared light to instantly measure and then analyze the emissions of cars as they drive by on the highway. The Speer Avenue sign is attached to one of Stedman's devices. He says that cities should put half a dozen or so of his devices in vans, park them on freeway off-ramps around the city, and have a police car poised to pull over anyone who fails the test. A half-dozen vans could test thirty thousand cars a day. For the same twenty-five million dollars that Denver's motorists now spend on on-site testing, Stedman estimates, the city could identify and fix twenty-five thousand truly dirty vehicles every year, and within a few years cut automobile emissions in the Denver metropolitan area by somewhere between thirty-five and forty per cent. The city could stop managing its smog problem and start ending it.

Why don't we all adopt the Stedman method? There's no moral impediment here. We're used to the police pulling people over for having a blown headlight or a broken side mirror, and it wouldn't be difficult to have them add pollution-control devices to their list. Yet it does run counter to an instinctive social preference for thinking of pollution as a problem to which we all contribute equally. We have developed institutions that move reassuringly quickly and forcefully on collective problems. Congress passes a law. The Environmental Protection Agency promulgates a regulation. The auto industry makes its cars a little cleaner, and—presto—the air gets better. But Stedman doesn't much care about what happens in Washington and Detroit. The challenge of controlling air pollution isn't so much about the laws as it is about compliance with them. It's a policing problem, rather than a policy problem, and there is something ultimately unsatisfying about his proposed solution. He wants to end air pollution in Denver with a half-dozen vans outfitted with a contraption about the size of a suitcase. Can such a big problem have such a small-bore solution?

That's what made the findings of the Christopher Commission so unsatisfying. We put together blue-ribbon panels when we're faced with problems that seem too large for the normal mechanisms of bureaucratic repair. We want sweeping reforms. But what was the commission's most memorable observation? It was the story of an officer with a known history of doing things like beating up handcuffed suspects who nonetheless received a performance review from his superior stating that he "usually conducts himself in a manner that inspires respect for the law and instills public confidence." This is what you say about an officer when you haven't actually read his file, and the implication of the Christopher Commission's report was that the L.A.P.D. might help solve its problem simply by getting its police captains to read the files of their officers. The L.A.P.D.'s problem was a matter not of policy but of compliance. The department needed to adhere to the rules it already had in place, and that's not what a public hungry for institutional transformation wants to hear. Solving problems that have power-law distributions doesn't just violate our moral intuitions; it violates our political intuitions as well. It's hard not to conclude, in the end, that the reason we treated the homeless as one hopeless undifferentiated group for so long is not simply that we didn't know better. It's that we didn't want to know better. It was easier the old way.

Power-law solutions have little appeal to the right, because they involve special treatment for people who do not deserve special treatment; and they have little appeal to the left, because their emphasis on efficiency over fairness suggests the cold number-crunching of Chicago-school cost-benefit analysis. Even the promise of millions of dollars in savings or cleaner air or better police departments cannot entirely compensate for such discomfort. In Denver, John Hickenlooper, the city's enormously popular mayor, has worked on the homelessness issue tirelessly during the past couple of years. He spent more time on the subject in his annual State of the City address this past summer than on any other topic. He gave the speech, with deliberate symbolism, in the city's downtown Civic Center Park, where homeless people gather every day with their shopping carts and garbage bags. He has gone on local talk radio on many occasions to discuss what the city is doing about the issue. He has commissioned studies to show what a drain on the city's resources the homeless population has become. But, he says, "there are still people who stop me going into the supermarket and say, 'I can't believe you're going to help those homeless people, those bum's."

5.

Early one morning a year ago, Marla Johns got a call from her husband, Steve. He was at work. "He called and woke me up," Johns remembers. "He was choked up and crying on the phone. And I thought that something had happened with another police officer. I said, 'Oh, my gosh, what happened?' He said, 'Murray died last night.'" He died of intestinal bleeding. At the police department that morning, some of the officers gave Murray a moment of silence.

"There are not many days that go by that I don't have a thought of him," she went on. "Christmas comes—and I used to buy him a Christmas present. Make sure he had warm gloves and a blanket and a coat. There was this mutual respect. There was a time when another intoxicated patient jumped off the gurney and was coming at me, and Murray jumped off his gurney and shook his fist and said, 'Don't you touch my angel.' You know, when he was monitored by the system he did fabulously. He would be on house arrest and he would get a job and he would save money and go to work every day, and he wouldn't drink. He would do all the things he was supposed to do. There are some people who can be very successful members of society if someone monitors them. Murray needed someone to be in charge of him."

But, of course, Reno didn't have a place where Murray could be given the structure he needed. Someone must have decided that it cost too much.

"I told my husband that I would claim his body if no one else did," she said. "I would not have him in an unmarked grave."

No Name Woman

Maxine Hong Kingston

"You must not tell anyone," my mother said, "what I am about to tell you. In China your father had a sister who killed herself. She jumped into the family well. We say that your father has all brothers because it is as if she had never been born.

"In 1924 just a few days after our village celebrated seventeen hurry-up weddings—to make sure that every young man who went 'out on the road' would responsibly come home—your father and his brothers and your grandfather and his brothers and your aunt's new husband sailed for America, the Gold Mountain. It was your grandfather's last trip. Those lucky enough to get contracts waved goodbye from the decks. They fed and guarded the stowaways and helped them off in Cuba, New York, Bali, Hawaii. 'We'll meet in California next year,' they said. All of them sent money home.

"I remember looking at your aunt one day when she and I were dressing; I had not noticed before that she had such a protruding melon of a stomach. But I did not think, 'She's pregnant,' until she began to look like other pregnant women, her shirt pulling and the white tops of her black pants showing. She could not have been pregnant, you see, because her husband had been gone for years. No one said anything. We did not discuss it. In early summer she was ready to have the child, long after the time when it could have been possible.

"The village had also been counting. On the night the baby was to be born the villagers raided our house. Some were crying. Like a great saw, teeth strung with lights, files of people walked zigzag across our land, tearing the rice. Their lanterns doubled in the disturbed black water, which drained away through the broken bunds. As the villagers closed in, we could see that some of them, probably men and women we knew well, wore white masks. The people with long hair hung it over their faces. Women with short hair made it stand up on end. Some had tied white bands around their foreheads, arms, and legs.

At first they threw mud and rocks at the house. Then they threw eggs and began slaughtering our stock. We could hear the animals scream their deaths—the roosters, the pigs, a last great roar from the ox. Familiar wild heads flared in our night windows; the villagers encircled us. Some of the faces stopped to peer at us, their eyes rushing like searchlights. The hands flattened against the panes, framed heads, and left red prints.

"The villagers broke in the front and the back doors at the same time, even though we had not locked the doors against them. Their knives dripped with the blood of our animals. They smeared blood on the doors and walls. One woman swung a chicken, whose throat she had slit, splattering blood in red arcs about her. We stood together in the middle of our house, in the family hall with the pictures and tables of the ancestors around us, and looked straight ahead.

"At that time the house had only two wings. When the men came back, we would build two more to enclose our courtyard and a third one to begin a second courtyard. The villagers pushed through both wings, even your grandparents' rooms, to find your aunt's, which was also mine until the men returned. From this room a new wing for one of the younger families would grow. They ripped up her clothes and shoes and broke her combs, grinding them underfoot. They tore her work from the loom. They scattered the cooking fire and rolled the new weaving in it. We could hear them in the kitchen breaking our bowls and banging the pots. They overturned the great waist-high earthenware jugs; duck eggs, pickled fruits, vegetables burst out and mixed in acrid torrents. The old woman from the next field swept a broom through the air and loosed the spirits-of-the-broom over our heads. 'Pig.' 'Ghost.' 'Pig,' they sobbed and scolded while they ruined our house.

"When they left, they took sugar and oranges to bless themselves. They cut pieces from the dead animals. Some of them took bowls that were not broken and clothes that were not torn. Afterward we swept up the rice and sewed it back up into sacks. But the smells from the spilled preserves lasted. Your aunt gave birth in the pigsty that night. The next morning when I went for the water, I found her and the baby plugging up the family well.

"Don't let your father know that I told you. He denies her. Now that you have started to menstruate, what happened to her could happen to you. Don't humiliate us. You wouldn't like to be forgotten as if you had never been born. The villagers are watchful."

Whenever she had to warn us about life, my mother told stories that ran like this one, a story to grow up on. She tested our strength to establish realities. Those in the emigrant generations who could not reassert brute survival died young and far from home. Those of us in the first American generations have had to figure out how the invisible world the emigrants built around our childhoods fits in solid America.

The emigrants confused the gods by diverting their curses, misleading them with crooked streets and false names. They must try to confuse their offspring as well, who, I suppose, threaten them in similar ways—always trying to get things straight, always trying to name the unspeakable. The Chinese I know hide their names; sojourners take new names when their lives change and guard their real names with silence.

Chinese-Americans, when you try to understand what things in you are Chinese, how do you separate what is peculiar to childhood, to poverty, insanities, one family, your mother who marked your growing with stories, from what is Chinese? What is Chinese tradition and what is the movies?

If I want to learn what clothes my aunt wore, whether flashy or ordinary, I would have to begin, "Remember Father's drowned-in-the-well sister?" I cannot ask that. My mother has told me once and for all the useful parts. She will add nothing unless powered by Necessity, a riverbank that guides her life. She plants vegetable gardens rather than lawns; she carries the odd-shaped tomatoes home from the fields and eats food left for the gods.

Whenever we did frivolous things, we used up energy; we flew high kites. We children came up off the ground over the melting cones our parents brought home from work and the American movie on New Year's Day—*Oh, You Beautiful Doll* with Betty Grable one year, and *She Wore a Yellow Ribbon* with John Wayne another year. After the one carnival ride each, we paid in guilt; our tired father counted his change on the dark walk home.

Adultery is extravagance. Could people who hatch their own chicks and eat the embryos and the heads for delicacies and boil the feet in vinegar for party food, leaving only the gravel, eating even the gizzard lining—could such people engender a prodigal aunt? To be a woman, to have a daughter in starvation time was a waste enough. My aunt could not have been the lone romantic who gave up everything for sex. Women in the old China did not choose. Some man had commanded her to lie with him and be his secret evil. I wonder whether he masked himself when he joined the raid on her family.

Perhaps she had encountered him in the fields or on the mountain where the daughters-in-law collected fuel. Or perhaps he first noticed her in the marketplace. He was not a stranger because the village housed no strangers. She had to have dealings with him other than sex. Perhaps he worked an adjoining field, or he sold her the cloth for the dress she sewed and wore. His demand must have surprised, then terrified her. She obeyed him; she always did as she was told.

When the family found a young man in the next village to be her husband, she had stood tractably beside the best rooster, his proxy, and promised before they met that she would be his forever. She was lucky that he was her age and she would be the first wife, an advantage secure now. The night she first saw him, he had sex with her. Then he left for America. She had almost forgotten what he looked like. When she tried to envision him, she only saw the black and white face in the group photograph the men had had taken before leaving.

The other man was not, after all, much different from her husband. They both gave orders: she followed. "If you tell your family, I'll beat you. I'll kill you. Be here again next week." No one talked sex, ever. And she might have separated the rapes from the rest of living if only she did not have to buy her oil from him or gather wood in the same forest. I want her fear to have lasted just as long as rape lasted so that the fear could have been contained. No drawn-out fear. But women at sex hazarded birth and hence lifetimes. The fear did not stop but permeated everywhere. She told the man, "I think I'm pregnant!" He organized the raid against her.

On nights when my mother and father talked about their life back home, sometimes they mentioned an "outcast table" whose business they still seemed to be settling, their voices tight. In a commensal tradition, where food is precious, the powerful older people made wrongdoers eat alone. Instead of letting them start separate new lives like the Japanese, who could become samurais and geishas, the Chinese family, faces averted but eyes glowering sideways, hung on to the offenders and fed them leftovers. My aunt must have lived in the same house as my parents and eaten at an outcast table. My mother spoke about the raid as if she had seen it, when she and my aunt, a daughter-in-law to a different household, should not have been living together at all. Daughters-in-law lived with their husbands' parents, not their own; a synonym for marriage in

Chinese is "taking a daughter-in-law!" Her husband's parents could have sold her, mortgaged her, stoned her. But they had sent her back to her own mother and father, a mysterious act hinting at disgraces not told me. Perhaps they had thrown her out to deflect the avengers.

She was the only daughter; her four brothers went with her father, husband, and uncles "out on the road" and for some years became western men. When the goods were divided among the family, three of the brothers took land, and the youngest, my father, chose an education. After my grandparents gave their daughter away to her husband's family, they had dispensed all the adventure and all the property. They expected her alone to keep the traditional ways, which her brothers, now among the barbarians, could fumble without detection. The heavy, deep-rooted women were to maintain the past against the flood, safe for returning. But the rare urge west had fixed upon our family, and so my aunt crossed boundaries not delineated in space.

The work of preservation demands that the feelings playing about in one's guts not be turned into action. Just watch their passing like cherry blossoms. But perhaps my aunt, my forerunner, caught in a slow life, let dreams grow and fade and after some months or years went toward what persisted. Fear at the enormities of the forbidden kept her desires delicate, wire and bone. She looked at a man because she liked the way the hair was tucked behind his ears, or she liked the question-mark line of a long torso curving at the shoulder and straight at the hip. For warm eyes or a soft voice or a slow walk—that's all—a few hairs, a line, a brightness, a sound, a pace, she gave up family. She offered us up for a charm that vanished with tiredness, a pigtail that didn't toss when the wind died. Why, the wrong lighting could erase the dearest thing about him.

It could very well have been, however, that my aunt did not take subtle enjoyment of her friend, but, a wild woman, kept rollicking company. Imagining her free with sex doesn't fit, though. I don't know any women like that, or men either. Unless I see her life branching into mine, she gives me no ancestral help.

To sustain her being in love, she often worked at herself in the mirror, guessing at the colors and shapes that would interest him, changing them frequently in order to hit on the right combination. She wanted him to look back.

On a farm near the sea, a woman who tended her appearance reaped a reputation for eccentricity. All the married women blunt-cut their hair in flaps about their ears or pulled it back in tight buns. No nonsense. Neither style blew easily into heart-catching tangles. And at their weddings they displayed themselves in their long hair for the last time. It brushed the backs of my knees," My mother tells me. "It was braided, and even so, it brushed the backs of my knees!"

At the mirror my aunt combed individuality into her bob. A bun could have been contrived to escape into black streamers blowing in the wind or in quiet wisps about her face, but only the older women in our picture album wear buns. She brushed her hair back from her forehead, tucking the flaps behind her ears. She looped a piece of thread, knotted into a circle between her index fingers and thumbs, and ran the double strand across her forehead. When she closed her fingers as if she were making a pair of shadow geese bite, the string twisted together catching the little hairs. Then she pulled the thread away from her skin, ripping the hairs out neatly, her eyes watering from the needles of pain. Opening her fingers, she cleaned the thread, then rolled it along her hairline and the tops of her eyebrows. My mother did the same to me and my sisters and herself. I used to believe that the expression "caught by the short hairs" meant a captive held with a depilatory string. It especially hurt at the temples, but my mother said we were lucky we didn't have to have our feet bound when we were seven. Sisters used to sit on their beds and cry together, she said, as their mothers or their slaves removed the bandages for a few minutes each night and let the blood gush back into their veins. I hope that the man my aunt loved appreciated a smooth brow, that he wasn't just a tits-and-ass man.

Once my aunt found a freckle on her chin, at a spot that the almanac said predestined her for unhappiness. She dug it out with a hot needle and washed the wound with peroxide.

More attention to her looks than these pullings of hairs and pickings at spots would have caused gossip among the villagers. They owned work clothes and good clothes, and they wore good clothes for feasting the new seasons. But since a woman combing her hair hexes beginnings, my aunt rarely found an occasion to look her best. Women looked like great sea snails—the corded wood, babies, and laundry they carried were the whorls on their backs. The Chinese did not admire a bent back; goddesses and warriors stood straight. Still there must have been a marvelous freeing of beauty when a worker laid down her burden and stretched and arched.

Such commonplace loveliness, however, was not enough for my aunt. She dreamed of a lover for the fifteen days of New Year's, the time for families to exchange visits, money, and food. She plied her secret comb. And sure enough she cursed the year, the family, the village, and herself.

Even as her hair lured her imminent lover, many other men looked at her. Uncles, cousins, nephews, brothers would have looked, too, had they been home between journeys. Perhaps they had already been restraining their curiosity, and they left, fearful that their glances, like a field of nesting birds, might be startled and caught. Poverty hurt, and that was their first reason for leaving. But another, final reason for leaving the crowded house was the never-said.

She may have been unusually beloved, the precious only daughter, spoiled and mirror gazing because of the affection the family lavished on her. When her husband left, they welcomed the chance to take her back from the in-laws; she could live like the little daughter for just a while longer. There are stories that my grandfather was different from other people, "crazy ever since the little Jap bayoneted him in the head." He used to put his naked penis on the dinner table, laughing. And one day he brought home a baby girl, wrapped up inside his brown western-style greatcoat. He had traded one of his sons, probably my father, the youngest, for her. My grandmother made him trade back. When he finally got a daughter of his own, he doted on her. They must have all loved her, except perhaps my father, the only brother who never went back to China, having once been traded for a girl.

Brothers and sisters, newly men and women, had to efface their sexual color and present plain miens. Disturbing hair and eyes, a smile like no other, threatened the ideal of five generations living under one roof. To focus blurs, people shouted face to face and yelled from room to room. The immigrants I know have loud voices, unmodulated to American tones even after years away from the village where they called their friendships out across the fields. I have not been able to stop my mother's screams in public libraries or over telephones. Walking erect (knees straight, toes pointed forward, not pigeon-toed, which is Chinese-feminine) and speaking in an inaudible voice, I have tried to turn myself American-feminine. Chinese communication was loud, public. Only sick people had to whisper. But at the dinner table, where the family members came nearest one another, no one could talk, not the outcasts nor any eaters. Every word that falls from the mouth is a coin lost. Silently they gave and accepted food with both hands. A preoccupied child who took his bowl with one hand got a sideways glare. A complete moment of total attention is due everyone alike. Children and lovers have no singularity here, but my aunt used a secret voice, a separate attentiveness.

She kept the man's name to herself throughout her labor and dying; she did not accuse him that he be punished with her. To save her inseminator's name she gave silent birth.

He may have been somebody in her own household, but intercourse with a man outside the family would have been no less abhorrent. All the village were kinsmen, and the titles shouted in loud country voices never let kinship be forgotten. Any man within visiting distance would have been neutralized as a lover—"brother," "younger brother," "older brother"—one hundred and fifteen relationship titles. Parents researched birth charts probably not so much to assure good fortune as to circumvent incest in a population that has but one hundred surnames. Everybody has eight million relatives. How useless then sexual mannerisms, how dangerous.

As if it came from an atavism deeper than fear, I used to add "brother" silently to boys' names. It hexed the boys, who would or would not ask me to dance, and made them less scary and as familiar and deserving of benevolence as girls.

But, of course, I hexed myself also—no dates. I should have stood up, both arms waving, and shouted out across libraries, "Hey, you! Love me back." I had no idea, though, how to make attraction selective, how to control its direction and magnitude. If I made myself American-pretty so that the five or six Chinese boys in the class fell in love with me, everyone else—the Caucasian, Negro, and Japanese boys—would too. Sisterliness, dignified and honorable, made much more sense.

Attraction eludes control so stubbornly that whole societies designed to organize relationships among people cannot keep order, not even when they bind people to one another from childhood and raise them together. Among the very poor and the wealthy, brothers married their adopted sisters, like doves. Our family allowed some romance, paying adult brides' prices and providing dowries so that their sons and daughters could marry strangers. Marriage promises to turn strangers into friendly relatives—a nation of siblings.

In the village structure, spirits shimmered among the live creatures, balanced and held in equilibrium by time and land. But one human being flaring up into violence could open up a black hole, a maelstrom that pulled in the sky. The frightened villagers, who depended on one another to maintain the real, went to my aunt to show her a personal, physical representation of the break she had made in the "roundness." Misallying couples snapped off the future, which was to be embodied in true offspring. The villagers punished her for acting as if she could have a private life, secret and apart from them.

If my aunt had betrayed the family at a time of large grain yields and peace, when many boys were born, and wings were being built on many houses, perhaps she might have escaped such severe punishment. But the men—hungry, greedy, tired of planting in dry soil—had been forced to leave the village in order to send food-money home. There were ghost plagues, bandit plagues, wars with the Japanese, floods. My Chinese brother and sister had died of an unknown sickness. Adultery, perhaps only a mistake during good times, became a crime when the village needed food.

The round moon cakes and round doorways, the round tables of graduated sizes that fit one roundness inside another, round windows and rice bowls—these talismans had lost their power to warn this family of the law: a family must be whole, faithfully keeping the descent line by having sons to feed the old and the dead, who in turn look after the family. The villagers came to show my aunt and her lover-in-hiding a broken house. The villagers were speeding up the circling of events because she was too shortsighted to see that her infidelity had already harmed the village, that waves of consequences would return unpredictably, sometimes in disguise, as now, to hurt her. This roundness had to be made coin-sized so that she would see its circumference: punish her at the birth of her baby. Awaken her to the inexorable. People who refused fatalism because they could invent small resources insisted on culpability. Deny accidents and wrest fault from the stars.

After the villagers left, their lanterns now scattering in various directions toward home, the family broke their silence and cursed her. "Aiaa, we're going to die. Death is coming. Death is coming. Look what you've done. You've killed us. Ghost! Dead ghost! Ghost! You've never been born." She ran out into the fields, far enough from the house so that she could no longer hear their voices, and pressed herself against the earth, her own land no more. When she felt the birth coming, she thought that she had been hurt. Her body seized together. "They've hurt me too much," she thought. "This is gall, and it will kill me." With forehead and knees against the earth, her body convulsed and then relaxed. She turned on her back, lay on the ground. The black well of sky and stars went out and out and out forever; her body and her complexity seemed to disappear. She was one of the stars, a bright dot in blackness, without home, without a companion, in eternal cold and silence. An agoraphobia rose in her, speeding higher and higher, bigger and bigger; she would not be able to contain it; there would no end to fear.

Flayed, unprotected against space, she felt pain return, focusing her body. This pain chilled her—a cold, steady kind of surface pain. Inside, spasmodically, the other pain, the pain of the child, heated her. For hours she lay on the ground, alternately body and space. Sometimes a vision of normal comfort obliterated reality: she saw the family in the evening gambling at the dinner table, the young people massaging their elders' backs. She saw them congratulating one another, high joy on the mornings the rice shoots came up. When these pictures burst, the stars drew yet further apart. Black space opened.

She got to her feet to fight better and remembered that old-fashioned women gave birth in their pigsties to fool the jealous, pain-dealing gods, who do not snatch piglets. Before the next spasms could stop her, she ran to the pigsty, each step a rushing out into emptiness. She climbed over the fence and knelt in the dirt. It was good to have a fence enclosing her, a tribal person alone.

Laboring, this woman who had carried her child as a foreign growth that sickened her every day, expelled it at last. She reached down to touch the hot, wet, moving mass, surely smaller than anything human, and could feel that it was human after all—fingers, toes, nails, nose. She pulled it up on to her belly, and it lay curled there, butt in the air, feet precisely tucked one under the other. She opened her loose shirt and buttoned the child inside. After resting, it squirmed and thrashed and she pushed it up to her breast. It turned its head this way and that until it found her nipple. There, it made little snuffling noises. She clenched her teeth at its preciousness, lovely as a young calf, a piglet, a little dog.

She may have gone to the pigsty as a last act of responsibility: she would protect this child as she had protected its father. It would look after her soul, leaving supplies on her grave. But how would this tiny child without family find her grave when there would be no marker for her anywhere, neither in the earth nor the family hall? No one would give her a family hall name. She had taken the child with her into the wastes. At its birth the two of them had felt the same raw pain of separation, a wound that only the family pressing tight could close. A child with no descent line would not soften her life but only trail after her, ghostlike, begging her to give it purpose. At dawn the villagers on their way to the fields would stand around the fence and look.

Full of milk, the little ghost slept. When it awoke, she hardened her breasts against the milk that crying loosens. Toward morning she picked up the baby and walked to the well.

Carrying the baby to the well shows loving. Otherwise abandon it. Turn its face into the mud. Mothers who love their children take them along. It was probably a girl; there is some hope of forgiveness for boys.

"Don't tell anyone you had an aunt. Your father does not want to hear her name. She has never been born." I have believed that sex was unspeakable and words so strong and fathers so frail that "aunt" would do my father mysterious harm. I have thought that my family, having settled among immigrants who had also been their neighbors in the ancestral land, needed to clean their name, and a wrong word would incite the kinspeople even here. But there is more to this silence: they want me to participate in her punishment. And I have.

In the twenty years since I heard this story I have not asked for details nor said my aunt's name; I do not know it. People who can comfort the dead can also chase after them to hurt them further—a reverse ancestor worship. The real punishment was not the raid swiftly inflicted by the villagers, but the family's deliberately forgetting her. Her betrayal so maddened them, they saw to it that she would suffer forever, even after death. Always hungry, always needing, she would have to beg food from other ghosts, snatch and steal it from those whose living descendants give them gifts. She would have to fight the ghosts massed at crossroads for the buns a few thoughtful citizens leave to decoy her away from village and home so that the ancestral spirits could feast unharassed. At peace, they could act like gods, not ghosts, their descent lines providing them with paper suits and dresses, spirit money, paper houses, paper automobiles, chicken, meat, and rice into eternity—essences delivered up in smoke and flames, steam and incense rising from each rice bowl. In an attempt to make the Chinese care for people outside the family, Chairman Mao encourages us now to give our paper replicas to the spirits of outstanding soldiers and workers, no matter whose ancestors they may be. My aunt remains forever hungry. Goods are not distributed evenly among the dead.

My aunt haunts me—her ghost drawn to me because now, after fifty years of neglect, I alone devote pages of paper to her, though not origamied into houses and clothes. I do not think she always means me well. I am telling on her, and she was a spite suicide, drowning herself in the drinking water. The Chinese are always very frightened of the drowned one, whose weeping ghost, wet hair hanging and skin bloated, waits silently by the water to pull down a substitute.

Thirty-Eight Who Saw Murder Didn't Call the Police

Martin Gansberg

For more than half an hour thirty-eight respectable, law-abiding citizens in Queens watched a killer stalk and stab a woman in three separate attacks in Kew Gardens.

Twice their chatter and the sudden glow of their bedroom lights interrupted him and frightened him off. Each time he returned, sought her out, and stabbed her again. Not one person telephoned the police during the assault; one witness called after the woman was dead.

That was two weeks ago today.

Still shocked is Assistant Chief Inspector Frederick M. Lussen, in charge of the borough's detectives and a veteran of twenty-five years of homicide investigations. He can give a matter-of-fact recitation on many murders. But the Kew Gardens slaying baffles him—not because it is a murder, but because the "good people" failed to call the police.

"As we have reconstructed the crime," he said, "the assailant had three chances to kill this woman during a thirty-five-minute period. He returned twice to complete the job. If we had been called when he first attacked, the woman might not be dead now."

This is what the police say happened beginning at 3:20 A.M. in the staid, middle-class, tree-lined Austin Street area:

Twenty-eight-year-old Catherine Genovese, who was called Kitty by almost everyone in the neighborhood, was returning home from her job as manager of a bar in Hollis. She parked her red Fiat in a lot adjacent to the Kew Gardens Long Island Rail Road Station, facing Mowbray Place.

Like many residents of the neighborhood, she had parked there day after day since her arrival from Connecticut a year ago, although the railroad frowns on the practice.

She turned off the lights of her car, locked the door, and started to walk the one hundred feet to the entrance of her apartment at 82-70 Austin Street, which is in a Tudor building, with stores in the first floor and apartments on the second.

The entrance to the apartment is in the rear of the building because the front is rented to retail stores. At night the quiet neighborhood is shrouded in the slumbering darkness that marks most residential areas.

Miss Genovese noticed a man at the far end of the lot, near a seven-story apartment house at 82-40 Austin Street. She halted. Then, nervously, she headed up Austin Street toward Lefferts Boulevard, where there is a call box to the 102nd Police Precinct in nearby Richmond Hill.

She got as far as a street light in front of a bookstore before the man grabbed her. She screamed. Lights went on in the ten-story apartment house at 82-67 Austin Street, which faces the bookstore. Windows slid open and voices punctuated the early-morning stillness.

Miss Genovese screamed: "Oh, my God, he stabbed me! Please help me! Please help me!"

From one of the upper windows in the apartment house, a man called down: "Let that girl alone!"

The assailant looked up at him, shrugged, and walked down Austin Street toward a white sedan parked a short distance away. Miss Genovese struggled to her feet.

Lights went out. The killer returned to Miss Genovese, now trying to make her way around the side of the building by the parking lot to get to her apartment. The assailant stabbed her again.

"I'm dying!" she shrieked. "I'm dying!"

Windows were opened again, and lights went on in many apartments. The assailant got into his car and drove away. Miss Genovese staggered to her feet. A city bus, 0–10, the Lefferts Boulevard line to Kennedy International Airport, passed. It was 3:35 A.M.

The assailant returned. By then, Miss Genovese had crawled to the back of the building, where the freshly painted brown doors to the apartment house held out hope for safety. The killer tried the first door; she wasn't there. At the second door, 82-62 Austin Street, he saw her slumped on the floor at the foot of the stairs. He stabbed her a third time—fatally.

It was 3:50 by the time the police received their first call, from a man who was a neighbor of Miss Genovese. In two minutes they were at the scene. The neighbor, a seventy-year-old woman, and another woman were the only persons on the street. Nobody else came forward.

The man explained that he had called the police after much deliberation. He had phoned a friend in Nassau County for advice, and then he had crossed the roof of the building to the apartment of the elderly woman to get her to make the call.

"I didn't want to get involved," he sheepishly told police.

Six days later, the police arrested Winston Moseley, a twenty-nine-year-old business machine operator, and charged him with homicide. Moseley had no previous record. He is married, has two children, and owns a home at 133-19 Sutter Avenue, South Ozone Park, Queens. On Wednesday, a court committed him to Kings County Hospital for psychiatric observation.

When questioned by the police, Moseley also said that he had slain Mrs. Annie May Johnson, twenty-four, of 146-12 133d Avenue, Jamaica, on Feb. 29 and Barbara Kralik, fifteen, of 174-17 140th Avenue, Springfield Gardens, last July. In the Kralik case, the police are holding Alvin L. Mitchell, who is said to have confessed to that slaying.

The police stressed how simple it would have been to have gotten in touch with them. "A phone call," said one of the detectives, "would have done it." The police may be reached by dialing "0" for operator or SPring 7-3100.

Today witnesses from the neighborhood, which is made up of one-family homes in the $35,000 to $60,000 range with the exception of the two apartment houses near the railroad station, find it difficult to explain why they didn't call the police.

A housewife, knowingly if quite casually, said, "We thought it was a lovers' quarrel." A husband and wife both said, "Frankly, we were afraid." They seemed aware of the fact that events might have been different. A distraught woman, wiping her hands in her apron, said, "I didn't want my husband to get involved."

One couple, now willing to talk about that night, said they heard the first screams. The husband looked thoughtfully at the bookstore where the killer first grabbed Miss Genovese.

"We went to the window to see what was happening," he said, "but the light from our bedroom made it difficult to see the street." The wife, still apprehensive, added: "I put out the light and we were able to see better."

Asked why they hadn't called the police, she shrugged and replied: "I don't know."

A man peeked out from a slight opening in the doorway to his apartment and rattled off an account of the killer's second attack. Why hadn't he called the police at the time? "I was tired," he said without emotion. "I went back to bed."

It was 4:25 A.M. when the ambulance arrived to take the body of Miss Genovese. It drove off. "Then," a solemn police detective said, "the people came out."

The Back of the Bus

Mary Mebane

Historically, my lifetime is important because I was part of the last generation born into a world of total legal segregation in the Southern United States. When the Supreme Court outlawed segregation in the public schools in 1954, I was twenty-one. When Congress passed the Civil Rights Act of 1964, permitting blacks free access to public places, I was thirty-one. The world I was born into had been segregated for a long time—so long, in fact, that I never met anyone who had lived during the time when restrictive laws were not in existence, although some people spoke of parents and others who had lived during the "free" time. As far as anyone knew, the laws as they then existed would stand forever. They were meant to—and did—create a world that fixed black people at the bottom of society in all aspects of human life. It was a world without options.

Most Americans have never had to live with terror. I had had to live with it all my life—the psychological terror of segregation, in which there was a special set of laws governing your movements. You violated them at your peril, for you knew that if you broke one of them, knowingly or not, physical terror was just around the corner, in the form of policemen and jails, and in some cases and places white vigilante mobs formed for the exclusive purpose of keeping blacks in line.

It was Saturday morning, like any Saturday morning in dozens of Southern towns.

The town had a washed look. The street sweepers had been busy since six o'clock. Now, at eight, they were still slowly moving down the streets, white trucks with clouds of water coming from underneath the swelled tubular sides. Unwary motorists sometimes got a windowful of water as a truck passed by. As it moved on, it left in its wake a clear stream running in the gutters or splashed on the wheels of parked cars.

Homeowners, bent over industriously in the morning sun, were out pushing lawn mowers. The sun was bright, but it wasn't too hot. It was morning and it was May. Most of the mowers were glad that it was finally getting warm enough to go outside.

Traffic was brisk. Country people were coming into town early with their produce; clerks and service workers were getting to the job before the stores opened at ten o'clock. Though the big stores would not be open for another hour or so, the grocery stores, banks, open-air markets, dinettes, were already open and filling with staff and customers.

Everybody was moving toward the heart of Durham's downtown, which waited to receive them rather complacently, little knowing that in a decade the shopping centers far from the center of downtown Durham would create a ghost town in the midst of the busiest blocks on Main Street.

Some moved by car, and some moved by bus. The more affluent used cars, leaving the buses mainly to the poor, black and white, though there were some businesspeople who avoided the trouble of trying to find a parking place downtown by riding the bus.

I didn't mind taking the bus on Saturday. It wasn't so crowded. At night or on Saturday or Sunday was the best time. If there were plenty of seats, the blacks didn't have to worry about being asked to move so that a white person could sit down. And the knot of hatred and fear didn't come into my stomach.

I knew the stop that was the safety point, both going and coming. Leaving town, it was the Little Five Points, about five or six blocks north of the main downtown section. That was the last stop at which four or five people might get on. After the stop, the driver could sometimes pass two or three stops without taking on or letting off a passenger. So the number of seats on the bus usually remained constant on the trip from town to Braggtown. The nearer the bus got to the end of the line, the more I relaxed. For if a white passenger got on near the end of the line, often to catch the return trip back and avoid having to stand in the sun at the bus stop until the bus turned around, he or she would usually stand if there were not seats in the white section, and the driver would say nothing, knowing that the end of the line was near and that the standee would get a seat in a few minutes.

On the trip to town, the Mangum Street A&P was the last point at which the driver picked up more passengers than he let off. These people, though they were just a few blocks from the downtown section, preferred to ride the bus downtown. Those getting on at the A&P were usually on their way to work at the Duke University Hospital—past the downtown section, through a residential neighborhood, and then past the university, before they got to Duke Hospital.

So whether the driver discharged more passengers than he took on near the A&P on Mangum was of great importance. For if he took on more passengers than got off, it meant that some of the newcomers would have to stand. And if they were white, the driver was going to have to ask a black passenger to move so that a white passenger could sit down. Most of the drivers had a rule of thumb, though. By custom the seats behind the exit door had become "colored" seats, and no matter how many whites stood up, anyone sitting behind the exit door knew that he or she wouldn't have to move.

The disputed seat, though, was the one directly opposite the exit door. It was "no-man's-land." White people sat there, and black people sat there. It all depended on whose section was fuller. If the back section was full, the next black passenger who got on sat in the no-man's-land seat; but if the white section filled up, a white person would take the seat. Another thing about the white people: they could sit anywhere they chose, even in the "colored" section. Only the black passengers had to obey segregation laws.

On this Saturday morning Esther and I set out for town for our music lesson. We were going on our weekly big adventure, all the way across town, through the white downtown, then across the railroad tracks, then through the "colored" downtown, a section of run-down dingy shops, through some fading high class black neighborhoods, past North Carolina College, to Mrs. Shearin's house.

We walked the two miles from Wildwood to the bus line. Though it was a warm day, in the early morning there was dew on the grass and the air still had the night's softness. So we walked along and talked and looked back constantly, hoping someone we knew would stop and pick us up.

I looked back furtively, for in one of the few instances that I remembered my father criticizing me severely, it was for looking back. One day when I was walking from town he had passed in his old truck. I had been looking back and had seen him. "Don't look back," he had said. "People will think that you want them to pick you up." Though he said "people,"

I knew he meant men—not the men he knew, who lived in the black community, but the black men who were not part of the community, and all of the white men. To be picked up meant that something bad would happen to me. Still, two miles is a long walk and I occasionally joined Esther in looking back to see if anyone we knew was coming.

Esther and I got to the bus and sat on one of the long seats at the back that faced each other. There were three such long seats—one on each side of the bus and a third long seat at the very back that faced the front. I liked to sit on a long seat facing the side because then I didn't have to look at the expressions on the faces of the whites when they put their tokens in and looked at the blacks sitting in the back of the bus. Often I studied my music, looking down and practicing the fingering. I looked up at each stop to see who was getting on and to check on the seating pattern. The seating pattern didn't really bother me that day until the bus started to get unusually full for a Saturday morning. I wondered what was happening, where all these people were coming from. They got on and got on until the white section was almost full and the black section was full.

There was a black man in a blue windbreaker and a gray porkpie hat sitting in no-man's-land, and my stomach tightened. I wondered what would happen. I had never been on a bus on which a black person was asked to give a seat to a white person when there was no other seat empty. Usually, though, I had seen a black person automatically get up, and move to an empty seat farther back. But this morning the only empty seat was beside a black person sitting in no-man's-land.

The bus stopped at Little Five Points and one black got off. A young white man was getting on. I tensed. What would happen now? Would the driver ask the black man to get up and move to the empty seat farther back? The white man had a businessman's air about him: suit, shirt, tie, polished brown shoes. He saw the empty seat in the "colored" section and after just a little hesitation went to it, put his briefcase down, and sat with his feet crossed. I relaxed a little when the bus pulled off without the driver saying anything. Evidently he hadn't seen what had happened, or since he was just a few stops from Main Street, he figured the mass exodus there would solve all the problems. Still, I was afraid of a scene.

The next stop was an open-air fruit stand just after Little Five Points, and here another white man got on. Where would he sit? The only available seat was beside the black man. Would he stand the few stops to Main Street or would the driver make the black man move? The whole colored section tensed, but nobody said anything. I looked at Esther, who looked apprehensive. I looked at the other men and women, who studiously avoided my eyes and everybody else's as well, as they maintained a steady gaze at a far-distant land.

Just one woman caught my eye; I had noticed her before, and I had been ashamed of her. She was a stringy little black woman. She could have been forty; she could have been fifty. She looked as if she were a hard drinker. Flat black face with tight features. She was dressed with great insouciance in a tight boy's sweater with horizontal lines running across her flat chest. It pulled down over a nondescript skirt. Laced-up shoes, socks, and a head rag completed her outfit. She looked tense.

The white man who had just gotten on the bus walked to the seat in no-man's-land and stood there. He wouldn't sit down, just stood there. Two adult males, living in the most highly industrialized, most technologically advanced nation in the world, a nation that had devastated two other industrial giants in World War II and had flirted with taking on China in Korea. Both these men, either of whom could have fought for the United States in Germany or Korea, faced each other in mutual rage and hostility. The white one wanted to sit down, but he was going to exert his authority and force the black one to get up first. I watched the driver in the rearview mirror. He was about the same age as the antagonists. The driver wasn't looking for trouble, either.

"Say there, buddy, how about moving back," the driver said, meanwhile driving his bus just as fast as he could. The whole bus froze—whites at the front, blacks at the rear. They didn't want to believe what was happening was really happening.

The seated black man said nothing. The standing white man said nothing.

"Say, buddy, did you hear me? What about moving on back." The driver was scared to death. I could tell that.

"These is the niggers' seats!" the little lady in the strange outfit started screaming. I jumped. I had to shift my attention from the driver to the frieze of the black man seated and white man standing to the articulate little woman who had joined in the fray.

"The government gave us these seats! These is the niggers' seats." I was startled at her statement and her tone. "The president said that these are the niggers' seats!" I expected her to start fighting at any moment.

Evidently the bus driver did, too, because he was driving faster and faster. I believe that he forgot he was driving a bus and wanted desperately to pull to the side of the street and get out and run.

"I'm going to take you down to the station, buddy," the driver said.

The white man with the briefcase and the polished brown shoes who had taken a seat in the "colored" section looked as though he might die of embarrassment at any moment.

As scared and upset as I was, I didn't miss a thing.

By that time we had come to the stop before Main Street, and the black passenger rose to get off.

"You're not getting off, buddy. I'm going to take you downtown." The driver kept driving as he talked and seemed to be trying to get downtown as fast as he could.

"These are the niggers' seats! The government plainly said these are the niggers' seats!" screamed the little woman in rage.

I was embarrassed at the use of the word "nigger" but I was proud of the lady. I was also proud of the man who wouldn't get up.

The bus driver was afraid, trying to hold on to his job but plainly not willing to get into a row with the blacks.

The bus seemed to be going a hundred miles an hour and everybody was anxious to get off, though only the lady and the driver were saying anything.

The black man stood at the exit door; the driver drove right past the A&P stop. I was terrified. I was sure that the bus was going to the police station to put the black man in jail. The little woman had her hands on her hips and she never stopped yelling. The bus driver kept driving as fast as he could.

Then, somewhere in the back of his mind, he decided to forget the whole thing. The next stop was Main Street, and when he got there, in what seemed to be a flash of lightning, he flung both doors open wide. He and his black antagonist looked at each other in the rearview mirror; in a second the windbreaker and porkpie hat were gone. The little woman was standing, preaching to the whole bus about the government's gift of these seats to the blacks; the man with the brown shoes practically fell out of the door in his hurry; and Esther and I followed the hurrying footsteps.

We walked about three doors down the block, then caught a bus to the black neighborhood. Here we sat on one of the two long seats facing each other, directly behind the driver. It was the custom. Since this bus had a route from a black neighborhood to the downtown section and back, passing through no white residential areas, blacks could sit where they chose. One minute we had been on a bus in which violence was threatened over a seat near the exit door; the next minute we were sitting in the very front behind the driver.

The people who devised this system thought that it was going to last forever.

The Fourth of July

Audre Lorde

The first time I went to Washington, D.C., was on the edge of the summer when I was supposed to stop being a child. At least that's what they said to us all at graduation from the eighth grade. My sister Phyllis graduated at the same time from high school. I don't know what she was supposed to stop being. But as graduation presents for us both, the whole family took a Fourth of July trip to Washington, D.C., the fabled and famous capital of our country.

It was the first time I'd ever been on a railroad train during the day. When I was little, and we used to go to the Connecticut shore, we always went at night on the milk train, because it was cheaper.

Preparations were in the air around our house before school was even over. We packed for a week. There were two very large suitcases that my father carried, and a box filled with food. In fact, my first trip to Washington was a mobile feast; I started eating as soon as we were comfortably ensconced in our seats, and did not stop until somewhere after Philadelphia. I remember it was Philadelphia because I was disappointed not to have passed by the Liberty Bell.

My mother had roasted two chickens and cut them up into dainty bite-size pieces. She packed slices of brown bread and butter and green pepper and carrot sticks. There were little violently yellow iced cakes with scalloped edges called "marigolds," that came from Cushman's Bakery. There was a spice bun and rock-cakes from Newton's, the West Indian bakery across Lenox Avenue from St. Mark's School, and iced tea in a wrapped mayonnaise jar. There were sweet pickles for us and dill pickles for my father, and peaches with the fuzz still on them, individually wrapped to keep them from bruising. And, for neatness, there were piles of napkins and a little tin box with a washcloth dampened with rose-water and glycerine for wiping sticky mouths.

I wanted to eat in the dining car because I had read all about them, but my mother reminded me for the umpteenth time that dining car food always cost too much money and besides, you never could tell whose hands had been playing all over that food, nor where those same hands had been just before. My mother never mentioned that black people were not allowed into railroad dining cars headed south in 1947. As usual, whatever my mother did not like and could not change, she ignored. Perhaps it would go away, deprived of her attention.

I learned later that Phyllis's high school senior class trip had been to Washington, but the nuns had given her back her deposit in private, explaining to her that the class, all of whom were white, except Phyllis, would be staying in a hotel where Phyllis "would not be happy," meaning, Daddy explained to her, also in private, that they did not rent rooms to Negroes. "We will take you to Washington, ourselves," my father had avowed, "and not just for an overnight in some measly fleabag hotel."

American racism was a new and crushing reality that my parents had to deal with every day of their lives once they came to this country. They handled it as a private woe. My mother and father believed that they could best protect their children from the realities of race in America and the fact of American racism by never giving them name, much less discussing their nature. We were told we must never trust white people, but *why* was never explained, nor the nature of their ill will. Like so many other vital pieces of information in my childhood, I was supposed to know without being told. It always seemed like a very strange injunction coming from my mother, who looked so much like one of those people we were never supposed to trust. But something always warned me not to ask my mother why she wasn't white, and why Auntie Lillah and Auntie Etta weren't, even though they were all that same problematic color so different from my father and me, even from my sisters, who were somewhere in-between.

In Washington, D.C., we had one large room with two double beds and an extra cot for me. It was a back-street hotel that belonged to a friend of my father's who was in real estate, and I spent the whole next day after Mass squinting up at the Lincoln Memorial where Marian Anderson had sung after the D.A.R. refused to allow her to sing in their auditorium because she was black. Or because she was "Colored," my father said as he told us the story. Except that what he probably said was "Negro," because for his times, my father was quite progressive.

I was squinting because I was in that silent agony that characterized all of my childhood summers, from the time school let out in June to the end of July, brought about by my dilated and vulnerable eyes exposed to the summer brightness.

I viewed Julys through an agonizing corolla of dazzling whiteness and I always hated the Fourth of July, even before I came to realize the travesty such a celebration was for black people in this country.

My parents did not approve of sunglasses, nor of their expense.

I spent the afternoon squinting up at monuments to freedom and past presidencies and democracy, and wondering why the light and heat were both so much stronger in Washington, D.C., than back home in New York City. Even the pavement on the streets was a shade lighter in color than back home.

Late that Washington afternoon my family and I walked back down Pennsylvania Avenue. We were a proper caravan, mother bright and father brown, the three of us girls step-standards in-between. Moved by our historical surroundings and the heat of early evening, my father decreed yet another treat. He had a great sense of history, a flair for the quietly dramatic and the sense of specialness of an occasion and a trip.

"Shall we stop and have a little something to cool off, Lin?"

Two blocks away from our hotel, the family stopped for a dish of vanilla ice cream at a Breyer's ice cream and soda fountain. Indoors, the soda fountain was dim and fan-cooled, deliciously relieving to my scorched eyes.

Corded and crisp and pinafored, the five of us seated ourselves one by one at the counter. There was I between my mother and father, and my two sisters on the other side of my mother. We settled ourselves along the white mottled marble counter, and when the waitress spoke at first no one understood what she was saying, and so the five of us just sat there.

The waitress moved along the line of us closer to my father and spoke again. "I said I kin give you to take out, but you can't eat here. Sorry." Then she dropped her eyes looking very embarrassed, and suddenly we heard what it was she was saying all at the same time, loud and clear.

Straight-backed and indignant, one by one, my family and I got down from the counter stools and turned around and marched out of the store, quiet and outraged, as if we had never been black before. No one would answer my emphatic questions with anything other than a guilty silence. "But we hadn't done anything!" This wasn't right or fair! Hadn't I written poems about Bataan and freedom and democracy for all?

My parents wouldn't speak of this injustice, not because they had contributed to it, but because they felt they should have anticipated it and avoided it. This made me even angrier. My fury was not going to be acknowledged by a like fury. Even my two sisters copied my parents' pretense that nothing unusual and anti-American had occurred. I was left to write my angry letter to the president of the United States all by myself, although my father did promise I could type it out on the office typewriter next week, after I showed it to him in my copybook diary.

The waitress was white, and the counter was white, and the ice cream I never ate in Washington, D.C., that summer I left childhood was white, and the white heat and the white pavement and the white stone monuments of my first Washington summer made me sick to my stomach for the whole rest of that trip and it wasn't much of a graduation present after all.

Description

Description

"Write like Hemingway," editors often told cub reporters because Ernest Hemingway's concise style was shaped by his experience as a war correspondent sending his stories over the telegraph. While conciseness was one of Hemingway's virtues, his other virtue was to write using concrete words and significant details to make his writing come alive and to connect with the reader's senses of hearing, sight, smell, taste, and touch.

Like narration, description is familiar to us and a frequent element in our conversations. We readily describe the steepness of the mountain trail we hiked, the stomach-dropping thrill of bungee-cord jumping for the first time, the palate pleasures of a good meal, or acrid odors of a failed attempt at barbecuing. Description has its place in essay writing because the specific details used bring a sense of immediacy, enliven the writing, and invite the reader in.

The Process

Purpose

Because of its involvement with the senses, description is used to communicate a particular experience by creating a dominant impression that the details relate to. For example, Joan Didion in "The Santa Ana" conveys a particular impression of the Santa Ana winds of Los Angeles when she chooses to write the following details:

> The Pacific turned ominously glossy during a Santa Ana period, and one woke in the night troubled not only by the peacocks screaming in the olive trees but by the eerie absence of surf. The heat was surreal. The sky had a yellow cast, the kind of light sometimes called "earthquake weather.

By choosing her details carefully, Didion presents the reader not only with a clear description of the physical manifestations of the wind but also its emotional tone.

As with narration, you must decide what your purpose is in writing a description essay about your subject—which could be an object, a person, a place, a natural phenomenon, an emotion—what your involvement with the subject is, and what audience you want to reach. What do you want to accomplish for the readers? What do you want readers to experience? What perceptions do you want to share with readers? The answers to these questions will determine if you will write an objective description or a subjective description.

An *objective* description is factual without an emotion connection whereas a *subjective* description filters the information through the writer's feelings or the feelings the writer wants to convey. A description of Mount Washington in New Hampshire and its geological formation would provide descriptive detail but objectively, without any personal inferences. A description of a hike up Tuckerman's Ravine with its challenges and achievements that were life-changing for the writer, however, would convey sensory details subjectively, drawing clearly on the emotions of a first-hand experience.

Thesis

Once you have determined the purpose of your essay and what impression you want to create for the reader, make it clear in a sentence that will serve as your thesis. As with all essays, the thesis presents the main idea or point you are making and also serves as a guide for choosing the information and descriptions that support your main idea.

The thesis should evoke a sensory image as these examples do.

Objective: Mount Washington's rocky peak dominates the Presidential Range, enveloped in its own atmosphere, the massive quartz and mica schist boulders of Tuckerman's Ravine a devil to climb.

Subjective: Bruised, tired, muscles screaming, and snow swirling around me, I looked down from the summit of the "Home of the World's Worst Weather" at the four grueling, vertical miles of massive boulders that comprise the mountain top.

Organization

With a sense of purpose and a clear thesis as a guide, you need to examine your subject in all its and aspects to determine what details are important to the impression you want to convey and what details are needed for readers who may not be familiar with your subject. The challenge will be in choosing where detail will have the most significance in serving your purpose and supporting your dominant impression. You do not want to use detail everywhere or the effect will be lessoned and the essay will be tiresome to read. You also want to avoid vagueness by choosing details that are concrete and have power. *Concrete* means things you can perceive with the five senses—tastes, smells, sounds, sights, touches. The opposite of concrete is *abstract*. Thoughts, opinions, feelings, ideas are abstract; you cannot perceive them with the five senses.

Concrete language uses words or passages that evoke sensation—they make you feel like you are smelling, seeing, hearing, etc., when you read them. Abstract words don't. Here is an example of how to make writing concrete and more alive.

Abstract: He was nervous.

Concrete: His eyes were twitching, his hands were trembling, his brow was coated with sweat, and he kept pacing back and forth mumbling to himself.

To master the technique of using concrete words, ask yourself:

- Can I see it clearly in my mind?
- Can I hear just how it sounds?
- Can I get a sense for how it feels?
- What does it sound like?
- Can I taste it?

The Feedlot

Making Meat
(54,000 Kernels)

Michael Pollan

1. Cattle Metropolis

The landscape that corn has made in the American Middle West is unmistakable: It forms a second great American lawn, unfurling through the summer like an absurdly deep-pile carpet of green across the vast lands drained by the Mississippi River. Corn the plant has colonized some 125,000 square miles of the American continent, an area twice the size of New York State; even from outer space you can't miss it. It takes a bit more looking, however, to see some of the other landscapes that corn-the-commodity has created, in obscure places like Garden City, Kansas. Here in the high plains of western Kansas is where America's first feedlots were built, beginning in the early fifties.

You'll be speeding down one of Finney County's ramrod roads when the empty, dun-colored January prairie suddenly turns black and geometric, an urban grid of steel-fenced rectangles as far as the eye can see—which in Kansas is really far. I say "suddenly" but in fact the swiftly rising odor—an aroma whose Proustian echoes are decidedly more bus station men's room than cows in the country—has been heralding the feedlot's approach for more than a mile. And then it's upon you: Poky Feeders, population, thirty-seven thousand. A sloping subdivision of,cattle pens stretches to the horizon, each one home to a hundred or so animals standing dully or lying around in a grayish mud that, it eventually dawns on you, isn't mud at all. The pens line a network of unpaved roads that loop around vast waste lagoons on their way to the feedyard's thunderously beating heart and dominating landmark: a rhythmically chugging feed mill that rises, soaring and silvery in the early morning light, like an industrial cathedral in the midst of a teeming metropolis of meat. As it does twelve hours a day seven days a week, the mill is noisily converting America's river of corn into cattle feed.

I'd traveled to Poky early one January with the slightly improbable notion of visiting one particular resident, though as I nosed my rental car through the feedlot's rolling black sea of bovinity I began to wonder if this was realistic. I was looking for a young black steer with three white blazes on his face that I'd met the previous fall on a ranch in Vale, South Dakota, five hundred miles due north of here. In fact, the steer I hoped to find belonged to me: I'd purchased him as an eight-month-old calf from the Blair Ranch for $598. I was paying Poky Feeders $1.60 a day for his room and board (all the corn he could eat) and meds.

My interest in this steer was not strictly financial, or even gustatory. No, my primary interest in this animal was educational. I wanted to learn how the industrial food chain transforms bushels of corn into steaks. How do you enlist so unlikely a creature—for the cow is a herbivore by nature—to help dispose of America's corn surplus? By far the biggest portion of a bushel of American commodity corn (about 60 percent of it, or some fifty-four thousand kernels) goes to feeding livestock, and much of that goes to feeding America's 100 million beef cattle—cows and bulls and steers that in times past spent most of their lives grazing on grasses out on the prairie.

America's food animals have undergone a revolution in lifestyle in the years since World War II. At the same time as much of America's human population found itself leaving the city for the suburbs, our food animals found themselves traveling in the opposite direction, leaving widely dispersed farms in places like Iowa to live in densely populated new animal cities. These places are so different from farms and ranches that a new term was needed to denote them: CAFO—Concentrated Animal Feeding Operation. The new animal and human landscapes were both products of government policy. The postwar suburbs would never have been built if not for the interstate highway system, as well as the G.I. Bill and federally subsidized mortgages. The urbanization of America's animal population would never have taken place if not for the advent of cheap, federally subsidized corn.

Corn itself profited from the urbanization of livestock twice. As the animals left the farm, more of the farm was left for corn, which rapidly colonized the paddocks and pastures and even the barnyards that had once been the animals' territory. The animals left because the farmers simply couldn't compete with the CAFOs. It cost a farmer more to grow feed corn than it cost a CAFO to buy it, for the simple reason that commodity corn now was routinely sold for less than it cost to grow. Corn profited again as the factory farms expanded, absorbing increasing amounts of its surplus. Corn found its way into the diet of animals that never used to eat very much of it (like cattle) or any corn at all, like the farmed salmon now being bred to tolerate grain. All that excess biomass has to go somewhere.

The economic logic of gathering so many animals together to feed them cheap corn in CAFOs is hard to argue with; it has made meat, which used to be a special occasion in most American homes, so cheap and abundant that many of us now eat it three times a day. Not so compelling is the biological logic behind this cheap meat. Already in their short history CAFOs have produced more than their share of environmental and health problems: polluted water and air, toxic wastes, novel and deadly pathogens.

Raising animals on old-fashioned mixed farms such as the Naylors' used to make simple biological sense: You can feed them the waste products of your crops, and you can feed their waste products *to* your crops. In fact, when animals live on farms the very idea of waste ceases to exist; what you have instead is a closed ecological loop—what in retrospect you might call a solution. One of the most striking things that animal feedlots do (to paraphrase Wendell Berry) is to take this elegant solution and neatly divide it into two new problems: a fertility problem on the farm (which must be remedied with chemical fertilizers) and a pollution problem on the feedlot (which seldom is remedied at all).

This biological absurdity, characteristic of all CAFOs, is compounded in the cattle feedyard by a second absurdity. Here animals exquisitely adapted by natural selection to live on grass must be adapted by us—at considerable cost to their health, to the health of the land, and ultimately to the health of their eaters—to live on corn, for no other reason than it offers the cheapest calories around and because the great pile must be consumed. This is why I decided to follow the trail of industrial corn through a single steer rather than, say, a chicken or a pig, which can get by just fine on a diet of grain: The short, unhappy life of a corn-fed feedlot steer represents the ultimate triumph of industrial thinking over the logic of evolution.

2. Pastoral: Vale, South Dakota

The Blair Ranch occupies fifty-five hundred acres of rolling shortgrass prairie a few miles outside Sturgis, South Dakota, and directly in the shadow of Bear Butte. The Bismarck-Deadwood trail crossed its land just to the north of the butte, which rises dramatically from the plains like a chubby ten-story exclamation mark. You can still make out ruts in the turf dug by stagecoaches and cattle drives the century before last. The turf itself in November, when I visited, forms a luxuriant pelt of grass oscillating yellow and gold in the constant wind and sprinkled with perambulating black dots: Angus cows and calves, grazing.

Ed and Rich Blair run what's called a "cow-calf" operation, the first stage in the production of a hamburger and the stage least changed by the modern industrialization of meat. While the pork and chicken industries have consolidated the life cycle of those animals under a single roof, beef cattle still get born on hundreds of thousands of independently owned ranches scattered mainly across the West. Although a mere four giant meatpacking companies (Tyson subsidiary IBP, Cargill subsidiary Excel, Swift & Company, and National) now slaughter and market four of every five beef cattle born in this country, that concentration represents the narrow end of a funnel that starts out as wide as the Great Plains. These corporations have concluded that it takes so much land (and therefore capital) to produce a calf ready for the feedlot—ten acres per head at a minimum—that they're better off leaving the ranching (and the risk) to the ranchers.

Steer number 534 spent his first six months in these lush pastures alongside his mother, 9534. The number signifies she was the thirty-fourth cow born in 1995; since none of her male offspring stick around long enough to meet, they're all named 534. His father was a registered Angus by the name of Gar Precision 1680, a bull distinguished by the size and marbling of his offsprings' rib-eye steaks. Gar Precision's only contact with 9534 came by way of a fifteen-dollar mail-order straw of his semen.

Born on March 13, 2001, in the birthing shed across the road, 534 and his mother were turned out on pasture just as soon as the eighty-pound calf stood up and began nursing. Within a few weeks the calf began supplementing his mother's milk by nibbling on a salad bar of mostly native grasses: western wheatgrass, little bluestem, buffalo grass, green needlegrass.

Apart from the trauma of the Saturday in April when he was branded and castrated, one could imagine 534 looking back on those six months as the good old days. It might be foolish for us to presume to know what a cow experiences, yet we can say that a calf grazing on grass is at least doing what he has been supremely well suited by evolution to do. Oddly enough, though, eating grass is something that after October my steer will never have the opportunity to do again.

The coevolutionary relationship between cows and grass is one of nature's underappreciated wonders; it also happens to be the key to understanding just about everything about modern meat. For the grasses, which have evolved to withstand the grazing of ruminants, the cow maintains and expands their habitat by preventing trees and shrubs from gaining a foothold and hogging the sunlight; the animal also spreads grass seed, plants it with his hooves, and then fertilizes it with his manure. In exchange for these services the grasses offer ruminants a plentiful and exclusive supply of lunch. For cows (like sheep, bison, and other ruminants) have evolved the special ability to convert grass—which single-stomached creatures like us can't digest—into high-quality protein. They can do this because they possess what is surely the most highly evolved digestive organ in nature: the rumen. About the size of a medicine ball, the organ is essentially a twenty-gallon fermentation tank in which a resident population of bacteria dines on grass. Living their unseen lives at the far end of the food chain that culminates in a hamburger, these bacteria have, like the grasses, coevolved with the cow, whom they feed.

Truly this is an excellent system for all concerned: for the grasses, for the bacteria, for the animals, and for us, the animals' eaters. While it is true that overgrazing can do ecological harm to a grassland, in recent years ranchers have adopted rotational grazing patterns that more closely mimic the patterns of the bison, a ruminant that sustainably grazed these same grasses for thousands of years before the cow displaced it. In fact, a growing number of ecologists now believe the rangelands are healthier with cattle on them, provided they're moved frequently. Today the most serious environmental harm associated with the cattle industry takes place on the feedlot.

In fact, growing meat on grass makes superb ecological sense: It is a sustainable, solar-powered food chain that produces food by transforming sunlight into protein. Row crops could accomplish this trick too, but not around here: In places like western South Dakota the land is far too arid, thin, and hilly to grow crops without large amounts of irrigation, chemicals, and erosion. "My cattle can take low-quality forage and convert it into a pretty desirable product," Rich Blair pointed out. "If you didn't have ruminant animals, all this"—he gestures to the high plains rolling out from his ranch in every direction—"would be the great American desert."

So then why is it that steer number 534 hasn't tasted a blade of prairie grass since October? Speed, in a word, or, in the industry's preferred term, "efficiency." Cows raised on grass simply take longer to reach slaughter weight than cows raised on a richer diet, and for half a century now the industry has devoted itself to shortening a beef animal's allotted span on earth. "In my grandfather's time, cows were four or five years old at slaughter," Rich explained. "In the fifties, when my father was ranching, it was two or three years old. Now we get there at fourteen to sixteen months." Fast food, indeed. What gets a steer from 80 to 1,100 pounds in fourteen months is tremendous quantities of corn, protein and fat supplements, and an arsenal of new drugs.

Weaning marks the fateful moment when the natural, evolutionary logic represented by a ruminant grazing on grass bumps up against the industrial logic that will propel the animal on the rest of its swift journey to a wholesale box of beef. This industrial logic is rational and even irresistible—after all, it has succeeded in making beef everyday fare for millions of people for whom it once represented a luxury. And yet the further you follow it, the more likely you are to begin wondering if that rational logic might not also be completely mad.

In October, two weeks before I made his acquaintance, steer number 534 was weaned from his mother. Weaning is perhaps the most traumatic time on a ranch for animals and ranchers alike; cows separated from their calves will mope and bellow for days, and the calves, stressed by the change in circumstance and diet, are prone to getting sick. Calves are weaned for a couple of reasons: to free their mothers to have more calves (9534 had already been inseminated again in June), and to get the animals, now five or six hundred pounds, ready for life on the feedlot.

The animals are rounded up and herded into a "backgrounding" pen, where they'll spend a couple of months before boarding the truck for Poky Feeders. Think of backgrounding as prep school for feedlot life: The animals are, for the first time in their lives, confined to a pen, "bunk broken"—taught to eat from a trough—and gradually accustomed to eating what is for them a new and unnatural diet. Here is where the rumen first encounters corn.

It was in the backgrounding pen that I first made the acquaintance of 534. Before coming to Vale I'd told the Blairs I wanted to follow one of their steers through the life cycle; Ed Blair, the older of the brothers, suggested only half in jest that I might as well go whole hog and buy the animal, if I really wanted to appreciate the challenges of ranching. This immediately struck me as a promising idea.

Ed and Rich told me what to look for: a broad straight back and thick shoulders—basically, a sturdy frame on which to hang a lot of meat. I was also looking for a memorable face in this black Angus sea, one that I could pick out of the crowd at the feedlot. Almost as soon as I began surveying the ninety or so animals in the pen, 534 moseyed up to the railing and made eye contact. He had a wide stout frame and was brockle-faced—he had three easy-to-spot white blazes. Here was my boy.

3. Industrial: Garden City, Kansas

Traveling from the ranch to the feedyard, as 534 and I both did (in separate vehicles) the first week of January, feels a lot like going from the country to the big city. A feedlot is very much a premodern city, however, teeming and filthy and stinking, with open sewers, unpaved roads, and choking air rendered visible by dust.

The urbanization of the world's livestock being a fairly recent historical development, it makes a certain sense that cow towns like Poky Feeders would recall human cities centuries ago, in the days before modern sanitation. As in fourteenth-century London, say, the workings of the metropolitan digestion remain vividly on display, the foodstuffs coming in, the streams of waste going out. The crowding into tight quarters of recent arrivals from all over, together with the lack of sanitation, has always been a recipe for disease. The only reason contemporary animal cities aren't as plague-ridden or pestilential as their medieval human counterparts is a single historical anomaly: the modern antibiotic.

I spent the better part of a day at Poky Feeders, walking the streets, cattle watching, looking up my steer, and touring local landmarks like the towering feed mill. In any city it's easy to lose track of nature—of the transactions between various species and the land on which everything ultimately depends. Back on the ranch the underlying ecological relationship could not have been more legible: It is a local food chain built upon grass and the ruminants that can digest grass, and it draws its energy from the sun. But what about here?

As the long shadow of the mill suggests, the feedlot is a city built upon America's mountain of surplus corn—or rather, corn plus the various pharmaceuticals a ruminant must have if it is to tolerate corn. Yet, having started out from George Naylor's farm, I understood that the corn on which this place runs is implicated in a whole other set of ecological relationships powered by a very different source of energy—the fossil fuel it takes to grow all that corn. So if the modern CAFO is a city built upon commodity corn, it is a city afloat on an invisible sea of petroleum. How this peculiar state of affairs came to seem sensible is a question I spent my day at Poky trying to answer.

It was only natural that I start my tour at the feed mill, the feedlot's thundering hub, where three meals a day for thirty-seven thousand animals are designed and mixed by computer. A million pounds of feed pass through the mill each day. Every hour of every day a tractor trailer pulls up to the loading dock to deliver another fifty tons of corn. The driver opens a valve in the belly of the truck and a golden stream of grain—one thin rivulet of the great corn river coursing out of the Middle West—begins to flow, dropping down a chute into the bowels of the mill. Around to the other side of the building, tanker trucks back up to silo-shaped tanks into which they pump thousands of gallons of liquefied fat and protein supplements. In a shed attached to the mill sit vats of liquid vitamins and synthetic estrogen beside pallets stacked with fifty-pound sacks of antibiotics—Rumensin and Tylosin. Along with alfalfa hay and silage (for roughage), all these ingredients will be automatically blended and then piped into the parade of dump trucks that three times a day fan out from here to keep Poky's eight and a half miles of trough filled.

The feed mill's pulsing din is the sound of two giant steel rollers turning against one another twelve hours a day, crushing steamed corn kernels into warm and fragrant flakes. (Flaking the corn makes it easier for cattle to digest it.) This was the only feed ingredient I sampled, and it wasn't half bad; not as crisp as a Kellogg's flake, but with a cornier flavor. I passed on the other ingredients: the liquefied fat (which on today's menu is beef tallow, trucked in from one of the nearby slaughterhouses), and the protein supplement, a sticky brown goop consisting of molasses and urea. The urea is a form of synthetic nitrogen made from natural gas, similar to the fertilizer spread on George Naylor's fields.

Before being put on this highly concentrated diet, new arrivals to the feedyard are treated to a few days of fresh long-stemmed hay (They don't eat on the long ride and can lose up to one hundred pounds, so their rumens need to be carefully restarted.) Over the next several weeks they'll gradually step up to a daily ration of thirty-two pounds of feed, three-quarters of which is corn—nearly a half bushel a day.

What got corn onto the menu at this and almost every other American feedlot is price, of course, but also USDA policy, which for decades has sought to help move the mountain of surplus corn by passing as much of it as possible through the digestive tracts of food animals, who can convert it into protein.

We've come to think of "corn-fed" as some kind of old-fashioned virtue, which it may well be when you're referring to Midwestern children, but feeding large quantities of corn to cows for the greater part of their lives is a practice neither particularly old nor virtuous. Its chief advantage is that cows fed corn, a compact source of caloric energy, get fat quickly; their flesh also marbles well, giving it a taste and texture American consumers have come to like. Yet this corn-fed meat is demonstrably less healthy for us, since it contains more saturated fat and less omega-3 fatty acids than the meat of animals fed grass. A growing body of research suggests that many of the health problems associated with eating beef are really problems with corn-fed beef. (Modern-day hunter-gatherers who subsist on wild meat don't have our rates of heart disease.) In the same way ruminants are ill adapted to eating corn, humans in turn may be poorly adapted to eating ruminants that eat corn.

Yet the USDA's grading system has been designed to reward marbling (a more appealing term than "intramuscular fat," which is what it is) and thus the feeding of corn to cattle. Indeed, corn has become so deeply ingrained in the whole system of producing beef in America that whenever I raised any questions about it among ranchers or feed-lot operators or animal scientists, people looked at me as if I'd just arrived from another planet. (Or perhaps from Argentina, where excellent steaks are produced on nothing but grass.)

The economic logic behind corn is unassailable, and on a factory farm there is no other kind. Calories are calories, and corn is the cheapest, most convenient source of calories on the market. Of course, it was the same industrial logic—protein is protein—that made feeding rendered cow parts back to cows seem like a sensible thing to do, until scientists figured out that this practice was spreading bovine spongiform encephalopathy (BSE), more commonly known as mad cow disease. Rendered bovine meat and bonemeal represented the cheapest, most convenient way of satisfying a cow's protein requirement (never mind these animals were herbivores by evolution) and so appeared on the daily menus of Poky and most other feedyards until the Food and Drug Administration (FDA) banned the practice in 1997.

We now understand that while at a reductive, molecular level protein may indeed be protein, at an ecological or species level, this isn't quite true. As cannibal tribes have discovered, eating the flesh of one's own species carries special risks of infection. Kuru, a disease bearing a striking resemblance to BSE, spread among New Guinea tribesmen who ritually ate the brains of their dead kin. Some evolutionary biologists believe that evolution selected against cannibalism as a way to avoid such infections; animals' aversion to their own feces, and the carcasses of their species, may represent a similar strategy. Through natural selection animals have developed a set of hygiene rules, functioning much like taboos. One of the most troubling things about factory farms is how cavalierly they flout these evolutionary rules, forcing animals to overcome deeply ingrained aversions. We make them trade their instincts for antibiotics.

Though the industrial logic that made feeding cattle to cattle seem like a good idea has been thrown into doubt by mad cow disease, I was surprised to learn it hadn't been discarded. The FDA ban on feeding ruminant protein to ruminants makes an exception for blood products and fat; my steer will probably dine on beef tallow recycled from the very slaughterhouse he's heading to in June. ("Fat is fat," the feedlot manager shrugged, when I raised an eyebrow.) Though Poky doesn't do it, the rules still permit feedlots to feed nonruminant animal protein to ruminants. Feather meal and chicken litter (that is, bedding, feces, and discarded bits of feed) are accepted cattle feeds, as are chicken, fish, and pig meal. Some public health experts worry that since the bovine meat and bonemeal that cows used to eat is now being fed to chickens, pigs, and fish, infectious prions could find their way back into cattle when they're fed the protein of the animals that have been eating them.

Before mad cow disease remarkably few people in the cattle business, let alone the general public, comprehended the strange new semi-circular food chain that industrial agriculture had devised for the beef animal—and so, in turn, for the beef eater. When I mentioned to Rich Blair how surprised I'd been to learn cattle were eating cattle, he said, "To tell you the truth, it was kind of a shock to me, too."

Compared to all the other things we feed cattle these days, corn seems positively wholesome. And yet it too violates the biological or evolutionary logic of bovine digestion. During my day at Poky I spent a few hours with Dr. Mel Metzin, the staff veterinarian, learning more than any beef eater really should know about the gastrointestinal life of the modern cow. Dr. Mel, as he's known at Poky, oversees a team of eight cowboys who spend their days riding the yard's dusty streets, spotting sick animals and bringing them into Poky's three "hospitals" for treatment. Most of the health problems that afflict feedlot cattle can be traced either directly or indirectly to their diet. "They're made to eat forage," Dr. Metzin explained, "and we're making them eat grain."

"It's not that they can't adjust," he continues, "and now we're breeding cattle to do well in a feedyard." One way to look at the breeding work going on at ranches like the Blairs' is that the contemporary beef cow is being selected for the ability to eat large quantities of corn and efficiently convert it to protein without getting too sick. (These, after all, are precisely the genes prized in 534's father, Gar Precision 1680.) The species is evolving, in other words, to help absorb the excess biomass coming off America's cornfields. But the cow's not there quite yet, and a great many feedlot cattle—virtually all of them to one degree or another, according to several animal scientists I talked to—are simply sick.

Bloat is perhaps the most serious thing that can go wrong with a ruminant on corn. The fermentation in the rumen produces copious amounts of gas, which is normally expelled by belching during rumination. But when the diet contains too much starch and too little roughage, rumination all but stops, and a layer of foamy slime forms in the rumen that can trap the gas. The rumen inflates like a balloon until it presses against the animal's lungs. Unless action is taken promptly to relieve the pressure (usually by forcing a hose down the animal's esophagus), the animal suffocates.

A concentrated diet of corn can also give a cow acidosis. Unlike our own highly acid stomachs, the normal pH of a rumen is neutral. Corn renders it acidic, causing a kind of bovine heartburn that in some cases can kill the animal, but usually just makes him sick. Acidotic animals go off their feed, pant and salivate excessively, paw and scratch their bellies, and eat dirt. The condition can lead to diarrhea, ulcers, bloat, rumenitis, liver disease, and a general weakening of the immune system that leaves the animal vulnerable to the full panoply of feedlot diseases—pneumonia, coccidiosis, enterotoxemia, feedlot polio. Much like modern humans, modern cattle are susceptible to a set of relatively new diseases of civilization—assuming, that is, we're willing to put the modern feedlot under the rubric of civilization.

Cattle rarely live on feedlot diets for more than 150 days, which might be about as much as their systems can tolerate. "I don't know how long you could feed them this ration before you'd see problems," Dr. Metzin said; another vet told me the diet would eventually "blow out their livers" and kill them. Over time the acids eat away at the rumen wall, allowing bacteria to enter the animal's bloodstream. These microbes wind up in the liver, where they form abscesses and impair the liver's function. Between 15 percent and 30 percent of feedlot cows are found at slaughter to have abscessed livers; Dr. Mel told me that in some pens the figure runs as high as 70 percent.

What keeps a feedlot animal healthy—or healthy enough—are antibiotics. Rumensin buffers acidity in the rumen, helping to prevent bloat and acidosis, and Tylosin, a form of erythromycin, lowers the incidence of liver infection. Most of the antibiotics sold in America today end up in animal feed, a practice that, it is now generally acknowledged (except in agriculture), is leading directly to the evolution of new antibiotic-resistant superbugs. In the debate over the use of antibiotics in agriculture, a distinction is usually made between their clinical and nonclinical uses. Public health advocates don't object to treating sick animals with antibiotics; they just don't want to see the drugs lose their effectiveness because factory farms are feeding them to healthy animals to promote growth. But the use of antibiotics in feedlot cattle confounds this distinction. Here the drugs are plainly being used to treat sick animals, yet the animals probably wouldn't be sick if not for the diet of grain we feed them.

I asked Dr. Mel what would happen if drugs like Rumensin and Tylosin were banned from cattle feed, as some public health experts advocate. "We'd have a high death rate [it's currently about 3 percent, matching the industry average] and poorer performing cattle. We just couldn't feed them as hard. The whole system would have to change—and slow down.

"Hell, if you gave them lots of grass and space, I wouldn't have a job."

My first impression of pen 63, where my steer is spending his last five months, was, *Not a bad little piece of real estate, all considered.* The pen is far enough from the feed mill to be fairly quiet and it has a water view of what I thought was a pond or reservoir until I noticed the brown scum. The body of water is what is known, in the geography of CAFOs, as a manure lagoon. I asked the feedlot manager why they didn't just spray the liquefied manure on neighboring farms. The farmers don't want it, he explained. The nitrogen and phosphorus levels are so high that spraying the crops would kill them. He didn't say that feedlot wastes also contain heavy metals and hormone residues, persistent chemicals that end up in waterways downstream, where scientists have found fish and amphibians exhibiting abnormal sex characteristics. CAFOs like Poky transform what at the proper scale would be a precious source of fertility—cow manure—into toxic waste.

The pen 534 lives in is surprisingly spacious, about the size of a hockey rink, with a concrete feed bunk along the road, and a fresh water trough out back. I climbed over the railing and joined the ninety steers, which, en masse, retreated a few lumbering steps, and then stopped to see what I would do.

I had on the same carrot-colored sweater I'd worn to the ranch in South Dakota, hoping to elicit some glint of recognition from my steer. I couldn't find him at first; all the faces staring at me were either completely black or bore an unfamiliar pattern of white marks. And then I spotted him—the three white blazes—way off in the back. As I gingerly stepped toward him the quietly shuffling mass of black cowhide between us parted, and there stood 534 and I, staring dumbly at one another. Glint of recognition? None, none whatsoever. I told myself not to take it personally; 534 and his pen mates have been bred for their marbling, after all, not their ability to form attachments.

I noticed that 534's eyes looked a little bloodshot. Dr. Metzin had told me that some animals are irritated by feedlot dust. The problem is especially serious in the summer months, when the animals kick up clouds of the stuff and workers have to spray the pens with water to keep it down. I had to remind myself that this is not ordinary dirt dust, inasmuch as the dirt in a feedyard is not ordinary dirt; no, this is fecal dust. But apart from the air quality, how did feedlot life seem to be agreeing with 534? I don't know enough about the emotional life of a steer to say with confidence that 534 was miserable, bored, or indifferent, but I would not say he looked happy.

He's clearly eating well, though. My steer had put on a couple hundred pounds since we'd last met, and he looked it: thicker across the shoulder and round as a barrel through the middle. He carried himself more like a steer now than a calf, even though his first birthday was still two months away. Dr. Metzin complimented me on his size and conformation. "That's a handsome-looking beef you got there." (Shucks.)

If I stared at my steer hard enough, I could imagine the white lines of the butcher's chart dissecting his black hide: rump roast, flank steak, standing rib, tenderloin, brisket. One way of looking at 534—the feed-lot way, the industrial way—was as a most impressive machine for turning number 2 field corn into cuts of beef. Every day between now and his slaughter in six months, 534 will convert thirty-two pounds of feed into four pounds of gain—new muscle, fat, and bone. This at least is how 534 appears in the computer program I'd seen at the mill: the ratio of feed to gain that determines his efficiency. (Compared to other food animals, cattle are terribly inefficient: The ratio of feed to flesh in chicken, the most efficient animal by this measure, is two pounds of corn to one of meat, which is why chicken costs less than beef.) Poky Feeders is indeed a factory, transforming—as fast as bovinely possible—cheap raw materials into a less cheap finished product, through the mechanism of bovine metabolism.

Yet metaphors of the factory and the machine obscure as much as they reveal about the creature standing before me. He has, of course, another, quite different identity—as an animal, I mean, connected as all animals must be to certain other animals and plants and microbes, as well as to the earth and the sun. He's a link in a food chain, a thread in a far-reaching web of ecological relationships. Looked at from this perspective, everything going on in this cattle pen appears quite different, and not nearly as far removed from our world as this manure-encrusted patch of ground here in Nowhere, Kansas, might suggest.

For one thing, the health of these animals is inextricably linked, to our own by that web of relationships. The unnaturally rich diet of corn that undermines a steer's health fattens his flesh in a way that undermines the health of the humans who will eat it. The antibiotics these animals consume with their corn at this very moment are selecting, in their gut and wherever else in the environment they end up, for new strains of resistant bacteria that will someday infect us and withstand the drugs we depend on to treat that infection. We inhabit the same microbial ecosystem as the animals we eat, and whatever happens in it also happens to us.

Then there's the deep pile of manure on which I stand, in which 534 sleeps. We don't know much about the hormones in it—where they will end up, or what they might do once they get there—but we do know something about the bacteria, which can find their way from the manure on the ground to his hide and from there into our hamburgers. The speed at which these animals will be slaughtered and processed—four hundred an hour at the plant where 534 will go—means that sooner or later some of the manure caked on these hides gets into the meat we eat. One of the bacteria that almost certainly resides in the manure I'm standing in is particularly lethal to humans. *Escherichia coli* O157:H7 is a relatively new strain of the common intestinal bacteria (no one had seen it before 1980) that thrives in feedlot cattle, 40 percent of which carry it in their gut. Ingesting as few as ten of these microbes can cause a fatal infection; they produce a toxin that destroys human kidneys.

Most of the microbes that reside in the gut of a cow and find their way into our food get killed off by the strong acids in our stomachs, since they evolved to live in the neutral pH environment of the rumen. But the rumen of a corn-fed feedlot steer is nearly as acidic as our own stomachs, and in this new, man-made environment new acid-resistant strains of *E. coli,* of which O157:H7 is one, have evolved—yet another creature recruited by nature to absorb the excess biomass coming off the Farm Belt. The problem with these bugs is that they can shake off the acid bath in our stomachs—and then go on to kill us. By acidifying the rumen with corn we've broken down one of our food chain's most important barriers to infection. Yet another solution turned into a problem.

We've recently discovered that this process of acidification can be reversed, and that doing so can greatly diminish the threat from *E. coli* O 157:H7. Jim Russell, a USDA microbiologist on the faculty at Cornell, has found that switching a cow's diet from corn to grass or hay for a few days prior to slaughter reduces the population of *E. coli* O157:H7 in the animal's gut by as much as 80 percent. But such a solution *(Grass?!)* is considered wildly impractical by the cattle industry and (therefore) by the USDA. Their preferred solution for dealing with bacterial contamination is irradiation—essentially, to try to sterilize the manure getting into the meat.

So much comes back to corn, this cheap feed that turns out in so many ways to be not cheap at all. While I stood in pen 63 a dump truck pulled up alongside the feed bunk and released a golden stream of feed. The black mass of cowhide moved toward the trough for lunch. The $1.60 a day I'm paying for three meals a day here is a bargain only by the narrowest of calculations. It doesn't take into account, for example, the cost to the public health of antibiotic resistance or food poisoning by *E. coli* O 157:H7. It doesn't take into account the cost to taxpayers of the farm subsidies that keep Poky's raw materials cheap. And it certainly doesn't take into account all the many environmental costs incurred by cheap corn.

I stood alongside 534 as he lowered his big head into the stream of fresh grain. How absurd, I thought, the two of us standing hock-deep in manure in this godforsaken place, overlooking a manure lagoon in the middle of nowhere somewhere in Kansas. Godforsaken perhaps, and yet not apart, I realized, as I thought of the other places connected to this place by the river of commodity corn. Follow the corn from this bunk back to the fields where it grows and I'd find myself back in the middle of that 125,000-mile-square monoculture, under a steady rain of pesticide and fertilizer. Keep going, and I could follow the nitrogen runoff from that fertilizer all the way down the Mississippi into the Gulf of Mexico, adding its poison to an eight-thousand-square-mile zone so starved of oxygen nothing but algae can live in it. And then go farther still, follow the fertilizer (and the diesel fuel and the petrochemical pesticides) needed to grow the corn all the way to the oil fields of the Persian Gulf.

I don't have a sufficiently vivid imagination to look at my steer and see a barrel of oil, but petroleum is one of the most important ingredients in the production of modern meat, and the Persian Gulf is surely a link in the food chain that passes through this (or any) feedlot. Steer 534 started his life part of a food chain that derived all of its energy from the sun, which nourished the grasses that nourished him and his mother. When 534 moved from ranch to feedlot, from grass to corn, he joined an industrial food chain powered by fossil fuel—and therefore defended by the U.S. military, another never-counted cost of cheap food. (One-fifth of America's petroleum consumption goes to producing and transporting our food.) After I got home from Kansas, I asked an economist who specializes in agriculture and energy if it might be possible to calculate precisely how much petroleum it will take to grow my steer to slaughter weight. Assuming 534 continues to eat twenty-five pounds of corn a day and reaches a weight of twelve hundred pounds, he will have consumed in his lifetime the equivalent of thirty-five gallons of oil—nearly a barrel.

So this is what commodity corn can do to a cow: industrialize the miracle of nature that is a ruminant, taking this sunlight and prairie grass-powered organism and turning it into the last thing we need: another fossil fuel machine. This one, however, is able to suffer.

Standing there in the pen alongside my steer, I couldn't imagine ever wanting to eat the flesh of one of these protein machines. Hungry was the last thing I felt. Yet I'm sure that after enough time goes by, and the stink of this place is gone from my nostrils, I will eat feedlot beef again. Eating industrial meat takes an almost heroic act of not knowing or, now, forgetting. But I left Poky determined to follow this meat to a meal on a table somewhere, to see this food chain at least that far. I was curious to know what feedlot beef would taste like now, if I could taste the corn or even, since taste is as much a matter of what's in the head as it is about molecules dancing on the tongue, some hint of the petroleum. "You are what you eat" is a truism hard to argue with, and yet it is, as a visit to a feedlot suggests, incomplete, for you are what what you eat eats, too. And what we are, or have become, is not just meat but number 2 corn and oil.

Shooting Dad

Sarah Vowell

If you were passing by the house where I grew up during my teenage years and it happened to be before Election Day, you wouldn't have needed to come inside to see that it was a house divided. You could have looked at the Democratic campaign poster in the upstairs window and the Republican one in the downstairs window and seen our home for the Civil War battleground it was. I'm not saying who was the Democrat or who was the Republican—my father or I—but I will tell you that I have never subscribed to *Guns & Ammo*, that I did not plaster the family vehicle with National Rifle Association stickers, and that hunter's orange was never my color.

About the only thing my father and I agree on is the Constitution, though I'm partial to the First Amendment, while he's always favored the Second.

I am a gunsmith's daughter. I like to call my parents' house, located on a quiet residential street in Bozeman, Montana, the United States of Firearms. Guns were everywhere: the so-called pretty ones like the circa 1850 walnut muzzleloader hanging on the wall, Dad's clients' fixer-uppers leaning into corners, an entire rack right next to the TV. I had to move revolvers out of my way to make room for a bowl of Rice Krispies on the kitchen table.

I was eleven when we moved into that Bozeman house. We had never lived in town before, and this was a college town at that. We came from Oklahoma—a dusty little Muskogee County nowhere called Braggs. My parents' property there included an orchard, a horse pasture, and a couple of acres of woods. I knew our lives had changed one morning not long after we moved to Montana when, during breakfast, my father heard a noise and jumped out of his chair. Grabbing a BB gun, he rushed out the front door. Standing in the yard, he started shooting at crows. My mother sprinted after him screaming, "Pat, you might ought to check, but I don't think they do that up here!" From the look on his face, she might as well have told him that his American citizenship had been revoked. He shook his head, mumbling, "Why, shooting crows is a national pastime, like baseball and apple pie." Personally, I preferred baseball and apple pie. I looked up at those crows flying away and thought, I'm going to like it here.

Dad and I started bickering in earnest when I was fourteen, after the 1984 Democratic National Convention. I was so excited when Walter Mondale chose Geraldine Ferraro as his running mate that I taped the front page of the newspaper with her picture on it to the refrigerator door. But there was some sort of mysterious gravity surge in the kitchen. Somehow, that picture ended up in the trash all the way across the room.

Nowadays, I giggle when Dad calls me on Election Day to cheerfully inform me that he has once again canceled out my vote, but I was not always so mature. There were times when I found the fact that he was a gunsmith horrifying. And just *weird*. All he ever cared about were guns. All I ever cared about was art. There were years and years when he hid out by himself in the garage making rifle barrels and I holed up in my room reading Allen Ginsberg poems, and we were incapable of having a conversation that didn't end in an argument.

Our house was partitioned off into territories. While the kitchen and the living room were well within the DMZ, the respective work spaces governed by my father and me were jealously guarded totalitarian states in which each of us declared ourselves dictator. Dad's shop was a messy disaster area, a labyrinth of lathes. Its walls were hung with the mounted antlers of deer he'd bagged, forming a makeshift museum of death. The available flat surfaces were buried under a million scraps of paper on which he sketched his mechanical inventions in blue ballpoint pen. And the floor, carpeted with spiky metal shavings, was a tetanus shot waiting to happen. My domain was the cramped, cold space known as the music room. It was also a messy disaster area, an obstacle course of musical instruments—piano, trumpet, baritone horn, valve trombone, various percussion doodads (bells!), and recorders. A framed portrait of the French composer Claude Debussy was nailed to the wall. The available flat surfaces were buried under piles of staff paper, on which I penciled in the pompous orchestra music given titles like "Prelude to the Green Door" (named after an O. Henry short story by the way, not the watershed porn flick *Behind the Green Door*) I started writing in junior high.

It has been my experience that in order to impress potential suitors, skip the teen Debussy anecdotes and stick with the always attention-getting line "My dad makes guns." Though it won't cause the guy to like me any better, it will make him handle the inevitable breakup with diplomacy—just in case I happen to have any loaded family heirlooms lying around the house.

But the fact is, I have only shot a gun once and once was plenty. My twin sister, Amy, and I were six years old—six—when Dad decided that it was high time we learned how to shoot. Amy remembers the day he handed us the gun for the first time differently. She liked it.

Amy shared our father's enthusiasm for firearms and the quick-draw cowboy mythology surrounding them. I tended to daydream through Dad's activities—the car trip to Dodge City's Boot Hill, his beloved John Wayne Westerns on TV. My sister, on the other hand, turned into Rooster Cogburn Jr., devouring Duke movies with Dad. In fact, she named her teddy bear Duke, hung a colossal John Wayne portrait next to her bed, and took to wearing one of those John Wayne shirts that button on the side. So when Dad led us out to the backyard when we were six and, to Amy's delight, put the gun in her hand, she says she felt it meant that Daddy trusted us and that he thought of us as "big girls."

But I remember holding the pistol only made me feel small. It was so heavy in my hand. I stretched out my arm and pointed it away and winced. It was a very long time before I had the nerve to pull the trigger and I was so scared I had to close my eyes. It felt like it just went off by itself, as if I had no say in the matter, as if the gun just had this need. The sound it made was as big as God. It kicked little me back to the ground like a bully, like a foe. It hurt. I don't know if I dropped it or just handed it back over to my dad, but I do know that I never wanted to touch another one again. And, because I believed in the devil, I did what my mother told me to do every time I felt an evil presence. I looked at the smoke and whispered under my breath, "Satan, I rebuke thee."

It's not like I'm saying I was traumatized. It's more like I was decided. Guns: Not For Me. Luckily, both my parents grew up in exasperating households where children were considered puppets and/or slaves. My mom and dad were hell-bent on letting my sister and me make our own choices. So if I decided that I didn't want my father's little death sticks to kick me to the ground again, that was fine with him. He would go hunting with my sister, who started calling herself "the loneliest twin in history" because of my reluctance to engage in family activities.

Of course, the fact that I was allowed to voice my opinions did not mean that my father would silence his own. Some things were said during the Reagan administration that cannot be taken back. Let's just say that I blamed Dad for nuclear proliferation and Contra aid. He believed that if I had my way, all the guns would be confiscated and it would take the commies about fifteen minutes to parachute in and assume control.

We're older now, my dad and I. The older I get, the more I'm interested in becoming a better daughter. First on my list: Figure out the whole gun thing.

Not long ago, my dad finished his most elaborate tool of death yet. A cannon. He built a nineteenth-century cannon. From scratch. It took two years.

My father's cannon is a smaller replica of a cannon called the Big Horn Gun in front of Bozeman's Pioneer Museum. The barrel of the original has been filled with concrete ever since some high school kids in the '50s pointed it at the school across the street and shot out its windows one night as a prank. According to Dad's historical source, a man known to scholars as A Guy at the Museum, the cannon was brought to Bozeman around 1870, and was used by local white merchants to fire at the Sioux and Cheyenne Indians who blocked their trade access to the East in 1874.

"Bozeman was founded on greed," Dad says. The courthouse cannon, he continues, "definitely killed Indians. The merchants filled it full of nuts, bolts, and chopped-up horseshoes. Sitting Bull could have been part of these engagements. They definitely ticked off the Indians, because a couple of years later, Custer wanders into them at Little Bighorn. The Bozeman merchants were out to cause trouble. They left fresh baked bread with cyanide in it on the trail to poison a few Indians."

Because my father's sarcastic American history yarns rarely go on for long before he trots out some nefarious ancestor of ours—I come from a long line of moonshiners, Confederate soldiers, murderers, even Democrats—he cracks that the merchants hired some "community-minded Southern soldiers from North Texas." These soldiers had, like my great-great-grandfather John Vowell, fought under pro-slavery guerrilla William C. Quantrill. Quantrill is most famous for riding into Lawrence, Kansas, in 1863 flying a black flag and commanding his men pharaohlike to "kill every male and burn down every house."

"John Vowell," Dad says, "had a little rep for killing people." And since he abandoned my great-grandfather Charles, whose mother died giving birth to him in 1870, and wasn't seen again until 1912, Dad doesn't rule out the possibility that John Vowell could have been one of the hired guns on the Bozeman Trail. So the cannon isn't just another gun to my dad. It's a map of all his obsessions—firearms, certainly, but also American history and family history, subjects he's never bothered separating from each other.

After tooling a million guns, after inventing and building a rifle barrel boring machine, after setting up that complicated shop filled with lathes and blueing tanks and outmoded blacksmithing tools, the cannon, is his most ambitious project ever. I thought that if I was ever going to understand the ballistic bee in his bonnet, this was my chance. It was the biggest gun he ever made and I could experience it and spend time with it with the added bonus of not having to actually pull a trigger myself.

I called Dad and said that I wanted to come to Montana and watch him shoot off the cannon. He was immediately suspicious. But I had never taken much interest in his work before and he would take what he could get. He loaded the cannon into the back of his truck and we drove up into the Bridger Mountains. I was a little worried that the National Forest Service would object to us lobbing fiery balls of metal onto its property. Dad laughed, assuring me that "you cannot shoot fireworks, but this is considered a fire*arm*."

It is a small cannon, about as long as a baseball bat and as wide as a coffee can. But it's heavy—110 pounds. We park near the side of the hill. Dad takes his gunpowder and other tools out of this adorable wooden box on which he has stenciled "PAT G. VOWELL CANNONWORKS." Cannonworks: So that's what NRA members call a metal-strewn garage.

Dad plunges his homemade bullets into the barrel, points it at an embankment just to be safe, and lights the fuse. When the fuse is lit, it resembles a cartoon. So does the sound, which warrants Ben Day dot words along the lines of *ker-pow*! There's so much Fourth of July smoke everywhere I feel compelled to sing the national anthem.

I've given this a lot of thought—how to convey the giddiness I felt when the cannon shot off. But there isn't a sophisticated way to say this. It's just really, really cool. My dad thought so, too.

Sometimes, I put together stories about the more eccentric corners of the American experience for public radio. So I happen to have my tape recorder with me, and I've never seen levels like these. Every time the cannon goes off, the delicate needles which keep track of the sound quality lurch into the bad, red zone so fast and so hard I'm surprised they don't break.

The cannon was so loud and so painful, I had to touch my head to make sure my skull hadn't cracked open. One thing that my dad and I share is that we're both a little hard of hearing—me from Aerosmith, him from gunsmith.

He lights the fuse again. The bullet knocks over the log he was aiming at. I instantly utter a sentence I never in my entire life thought I would say. I tell him, "Good shot, Dad."

Just as I'm wondering what's coming over me, two hikers walk by. Apparently, they have never seen a man set off a homemade cannon in the middle of the wilderness while his daughter holds a foot-long microphone up into the air recording its terrorist boom. One hiker gives me a puzzled look and asks, "So you work for the radio and that's your dad?"

Dad shoots the cannon again so that they can see how it works. The other hiker says, "That's quite the machine you got there." But he isn't talking about the cannon. He's talking about my tape recorder and my microphone—which is called a *shotgun* mike. I stare back at him, then I look over at my father's cannon, then down at my microphone, and I think, Oh. My. God. My dad and I are the same person. We're both smart-alecky loners with goofy projects and weird equipment. And since this whole target practice outing was my idea, I was no longer his adversary. I was his accomplice. What's worse, I was liking it.

I haven't changed my mind about guns. I can get behind the cannon because it is a completely ceremonial object. It's unwieldy and impractical, just like everything else I care about. Try to rob a convenience store with this 110-pound Saturday night special, you'd still be dragging it in the door Sunday afternoon.

I love noise. As a music fan, I'm always waiting for that moment in a song when something just flies out of it and explodes in the air. My dad is a one-man garage band, the kind of rock 'n' roller who slaves away at his art for no reason other than to make his own sound. My dad is an artist—a pretty driven, idiosyncratic one, too. He's got his last *Gesamtkunstwerk* all planned out. It's a performance piece. We're all in it—my mom, the loneliest twin in history, and me.

When my father dies, take a wild guess what he wants done with his ashes. Here's a hint: It requires a cannon.

"You guys are going to love this," he smirks, eyeballing the cannon. "You get to drag this thing up on top of the Gravellies on opening day of hunting season. And looking off at Sphinx Mountain, you get to put me in little paper bags. I can take my last hunting trip on opening morning."

I'll do it, too. I will have my father's body burned into ashes. I will pack these ashes into paper bags. I will go to the mountains with my mother, my sister, and the cannon. I will plunge his remains into the barrel and point it into a hill so that he doesn't take anyone with him. I will light the fuse. But I will not cover my ears. Because when I blow what used to be my dad into the earth, I want it to hurt.

Stadium Pal

David Sedaris

I've always liked the idea of accessories, those little pick-me-ups designed to invigorate what has come to feel drab and predictable. A woman might rejuvenate her outfit with a vintage Hermès scarf or jaunty rope belt, but the options for men aren't nearly so interesting. I have no use for cuff links or suspenders, and while I'll occasionally pick up a new tie it hardly leaves me feeling "kicky." Hidden accessories can do the trick, but again they're mainly the province of women. Garter belt and lingerie—yes. Sock garter and microbrief—no.

It was my search for something discreet, masculine, and practical that led me to the Stadium Pal, an external catheter currently being marketed to sports fans, truck drivers, and anyone else who's tired of searching for a bathroom. At first inspection, the device met all my criteria:

Was it masculine? Yes, and proudly so. Knowing that no sensible female would ever voluntarily choose to pee in her pants, the manufacturers went ahead and designed the product exclusively for men. Unlike a regular catheter, which is inserted directly into the penis, the Stadium Pal connects by way of a self-adhesive condom, which is then attached to a flexible rubber tube. Urine flows through the tube and collects in the "freedom leg bag," conveniently attached to the user's calf. The bag can be emptied and reused up to twelve times, making it both disgusting *and* cost effective. And what could be manlier?

Was it discreet? According to the brochure, unless you wore it with shorts, no one needed to know anything about it.

Was it practical? At the time, yes. I don't drive or attend football games, but I did have a book tour coming up, and the possibilities were endless. Five glasses of iced tea followed by a long public reading?

Thanks, Stadium Pal! The window seat on an overbooked coast-to-coast flight? *Don't mind if I do!*

I ordered myself a Stadium Pal and realized that while it might make sense in a hospital, it really wasn't very practical for day-to-day use. In an open-air sporting arena, a piping hot thirty-two-ounce bag of urine might go unnoticed, but not so in a stuffy airplane or small, crowded bookstore. An hour after christening it, I smelled like a nursing home. On top of that, I found that it was hard to pee and do other things at the same time. Reading out loud, discussing my beverage options with the flight attendant, checking into a fine hotel: each activity required its own separate form of concentration, and while no one knew exactly what I was up to, it was pretty clear that something was going on. I think it was my face that gave me away. That and my oddly swollen calf.

What ultimately did me in was the self-adhesive condom. Putting it on was no problem, but its removal qualified as what, in certain cultures, is known as a *bris.* Wear it once, and you'll need a solid month to fully recover. It will likely be a month in which you'll weigh the relative freedom of peeing in your pants against the unsightly discomfort of a scab-covered penis, ultimately realizing that, in terms of a convenient accessory, you're better off with a new watchband.

Arm Wrestling with My Father

Brad Manning

"Now you say when" is what he always said before an arm-wrestling match. He liked to put the responsibility on me, knowing that he would always control the outcome. "When!" I'd shout, and it would start. And I would tense up, concentrating and straining and trying to push his wrist down to the carpet with all my weight and strength. But Dad would always win; I always had to lose. "Want to try it again?" he would ask, grinning. He would see my downcast eyes, my reddened, sweating face, and sense my intensity. And with squinting eyes he would laugh at me, a high laugh, through his perfect white teeth. Too bitter to smile, I would not answer or look at him, but I would just roll over on my back and frown at the ceiling. I never thought it was funny at all.

That was the way I felt for a number of years during my teens, after I had lost my enjoyment of arm wrestling and before I had given up that same intense desire to beat my father. Ours had always been a physical relationship, I suppose, one determined by athleticism and strength. We never communicated as well in speech or in writing as in a strong hug, battling to make the other gasp for breath. I could never find him at one of my orchestra concerts. But at my lacrosse games, he would be there in the stands, with an angry look, ready to coach me after the game on how I could do better. He never helped me write a paper or a poem. Instead, he would take me outside and show me a new move for my game, in the hope that I would score a couple of goals and gain confidence in my ability. Dad knew almost nothing about lacrosse and his movements were all wrong and sad to watch. But at those times I could just feel how hard he was trying to communicate, to help me, to show the love he had for me, the love I could only assume was there.

His words were physical. The truth is, I have never read a card or a letter written in his hand because he never wrote to me. Never. Mom wrote me all the cards and letters when I was away from home. The closest my father ever came, that I recall, was in a newspaper clipping Mom had sent with a letter. He had gone through and underlined all the important words about the dangers of not wearing a bicycle helmet. Our communication was physical, and that is why we did things like arm wrestle. To get down on the floor and grapple, arm against arm, was like having a conversation.

This ritual of father-son competition in fact had started early in my life, back when Dad started the matches with his arm almost horizontal, his wrist an inch from defeat, and still won. I remember in those battles how my tiny shoulders would press over our locked hands, my whole upper body pushing down in hope of winning that single inch from his calm, unmoving forearm. "Say when," he'd repeat, killing my concentration and causing me to squeal, "I did, I did!" And so he'd grin with his eyes fixed on me, not seeming to notice his own arm, which would begin to rise slowly from its starting position. My greatest efforts could not slow it down. As soon as my hopes had disappeared I'd start to cheat and use both hands. But the arm would continue to move steadily along its arc toward the carpet. My brother, if he was watching, would sometimes join in against the arm. He once even wrapped his little legs around our embattled wrists and pulled back with everything he had. But he did not have much and, regardless of the opposition, the man would win. My arm would lie at rest, pressed into the carpet beneath a solid, immovable arm. In that pinned position, I could only giggle, happy to have such a strong father.

My feelings have changed, though. I don't giggle anymore, at least not around my father. And I don't feel pressured to compete with him the way I thought necessary for years. Now my father is not really so strong as he used to be and I am getting stronger. This change in strength comes at a time when I am growing faster mentally than at any time before. I am becoming less my father and more myself. And as a result, there is less of a need to be set apart from him and his command. I am no longer a rebel in the household, wanting to stand up against the master with clenched fists and tensing jaws, trying to impress him with my education or my views on religion. I am no longer a challenger, quick to correct his verbal mistakes, determined to beat him whenever possible in physical competition.

I am not sure when it was that I began to feel less competitive with my father, but it all became clearer to me one day this past January. I was home in Virginia for a week between exams, and Dad had stayed home from work because the house was snowed in deep. It was then that I learned something I never could have guessed.

I don't recall who suggested arm wrestling that day. We hadn't done it for a long time, for months. But there we were, lying flat on the carpet, face to face, extending our right arms. Our arms were different. His still resembled a fat tree branch, one which had leveled my wrist to the ground countless times before. It was hairy and white with some pink moles scattered about. It looked strong, to be sure, though not so strong as it had in past years. I expect that back in his youth it had looked even stronger. In high school he had played halfback and had been voted "best-built body" of the senior class. Between college semesters he had worked on road crews and on Louisiana dredges. I admired him for that. I had begun to row crew in college and that accounted for some small buildup along the muscle lines, but it did not seem to be enough. The arm I extended was lanky and featureless. Even so, he insisted that he would lose the match, that he was certain I'd win. I had to ignore this, however, because it was something he always said, whether or not he believed it himself.

Our warm palms came together, much the same way we had shaken hands the day before at the airport. Fingers twisted and wrapped about once again, testing for a better grip. Elbows slid up and back making their little indentations on the itchy carpet. My eyes pinched closed in concentration as I tried to center as much of my thought as possible on the match. Arm wrestling, I knew, was a competition that depended less on talent and experience than on one's mental control and confidence. I looked up into his eyes and was ready. He looked back, smiled at me, and said softly (did he sound nervous?), "You say when."

It was not a long match. I had expected him to be stronger, faster. I was conditioned to lose and would have accepted defeat easily. However, after some struggle, his arm yielded to my efforts and began to move unsteadily toward the carpet. I worked against his arm with all the strength I could find. He was working hard as well, straining, breathing heavily. It seemed that this time was different, that I was going to win. Then something occurred to me, something unexpected. I discovered that I was feeling sorry for my father. I wanted to win but I did not want to see him lose.

It was like the thrill I had once experienced as a young boy at my grandfather's lake house in Louisiana when I hooked my first big fish. There was that sudden tug that made me leap. The red bobber was sucked down beneath the surface and I pulled back against it, reeling it in excitedly. But when my cousin caught sight of the fish and shouted out, "It's a keeper," I realized that I would be happier for the fish if it were let go rather than grilled for dinner. Arm wrestling my father was now like this, like hooking "Big Joe," the old fish that Lake Quachita holds but you can never catch, and when you finally think you've got him, you want to let him go, cut the line, keep the legend alive.

Perhaps at that point I could have given up, letting my father win. But it was so fast and absorbing. How could I have learned so quickly how it would feel to have overpowered the arm that had protected and provided for me all of my life? His arms have always protected me and the family. Whenever I am near him I am unafraid, knowing his arms are ready to catch me and keep me safe, the way they caught my mother one time when she fainted halfway across the room, the way he carried me, full grown, up and down the stairs when I had mononucleosis, the way he once held my feet as I stood on his shoulders to put up a new basketball net. My mother may have had the words or the touch that sustained our family, but his were the arms that protected us. And his were the arms now that I had pushed to the carpet, first the right arm, then the left.

I might have preferred him to be always the stronger, the one who carries me. But this wish is impossible now; our roles have begun to switch. I do not know if I will ever physically carry my father as he has carried me, though I fear that someday I may have that responsibility. More than once this year I have hesitated before answering the phone late at night, fearing my mother's voice calling me back to help carry his wood coffin. When I am home with him and he mentions a sharp pain in his chest, I imagine him collapsing onto the floor. And in that second vision I see me rushing to him, lifting him onto my shoulders, and running.

A week after our match, we parted at the airport. The arm-wrestling match was by that time mostly forgotten. My thoughts were on school. I had been awake most of the night studying for my last exam, and by that morning I was already back into my college-student manner of reserve and detachment. To say goodbye, I kissed and hugged my mother and I prepared to shake my father's hand. A handshake had always seemed easier to handle than a hug. His hugs had always been powerful ones, intended I suppose to give me strength. They made me suck in my breath and struggle for control, and the way he would pound his hand on my back made rumbles in my ears. So I offered a handshake; but he offered a hug. I accepted it, bracing myself for the impact. Once our arms were wrapped around each other, however, I sensed a different message. His

was any basis for the effect it had on all of us, but it turns out to be another of those cases in which science bears out folk wisdom. The Santa Ana, which is named for one of the canyons it rushes through, is a *foehn* wind, like the *foehn* of Austria and Switzerland and the *hamsin* of Israel. There are a number of persistent malevolent winds, perhaps the best known of which are the mistral of France and the Mediterranean sirocco, but a *foehn* wind has distinct characteristics: it occurs on the leeward slope of a mountain range and, although the air begins as a cold mass, it is warmed as it comes down the mountain and appears finally as a hot dry wind. Whenever and wherever a *foehn* blows, doctors hear about headaches and nausea and allergies, about "nervousness," about "depression." In Los Angeles some teachers do not attempt to conduct formal classes during a Santa Ana, because the children become unmanageable. In Switzerland the suicide rate goes up during the *foehn,* and in the courts of some Swiss cantons the wind is considered a mitigating circumstance for crime. Surgeons are said to watch the wind, because blood does not clot normally during a *foehn*. A few years ago an Israeli physicist discovered that not only during such winds, but for the ten or twelve hours which precede them, the air carries an unusually high ratio of positive to negative ions. No one seems to know exactly why that should be; some talk about friction and others suggest solar disturbances. In any case the positive ions are there, and what an excess of positive ions does, in the simplest terms, is make people unhappy. One cannot get much more mechanistic than that.

Easterners commonly complain that there is no "weather" at all in Southern California, that the days and the seasons slip by relentlessly, numbingly bland. That is quite misleading. In fact the climate is characterized by infrequent but violent extremes: two periods of torrential subtropical rains which continue for weeks and wash out the hills and send subdivisions sliding toward the sea; about twenty scattered days a year of the Santa Ana, which, with its incendiary dryness, invariably means fire. At the first prediction of a Santa Ana, the Forest Service flies men and equipment from northern California into the southern forests, and the Los Angeles Fire Department cancels its ordinary non-firefighting routines. The Santa Ana caused Malibu to burn the way it did in 1956, and Bel Air in 1961, and Santa Barbara in 1964. In the winter of 1966–67 eleven men were killed fighting a Santa Ana fire that spread through the San Gabriel Mountains.

Just to watch the front-page news out of Los Angeles during a Santa Ana is to get very close to what it is about the place. The longest single Santa Ana period in recent years was in 1957, and it lasted not the usual three or four days but fourteen days, from November 21 until December 4. On the first day 25,000 acres of the San Gabriel Mountains were burning, with gusts reaching 100 miles an hour. In town, the wind reached Force 12, or hurricane force, on the Beaufort Scale; oil derricks were toppled and people ordered off the downtown streets to avoid injury from flying objects. On November 22 the fire in the San Gabriels was out of control. On November 24 six people were killed in automobile accidents, and by the end of the week the Los Angeles *Times* was keeping a box score of traffic deaths. On November 26 a prominent Pasadena attorney, depressed about money, shot and killed his wife, their two sons, and himself. On November 27 a South Gate divorcee, twenty-two, was murdered and thrown from a moving car. On November 30 the San Gabriel fire was still out of control, and the wind in town was blowing eighty miles an hour. On the first day of December four people died violently, and on the third the wind began to break.

It is hard for people who have not lived in Los Angeles to realize how radically the Santa Ana figures in the local imagination. The city burning is Los Angeles's deepest image of itself: Nathanael West perceived that, in *The Day of the Locust*; and at the time of the 1965 Watts riots what struck the imagination most indelibly were the fires. For days one could drive the Harbor Freeway and see the city on fire, just as we had always known it would be in the end. Los Angeles weather is the weather of catastrophe, of apocalypse, and, just as the reliably long and bitter winters of New England determine the way life is lived there, so the violence and the unpredictability of the Santa Ana affect the entire quality of life in Los Angeles, accentuate its impermanence, its unreliability. The wind shows us how close to the edge we are.

The Way to Rainy Mountain

N. Scott Momaday

A single knoll rises out of the plain in Oklahoma, north and west of the Wichita Range. For my people, the Kiowas, it is an old landmark, and they gave it the name Rainy Mountain. The hardest weather in the world is there. Winter brings blizzards, hot tornadic winds arise in the spring, and in summer the prairie is an anvil's edge. The grass turns brittle and brown, and it cracks beneath your feet. There are green belts along the rivers and creeks, linear groves of hickory and pecan, willow and witch hazel. At a distance in July or August the steaming foliage seems almost to writhe in fire. Great green and yellow grasshoppers are everywhere in the tall grass, popping up like corn to sting the flesh, and tortoises crawl about on the red earth, going nowhere in the plenty of time. Loneliness is an aspect of the land. All things in the plain are isolate; there is no confusion of objects in the eye, but *one* hill or *one* tree or *one* man. To look upon that landscape in the early morning, with the sun at your back, is to lose the sense of proportion. Your imagination comes to life, and this, you think, is where Creation was begun.

I returned to Rainy Mountain in July. My grandmother had died in the spring, and I wanted to be at her grave. She had lived to be very old and at last infirm. Her only living daughter was with her when she died, and I was told that in death her face was that of a child.

I like to think of her as a child. When she was born, the Kiowas were living the last great moment of their history. For more than a hundred years they had controlled the open range from the Smoky Hill River to the Red, from the headwaters of the Canadian to the fork of the Arkansas and Cimarron. In alliance with the Comanches, they had ruled the whole of the southern Plains. War was their sacred business, and they were among the finest horsemen the world has ever known. But warfare for the Kiowas was preeminently a matter of disposition rather than of survival, and they never understood the grim, unrelenting advance of the U.S. Cavalry. When at last, divided and ill-provisioned, they were driven onto the Staked Plains in the cold rains of autumn, they fell into panic. In Palo Duro Canyon they abandoned their crucial stores to pillage and had nothing then but their lives. In order to save themselves, they surrendered to the soldiers at Fort Sill and were imprisoned in the old stone corral that now stands as a military museum. My grandmother was spared the humiliation of those high gray walls by eight or ten years, but she must have known from birth the affliction of defeat, the dark brooding of old warriors.

Her name was Aho, and she belonged to the last culture to evolve in North America. Her forebears came down from the high country in western Montana nearly three centuries ago. They were a mountain people, a mysterious tribe of hunters whose language has never been positively classified in any major group. In the late seventeenth century they began a long migration to the south and east. It was a journey toward the dawn, and it led to a golden age. Along the way the Kiowas were befriended by the Crows, who gave them the culture and religion of the Plains. They acquired horses, and their ancient nomadic spirit was suddenly free of the ground. They acquired Tai-me, the sacred Sun Dance doll, from that moment the object and symbol of their worship, and so shared in the divinity of the sun. Not least, they acquired the sense of destiny, therefore courage and pride. When they entered upon the southern Plains they had been transformed. No longer were they slaves to the simple necessity of survival; they were a lordly and dangerous society of fighters and thieves, hunters and priests of the sun. According to their origin myth, they entered the world through a hollow log. From one point of view, their migration was the fruit of an old prophecy, for indeed they emerged from a sunless world.

Although my grandmother lived out her long life in the shadow of Rainy Mountain, the immense landscape of the continental interior lay like memory in her blood. She could tell of the Crows, whom she had never seen, and of the Black Hills, where she had never been. I wanted to see in reality what she had seen more perfectly in the mind's eye, and traveled fifteen hundred miles to begin my pilgrimage.

Yellowstone, it seemed to me, was the top of the world, a region of deep lakes and dark timber, canyons and waterfalls. But, beautiful as it is, one might have the sense of confinement there. The skyline in all directions is close at hand, the high wall of the woods and deep cleavages of shade. There is a perfect freedom in the mountains, but it belongs to the eagle and the elk, the badger and the bear. The Kiowas reckoned their stature by the distance they could see, and they were bent and blind in the wilderness.

Descending eastward, the highland meadows are a stairway to the plain. In July the inland slope of the Rockies is luxuriant with flax and buckwheat, stonecrop and larkspur. The earth unfolds and the limit of the land recedes. Clusters of trees, and animals grazing far in the distance, cause the vision to reach away and wonder to build upon the mind. The sun follows a longer course in the day, and the sky is immense beyond all comparison. The great billowing clouds that sail upon it are shadows that move upon the grain like water, dividing light. Farther down, in the land of the Crows and Blackfeet, the plain is yellow. Sweet clover takes hold of the hills and bends upon itself to cover and seal the soil. There the Kiowas paused on their way; they had come to the place where they must change their lives. The sun is at home on the plains. Precisely there does it have the certain character of a god. When the Kiowas came to the land of the Crows, they could see the dark lees of the hills at dawn across the Bighorn River, the profusion of light on the grain shelves, the oldest deity ranging after the solstices. Not yet would they veer southward to the caldron of the land that lay below; they must wean their blood from the northern winter and hold the mountains a while longer in their view. They bore Tai-me in procession to the east.

A dark mist lay over the Black Hills, and the land was like iron. At the top of a ridge I caught sight of Devil's Tower upthrust against the gray sky as if in the birth of time the core of the earth had broken through its crust and the motion of the world was begun. There are things in nature that engender an awful quiet in the heart of man; Devil's Tower is one of them. Two centuries ago, because they could not do otherwise, the Kiowas made a legend at the base of the rock. My grandmother said:

> Eight children were there at play, seven sisters and their brother. Suddenly the boy was struck dumb; he trembled and began to run upon his hands and feet. His fingers became claws, and his body was covered with fur. Directly there was a bear where the boy had been. The sisters were terrified; they ran, and the bear after them. They came to the stump of a great tree, and the tree spoke to them. It bade them climb upon it, and as they did so it began to rise into the air. The bear came to kill them, but they were just beyond its reach. It reared against the tree and scored the bark all around with its claws. The seven sisters were borne into the sky, and they became the stars of the Big Dipper.

From that moment, and so long as the legend lives, the Kiowas have kinsmen in the night sky. Whatever they were in the mountains, they could be no more. However tenuous their well-being, however much they had suffered and would suffer again, they had found a way out of the wilderness.

My grandmother had a reverence for the sun, a holy regard that now is all but gone out of mankind. There was a wariness in her, and an ancient awe. She was a Christian in her later years, but she had come a long way about, and she never forgot her birthright. As a child she had been to the Sun Dances; she had taken part in those annual rites, and by then she had learned the restoration of her people in the presence of Tai-me. She was about seven when the last Kiowa Sun Dance was held in 1887 on the Washita River above Rainy Mountain Creek. The buffalo were gone. In order to consummate the ancient sacrifice—to impale the head of a buffalo bull upon the medicine tree—a delegation of old men journeyed into Texas, there to beg and barter for an animal from the Goodnight herd. She was ten when the Kiowas came together for the last time as a living Sun Dance culture. They could find no buffalo; they had to hang an old hide from the sacred tree. Before the dance could begin, a company of soldiers rode out from Fort Sill under orders to disperse the tribe. Forbidden without cause the essential act of their faith, having seen the wild herds slaughtered and left to rot upon the ground, the Kiowas backed away forever from the medicine tree. That was July 20, 1890, at the great bend of the Washita. My grandmother was there. Without bitterness, and for as long as she lived, she bore a vision of deicide.

Now that I can have her only in memory, I see my grandmother in the several postures that were peculiar to her: standing at the wood stove on a winter morning and turning meat in a great iron skillet; sitting at the south window, bent above her beadwork, and afterwards, when her vision failed, looking down for a long time into the fold of her hands; going out upon a cane, very slowly as she did when the weight of age came upon her; praying. I remember her most often at prayer. She made long, rambling prayers out of suffering and hope, having seen many things. I was never sure that I had the right to hear, so exclusive were they of all mere custom and company. The last time I saw her she prayed standing by the side of her bed at night, naked to the waist, the light of a kerosene lamp moving upon her dark skin. Her long, black hair, always drawn and braided in the day, lay upon her shoulders and against her breasts like a shawl. I do not speak Kiowa, and I never understood her prayers, but there was something inherently sad in the sound, some merest hesitation upon the syllables of sorrow. She began in a high and descending pitch, exhausting her breath to silence; then again and again—and always the same intensity of effort, of something that is, and is not, like urgency in the human voice. Transported so in the dancing light among the shadows of her room, she seemed beyond the reach of time. But that was illusion; I think I knew then that I should not see her again.

Houses are like sentinels in the plain, old keepers of the weather watch. There, in a very little while, wood takes on the appearance of great age. All colors wear soon away in the wind and rain, and then the wood is burned gray and the grain appears and the nails turn red with rust. The windowpanes are black and opaque; you imagine there is nothing within, and indeed there are many ghosts, bones given up to the land. They stand here and there against the sky, and you approach them for a longer time than you expect. They belong in the distance; it is their domain.

Once there was a lot of sound in my grandmother's house, a lot of coming and going, feasting and talk. The summers there were full of excitement and reunion. The Kiowas are a summer people; they abide the cold and keep to themselves, but when the season turns and the land becomes warm and vital they cannot hold still; an old love of going returns upon them. The aged visitors who came to my grandmother's house when I was a child were made of lean and leather, and they bore themselves upright. They wore great black hats and bright ample shirts that shook in the wind. They rubbed fat upon their hair and wound their braids with strips of colored cloth. Some of them painted their faces and carried the scars of old and cherished enmities. They were an old council of warlords, come to remind and be reminded of who they were. Their wives and daughters served them well. The women might indulge themselves; gossip was at once the mark and compensation of their servitude. They made loud and elaborate talk among themselves, full of jest and gesture, fright and false alarm. They went abroad in fringed and flowered shawls, bright beadwork and German silver. They were at home in the kitchen, and they prepared meals that were banquets.

There were frequent prayer meetings, and great nocturnal feasts. When I was a child I played with my cousins outside, where the lamplight fell upon the ground and the singing of the old people rose up around us and carried away into the darkness. There were a lot of good things to eat, a lot of laughter and surprise. And afterwards, when the quiet returned, I lay down with my grandmother and could hear the frogs away by the river and feel the motion of the air.

Now there is a funeral silence in the rooms, the endless wake of some final word. The walls have closed in upon my grandmother's house. When I returned to it in mourning, I saw for the first time in my life how small it was. It was late at night, and there was a white moon, nearly full.

I sat for a long time on the stone steps by the kitchen door. From there I could see out across the land; I could see the long row of trees by the creek, the low light upon the rolling plains, and the stars of the Big Dipper. Once I looked at the moon and caught sight of a strange thing. A cricket had perched upon the handrail, only a few inches away from me. My line of vision was such that the creature filled the moon like a fossil. It had gone there, I thought, to live and die, for there, of all places, was its small definition made whole and eternal. A warm wind rose up and purled like the longing within me.

The next morning I awoke at dawn and went out on the dirt road to Rainy Mountain. It was already hot, and the grasshoppers began to fill the air. Still, it was early in the morning, and the birds sang out of the shadows. The long yellow grass on the mountain shone in the bright light, and a scissortail hied above the land. There, where it ought to be, at the end of a long and legendary way, was my grandmother's grave. Here and there on the dark stones were ancestral names. Looking back once, I saw the mountain and came away.

Living Like Weasels

Annie Dillard

A weasel is wild. Who knows what he thinks? He sleeps in his underground den, his tail draped over his nose. Sometimes he lives in his den for two days without leaving. Outside, he stalks rabbits, mice, muskrats, and birds, killing more bodies than he can eat warm, and often dragging the carcasses home. Obedient to instinct, he bites his prey at the neck, either splitting the jugular vein at the throat or crunching the brain at the base of the skull, and he does not let go. One naturalist refused to kill a weasel who was socketed into his hand deeply as a rattlesnake. The man could in no way pry the tiny weasel off, and he had to walk half a mile to water, the weasel dangling from his palm, and soak him off like a stubborn label.

And once, says Ernest Thompson Seton—once, a man shot an eagle out of the sky. He examined the eagle and found the dry skull of a weasel fixed by the jaws to his throat. The supposition is that the eagle had pounced on the weasel and the weasel swiveled and bit as instinct taught him, tooth to neck, and nearly won. I would like to have seen that eagle from the air a few weeks or months before he was shot: was the whole weasel still attached to his feathered throat, a fur pendant? Or did the eagle eat what he could reach, gutting the living weasel with his talons before his breast, bending his beak, cleaning the beautiful airborne bones?

I have been thinking about weasels because I saw one last week. I startled a weasel who startled me, and we exchanged a long glance.

Near my house in Virginia is a pond—Hollins Pond. It covers two acres of bottomland near Tinker Creek with six inches of water and six thousand lily pads. There is a fifty-five mph highway at one end of the pond, and a nesting pair of wood ducks at the other. Under every bush is a muskrat hole or a beer can. The far end is an alternating series of fields and woods, fields and woods, threaded everywhere with motorcycle tracks—in whose bare clay wild turtles lay eggs.

One evening last week at sunset, I walked to the pond and sat on a downed log near the shore. I was watching the lily pads at my feet tremble and part over the thrusting path of a carp. A yellow warbler appeared to my right and flew behind me. It caught my eye; I swiveled around—and the next instant, inexplicably, I was looking down at a weasel, who was looking up at me.

Weasel! I had never seen one wild before. He was ten inches long, thin as a curve, a muscled ribbon, brown as fruitwood, soft-furred, alert. His face was fierce, small and pointed as a lizard's; he would have made a good arrowhead. There was just a dot of chin, maybe two brown hairs' worth, and then the pure white fur began that spread down his underside. He had two black eyes I did not see, any more than you see a window.

The weasel was stunned into stillness as he was emerging from beneath an enormous shaggy wild-rose bush four feet away. I was stunned into stillness, twisted backward on the tree trunk. Our eyes locked, and someone threw away the key.

Our look was as if two lovers, or deadly enemies, met unexpectedly on an overgrown path when each had been thinking of something else: a clearing blow to the gut. It was also a bright blow to the brain, or a sudden beating of brains, with all the charge and intimate grate of rubbed balloons. It emptied our lungs. It felled the forest, moved the fields, and drained the pond; the world dismantled and tumbled into that black hole of eyes. If you and I looked at each other that way, our skulls would split and drop to our shoulders. But we don't. We keep our skulls.

He disappeared. This was only last week, and already I don't remember what shattered the enchantment. I think I blinked, I think I retrieved my brain from the weasel's brain, and tried to memorize what I was seeing, and the weasel felt the yank of separation, the careening splashdown into real life and the urgent current of instinct. He vanished under the wild rose. I waited motionless, my mind suddenly full of data and my spirit with pleadings, but he didn't return.

Please do not tell me about "approach-avoidance conflicts." I tell you I've been in that weasel's brain for sixty seconds, and he was in mine. Brains are private places, muttering through unique and secret tapes—

but the weasel and I both plugged into another tape simultaneously, for a sweet and shocking time. Can I help it if it was a blank?

What goes on in his brain the rest of the time? What does a weasel think about? He won't say. His journal is tracks in clay, a spray of feathers, mouse blood and bone: uncollected, unconnected, loose-leaf, and blown.

I would like to learn, or remember, how to live. I come to Hollins Pond not so much to learn how to live as, frankly, to forget about it. That is, I don't think I can learn from a wild animal how to live in particular—shall I suck warm blood, hold my tail high, walk with my footprints precisely over the prints of my hands?—but I might learn something of mindlessness, something of the purity of living in the physical senses and the dignity of living without bias or motive. The weasel lives in necessity and we live in choice, hating necessity and dying at the last ignobly in its talons. I would like to live as I should, as the weasel lives as he should. And I suspect that for me the way is like the weasel's: open to time and death painlessly, noticing everything, remembering nothing, choosing the given with a fierce and pointed will.

I missed my chance. I should have gone for the throat. I should have lunged for that streak of white under the weasel's chin and held on, held on through mud and into the wild rose, held on for a dearer life. We could live under the wild rose wild as weasels, mute and uncomprehending. I could very calmly go wild. I could live two days in the den, curled, leaning on mouse fur, sniffing bird bones, blinking, licking, breathing musk, my hair tangled in the roots of grasses. Down is a good place to go, where the mind is single. Down is out, out of your ever-loving mind and back to your careless senses. I remember muteness as a prolonged and giddy fast, where every moment is a feast of utterance received. Time and events are merely poured, unremarked, and ingested directly, like blood pulsed into my gut through a jugular vein. Could two live that way? Could two live under the wild rose, and explore by the pond, so that the smooth mind of each is as everywhere present to the other, and as received and as unchallenged, as falling snow?

We could, you know. We can live any way we want. People take vows of poverty, chastity, and obedience—even of silence—by choice. The thing is to stalk your calling in a certain skilled and supple way, to locate the most tender and live spot and plug into that pulse. This is yielding, not fighting. A weasel doesn't "attack" anything; a weasel lives as he's meant to, yielding at every moment to the perfect freedom of single necessity.

I think it would be well, and proper, and obedient, and pure, to grasp your one necessity and not let it go, to dangle from it limp wherever it takes you. Then even death, where you're going no matter how you live, cannot you part. Seize it and let it seize you up aloft even, till your eyes burn out and drop; let your musky flesh fall off in shreds, and let your very bones unhinge and scatter, loosened over fields, over fields and woods, lightly, thoughtless, from any height at all, from as high as eagles.

The Serpents of Paradise

Edward Abbey

The April mornings are bright, clear and calm. Not until the afternoon does the wind begin to blow, raising dust and sand in funnel-shaped twisters that spin across the desert briefly, like dancers, and then collapse—whirlwinds from which issue no voice or word except the forlorn moan of the elements under stress. After the reconnoitering dust-devils comes the real, the serious wind, the voice of the desert rising to a demented howl and blotting out sky and sun behind yellow clouds of dust, sand, confusion, embattled birds, last year's scrub-oak leaves, pollen, the husks of locusts, bark of juniper. . . .

Time of the red eye, the sore and bloody nostril, the sand-pitted windshield, if one is foolish enough to drive his car into such a storm. Time to sit indoors and continue that letter which is never finished—while the fine dust forms neat little windrows under the edge of the door and on the windowsills. Yet the springtime winds are as much a part of the canyon country as the silence and the glamorous distances; you learn, after a number of years, to love them also.

The mornings therefore, as I started to say and meant to say, are all the sweeter in the knowledge of what the afternoon is likely to bring. Before beginning the morning chores I like to sit on the sill of my doorway, bare feet planted on the bare ground and a mug of hot coffee in hand, facing the sunrise. The air is gelid, not far above freezing, but the butane heater inside the trailer keeps my back warm, the rising sun warms the front, and the coffee warms the interior.

Perhaps this is the loveliest hour of the day, though it's hard to choose. Much depends on the season. In midsummer the sweetest hour begins at sundown, after the awful heat of the afternoon. But now, in April, we'll take the opposite, that hour beginning with the sunrise. The birds, returning from wherever they go in winter, seem inclined to agree. The pinyon jays are whirling in garrulous, gregarious flocks from one stunted-tree to the next and back again, erratic exuberant games without any apparent practical function. A few big ravens hang around and croak harsh clanking statements of smug satisfaction from the rimrock, lifting their greasy wings now and then to probe for lice. I can hear but seldom see the canyon wrens singing their distinctive song from somewhere up on the cliffs: a flutelike descent—never ascent—of the whole-tone scale. Staking out new nesting claims, I understand. Also invisible but invariably present at some indefinable distance are the mourning doves whose plaintive call suggests irresistibly a kind of seeking-out, the attempt by separated souls to restore a lost communion:

Hello . . . they seem to cry, *who . . . are . . . you?*

And the reply from a different quarter. *Hello* . . . (pause) *where . . . are . . . you?*

No doubt this line of analogy must be rejected. It's foolish and unfair to impute to the doves, with serious concerns of their own, an interest in questions more appropriate to their human-kin. Yet their song, if not a mating call or a warning, must be what it sounds like, a brooding meditation on space, on solitude. The game.

Other birds, silent, which I have not yet learned to identify, are also lurking in the vicinity, watching me. What the ornithologist terms l.g.b.'s—little gray birds—they flit about from point to point on noiseless wings, their origins obscure.

As mentioned before, I share the housetrailer with a number of mice. I don't know how many but apparently only a few, perhaps a single family. They don't disturb me and are welcome to my crumbs and leavings. Where they came from, how they got into the trailer, how they survived before my arrival (for the trailer had been locked up for six months), these are puzzling matters I am not prepared to resolve. My only reservation concerning the mice is that they do attract rattlesnakes.

I'm sitting on my doorstep early one morning, facing the sun as usual, drinking coffee, when I happen to look down and see almost between my bare feet, only a couple of inches to the rear of my heels, the very thing I had in mind. No mistaking that wedgelike head, that tip of horny segmented tail peeping out of the coils. He's under the doorstep and in the shade where the ground and air remain very cold. In his sluggish condition he's not likely to strike unless I rouse him by some careless move of my own.

There's a revolver inside the trailer, a huge British Webley .45, loaded, but it's out of reach. Even if I had it in my hands I'd hesitate to blast a fellow creature at such close range, shooting between my own legs at a living target flat on solid rock thirty inches away. It would be like murder; and where would I set my coffee? My cherry-wood, walking stick leans against the trailerhouse wall only a few feet away but I'm afraid that in leaning over for it I might stir up the rattler or spill some hot coffee on his scales.

Other considerations come to mind. Arches National Monument is meant to be among other things a sanctuary for wildlife—for all forms of wildlife. It is my duty as a park ranger to protect, preserve and defend all living things within the park boundaries, making no exceptions. Even if this were not the case I have personal convictions to uphold. Ideals, you might say. I prefer not to kill animals. I'm a humanist; I'd rather kill a *man* than a snake.

What to do. I drink some more coffee and study the dormant reptile at my heels. It is not after all the mighty diamondback, *Crotalus atrox*, I'm confronted with but a smaller species known locally as the horny rattler or more precisely as the Faded Midget. An insulting name for a rattlesnake, which may explain the Faded Midget's alleged bad temper. But the name is apt: he is small and dusty-looking, with a little knob above each eye—the horns. His bite, though temporarily disabling, would not likely kill a full-grown man in normal health. Even so I don't really want him around. Am I to be compelled to put on boots or shoes every time I wish to step outside? The scorpions, tarantulas, centipedes, and black widows are nuisance enough.

I finish my coffee, lean back and swing my feet up and inside the doorway of the trailer. At once there is a buzzing sound from below and the rattler lifts his head from his coils, eyes brightening, and extends his narrow black tongue to test the air.

After thawing out my boots over the gas flame I pull them on and come back to the doorway. My visitor is still waiting beneath the doorstep, basking in the sun, fully alert. The trailerhouse has two doors. I leave by the other and get a long-handled spade out of the bed of the government pickup. With this tool I scoop the snake into the open. He strikes; I can hear the click of the fangs against steel, see the strain of venom. He wants to stand and fight, but I am patient; I insist on herding him well away from the trailer. On guard, head aloft—that evil slit-eyed weaving head shaped like the ace of spades—tail whirring, the rattler slithers sideways, retreating slowly before me until he reaches the shelter of a sandstone slab. He backs under it.

You better stay there, cousin, I warn him; if I catch you around the trailer again I'll chop your head off.

A week later he comes back. If not him, his twin brother. I spot him one morning under the trailer near the kitchen drain, waiting for a mouse. I have to keep my promise.

This won't do. If there are midget rattlers in the area there may be diamondbacks too—five, six or seven feet long, thick as a man's wrist, dangerous. I don't want *them* camping under my home. It looks as though I'll have to trap the mice.

However, before being forced to take that step I am lucky enough to capture a gopher snake. Burning garbage one morning at the park dump, I see a long slender yellow-brown snake emerge from a mound of old tin cans and plastic picnic plates and take off down the sandy bed of a gulch. There is a burlap sack in the cab of the truck which I carry when plucking Kleenex flowers from the brush and cactus along the road; I grab that and my stick, run after the snake and corner it beneath the exposed roots of a bush. Making sure it's a gopher snake and not something less useful, I open the neck of the sack and with a great deal of coaxing and prodding get the snake into it. The gopher snake, *Drymarchon corais couperi*, or bull snake, has a reputation as the enemy of rattlesnakes, destroying or driving them away whenever encountered.

Hoping to domesticate this sleek, handsome and docile reptile, I release him inside the trailerhouse and keep him there for several days. Should I attempt to feed him? I decide against it—let him eat mice. What little water he may need can also be extracted from the flesh of his prey.

The gopher snake and I get along nicely. During the day he curls up like a cat in the warm corner behind the heater and at night he goes about his business. The mice, singularly quiet for a change, make themselves scarce. The snake is passive, apparently contented, and makes no resistance when I pick him up with my hands and drape him over an arm or around my neck. When I take him outside into the wind and sunshine his favorite place seems to be inside my shirt, where he wraps himself around my waist and rests on my belt. In this position he sometimes sticks his head out between shirt buttons for a survey of the weather, astonishing and delighting any tourists who may happen to be with me at the time. The scales of a snake are dry and smooth, quite pleasant to the touch. Being a cold-blooded creature, of course, he takes his temperature from that of the immediate environment—in this case my body.

We are compatible. From my point of view, friends. After a week of close association I turn him loose on the warm sandstone at my doorstep and leave for patrol of the park. At noon when I return he is gone. I search everywhere beneath, nearby and inside the trailerhouse, but my companion has disappeared. Has he left the area entirely or is he hiding somewhere close by? At any rate I am troubled no more by rattlesnakes under the door.

The snake story is not yet ended.

In the middle of May, about a month after the gopher snake's disappearance, in the evening of a very hot day, with all the rosy desert cooling like a griddle with the fire turned off, he reappears. This time with a mate.

I'm in the stifling heat of the trailer opening a can of beer, barefooted, about to go outside and relax after a hard day watching cloud formations. I happen to glance out the little window near the refrigerator and see two gopher snakes on my verandah engaged in what seems to be a kind of ritual dance. Like a living caduceus they wind and unwind about each other in undulant, graceful, perpetual motion, moving slowly across a dome of sandstone. Invisible but tangible as music is the passion which joins them—sexual? combative? both? A shameless *voyeur*, I stare at the lovers, and then to get a closer view run outside and around the trailer to the back. There I get down on hands and knees and creep toward the dancing snakes, not wanting to frighten or disturb them. I crawl to within six feet of them and stop, flat on my belly, watching from the snake's-eye level. Obsessed with their ballet, the serpents seem unaware of my presence.

The two gopher snakes are nearly identical in length and coloring; I cannot be certain that either is actually my former household pet. I cannot even be sure that they are male and female, though their performance resembles so strongly a *pas de deux* by formal lovers. They intertwine and separate, glide side by side in perfect congruence, turn like mirror images of each other and glide back again, wind and unwind again. This is the basic pattern but there is a variation: at regular intervals the snakes elevate their heads, facing one another, as high as they can go, as if each is trying to outreach or overawe the other. Their heads and bodies rise, higher and higher, then topple together and the rite goes on.

I crawl after them, determined to see the whole thing. Suddenly and simultaneously they discover me, prone on my belly a few feet away. The dance stops. After a moment's pause the two snakes come straight toward me, still in flawless unison, straight toward my face, the forked tongues flickering, their intense wild yellow eyes staring directly into my eyes. For an instant I am paralyzed by wonder; then, stung by a fear too ancient and powerful to overcome I scramble back, rising to my knees. The snakes veer and turn and race away from me in parallel motion, their lean elegant bodies making a soft hissing noise as they slide over the sand and stone. I follow them for a short distance, still plagued by curiosity, before remembering my place and the requirements of common courtesy. For godsake let them go in peace, I tell myself. Wish them luck and (if lovers) innumerable offspring, a life of happily ever after. Not for their sake alone but for your own.

In the long hot days and cool evenings to come I will not see the gopher snakes again. Nevertheless I will feel their presence watching over me like totemic deities, keeping the rattlesnakes far back in the brush where I like them best, cropping off the surplus mouse population, maintaining useful connections with the primeval Sympathy, mutual aid, symbiosis, continuity.

How can I descend to such anthropomorphism? Easily—but is it, in this case, entirely false? Perhaps not. I am not attributing human motives to my snake and bird acquaintances. I recognize that when and where they serve purposes of mine they do so for beautifully selfish reasons of their own. Which is exactly the way it should be. I suggest, however, that it's a foolish, simple-minded rationalism which denies any form of emotion to all animals but man and his dog. This is no more justified than the Moslems are in denying souls to women. It seems to me possible, even probable, that many of the nonhuman undomesticated animals experience emotions unknown to us. What do the coyotes mean when they yodel at the moon? What are the dolphins trying so patiently to tell us? Precisely what did those two enraptured gopher snakes have in mind when they came gliding toward my eyes over the naked sandstone? If I had been as capable of trust as I am susceptible to fear I might have learned something new or some truth so very old we have all forgotten it.

> They do not sweat and whine about their condition,
> They do not lie awake in the dark and weep for their sins. . . .

All men are brothers, we like to say, half-wishing sometimes in secret it were not true. But perhaps it is true. And is the evolutionary line from protozoan to Spinoza any less certain? That also may be true. We are obliged, therefore, to spread the news, painful and bitter though it may be for some to hear, that all living things on earth are kindred.

Am I Blue?

"Ain't these tears in these eyes tellin' you?"

Alice Walker

For about three years my companion and I rented a small house in the country that stood on the edge of a large meadow that appeared to run from the end of our deck straight into the mountains. The mountains, however, were quite far away, and between us and them there was, in fact, a town. It was one of the many pleasant aspects of the house that you never really were aware of this.

It was a house of many windows, low, wide, nearly floor to ceiling in the living room, which faced the meadow, and it was from one of these that I first saw our closest neighbor, a large white horse, cropping grass, flipping its mane, and ambling about—not over the entire meadow, which stretched well out of sight of the house, but over the five or so fenced-in acres that were next to the twenty-odd that we had rented. I soon learned that the horse, whose name was Blue, belonged to a man who lived in another town, but was boarded by our neighbors next door. Occasionally, one of the children, usually a stocky teen-ager, but sometimes a much younger girl or boy, could be seen riding Blue. They would appear in the meadow, climb up on his back, ride furiously for ten or fifteen minutes, then get off, slap Blue on the flanks, and not be seen again for a month or more.

There were many apple trees in our yard, and one by the fence that Blue could almost reach. We were soon in the habit of feeding him apples, which he relished, especially because by the middle of summer the meadow grasses—so green and succulent since January—had dried out from lack of rain, and Blue stumbled about munching the dried stalks half-heartedly. Sometimes he would stand very still just by the apple tree, and when one of us came out he would whinny, snort loudly, or stamp the ground. This meant, of course: I want an apple.

It was quite wonderful to pick a few apples, or collect those that had fallen to the ground overnight, and patiently hold them, one by one, up to his large, toothy mouth. I remained as thrilled as a child by his flexible dark lips, huge, cubelike teeth that crunched the apples, core and all, with such finality, and his high, broad-breasted *enormity;* beside which, I felt small indeed. When I was a child, I used to ride horses, and was especially friendly with one named Nan until the day I was riding and my brother deliberately spooked her and I was thrown, head first, against the trunk of a tree. When I came to, I was in bed and my mother was bending worriedly over me; we silently agreed that perhaps horseback riding was not the safest sport for me. Since then I have walked, and prefer walking to horseback riding—but I had forgotten the depth of feeling one could see in horses' eyes.

I was therefore unprepared for the expression in Blue's. Blue was lonely. Blue was horribly lonely and bored. I was not shocked that this should be the case; five acres to tramp by yourself, endlessly, even in the most beautiful of meadows—and his was—cannot provide many interesting events, and once rainy season turned to dry that was about it. No, I was shocked that I had forgotten that human animals and nonhuman animals can communicate quite well; if we are brought up around animals as children we take this for granted. By the time we are adults we no longer remember. However, the animals have not changed. They are in fact *completed* creations (at least they seem to be, so much more than we) who are not likely to change; it is their nature to express themselves. What else are they going to express? And they do. And, generally speaking, they are ignored.

After giving Blue the apples, I would wander back to the house, aware that he was observing me. Were more apples not forthcoming then? Was that to be his sole entertainment for the day? My partner's small son had decided he wanted to learn how to piece a quilt; we worked in silence on our respective squares as I thought . . .

Well, about slavery: about white children, who were raised by black people, who knew their first all-accepting love from black women, and then, when they were twelve or so, were told they must "forget" the deep levels of communication between themselves and "mammy" that they knew. Later they would be able to relate quite calmly, "My old mammy was sold to another good family." "My old mammy was —— ——." Fill in the blank. Many more years later a white woman would say: "I can't understand these Negroes, these blacks. What do they want? They're so different from us."

And about the Indians, considered to be "like animals" by the "settlers" (a very benign euphemism for what they actually were), who did not understand their description as a compliment.

And about the thousands of American men who marry Japanese, Korean, Filipina, and other non-English-speaking women and of how happy they report they are, *"blissfully,"* until their brides learn to speak English, at which point the marriages tend to fall apart. What then did the men see, when they looked into the eyes of the women they married, before they could speak English? Apparently only their own reflections.

I thought of society's impatience with the young. "Why are they playing the music so loud?" Perhaps the children have listened to much of the music of oppressed people their parents danced to before they were born, with its passionate but soft cries for acceptance and love, and they have wondered why their parents failed to hear.

I do not know how long Blue had inhabited his five beautiful, boring acres before we moved into our house; a year after we had arrived—and had also traveled to other valleys, other cities, other worlds—he was still there.

But then, in our second year at the house, something happened in Blue's life. One morning, looking out the window at the fog that lay like a ribbon over the meadow, I saw another horse, a brown one, at the other end of Blue's field. Blue appeared to be afraid of it, and for several days made no attempt to go near. We went away for a week. When we returned, Blue had decided to make friends and the two horses ambled or galloped along together, and Blue did not come nearly as often to the fence underneath the apple tree.

When he did, bringing his new friend with him, there was a different look in his eyes. A look of independence, of self-possession, of inalienable *horse*ness. His friend eventually became pregnant. For months and months there was, it seemed to me, a mutual feeling between me and the horses of justice, of peace. I fed apples to them both. The look in Blue's eyes was one of unabashed "this is *it*ness."

It did not, however, last forever. One day, after a visit to the city, I went out to give Blue some apples. He stood waiting, or so I thought, though not beneath the tree. When I shook the tree and jumped back from the shower of apples, he made no move. I carried some over to him. He managed to half-crunch one. The rest he let fall to the ground. I dreaded looking into his eyes—because I had of course noticed that Brown, his partner, had gone—but I did look. If I had been born into slavery, and my partner had been sold or killed, my eyes would have looked like that. The children next door explained that Blue's partner had been "put with him" (the same expression that old people used, I had noticed, when speaking of an ancestor during slavery who had been impregnated by her owner) so that they could mate and she conceive. Since that was accomplished, she had been taken back by her owner, who lived somewhere else.

Will she be back? I asked.

They didn't know.

Blue was like a crazed person. Blue *was*, to me, a crazed person. He galloped furiously, as if he were being ridden, around and around his five beautiful acres. He whinnied until he couldn't. He tore at the ground with his hooves. He butted himself against his single shade tree. He looked always and always toward the road down which his partner had gone. And then, occasionally, when he came up for apples, or I took apples to him, he looked me. It was a look so piercing, so full of grief, a look so *human*, I almost laughed (I felt too sad to cry) to think there are people who do not know that animals suffer. People like me who have forgotten, and daily forget, all that animals try to tell us. "Everything you do to us will happen to you; we are your teachers, as you are ours. We are one lesson" is essentially it, I think. There are those who never once have even considered animals' rights: those who have been taught that animals actually want to be used and abused by us, as small children "love" to be frightened, or women "love" to be mutilated and raped. . . . They are the great-grandchildren of those who honestly thought, because someone taught them this: "Women can't think," and "niggers can't faint." But most disturbing of all, in Blue's large brown eyes was a new look, more painful than the look of despair: the look of disgust with human beings, with life; the look of hatred. And it was odd what the look of hatred did. It gave him, for the first time, the look of a beast. And what that meant was that he had put up a barrier within to protect himself from further violence; all the apples in the world wouldn't change that fact.

And so Blue remained, a beautiful part of our landscape, very peaceful to look at from the window, white against the grass. Once a friend came to visit and said, looking out on the soothing view. "And it *would* have to be a *white* horse; the very image of freedom." And I thought, yes, the animals are forced to become for us merely "images" of what they once so beautifully expressed. And we are used to drinking milk from containers showing "contented" cows, whose real lives we want to hear nothing about, eating eggs and drumsticks from "happy" hens, and munching hamburgers advertised by bulls of integrity who seem to command their fate.

As we talked of freedom and justice one day for all, we sat down to steaks. I am eating misery, I thought, as I took the first bite. And spit it out.

Exposition

Exposition

Exposition, according to *The American Heritage Dictionary*, means "the systematic explanation of a subject" (303). In other words, it is the process by which a writer conveys information so that the reader can understand the subject better, can make connections between the subject and his or her own experience, or can grasp the subject in a larger context. This method of writing requires analysis on the part of the writer as well as a decision about which mode of analysis is appropriate for the intended purpose. The modes that fall under exposition are example, definition, process analysis, cause and effect, comparison and contrast, and classification and division.

For instance, if the purpose is to inform readers about the short- and long-term influences of substance abuse, the writer would write using cause and effect. If the purpose is to examine the philosophical differences between the Democratic and Republican platforms, the writer would choose to write a comparison and contrast essay. If, again, the purpose is to explore what it means to be middle class in America today, the writer might decide to use definition to specify the essential nature or quality of what "middle class" means.

Each mode is featured in separate subsections with an explanation of the mode and selection of representative readings.

Exemplification

Essays are written compositions that present your thoughts and opinions about a topic backed by facts that shows the reader the logic of your position. Because you want readers to consider what you say, you need to show that your position is reasonable and worth considering. One way to support your position, or thesis statement, is through the use of examples. Examples provide specific information that illustrate or explain a general point or abstract concept. For example, you could make the general statement that reality shows have proliferated on TV, ranging from the ludicrous to the worthwhile. Then you would give examples of a few shows to show what you mean.

The method of using examples to illustrate a point is commonplace in all forms of writing and central to providing interest and clarity. Using examples makes writing effective because it makes the prose dynamic and eliminates confusion about concepts that are too general or vague. Think how many times you have read the words "for example" or "for instance" and how the examples that followed made the idea more understandable.

The Process

Purpose and Thesis

As described above, the purpose of an exemplification essay is to make a generalization clear but by providing specific examples that make it understandable and give proof. The thesis statement would provide the generalization, or main idea, and the remainder of the essay would provide the specifics that illustrate the point and make it clear. Here is an example of a thesis statement from an essay in this chapter:

> Sometimes I think we would be better off [in dealing with social problems] if we forgot about the broad strokes and concentrated on the details.
>
> –Anna Quindlen, "Homeless"

What does Quindlen mean? Her essay gives examples of what those details of "home" mean.

Quindlen's thesis proves the point that a thesis statement is a declarative sentence that reasonable people could disagree with. A reasonable person could disagree with Quindlen's takes on her subject.

As for the example of reality shows in the opening paragraph above, a thesis statement that illustrates a stand on the topic that might differ from someone else's is the following:

> Reality shows have proliferated across all television genres and range from the embarrassing and ludicrous to the inspirational and educational.

This general statement would be illustrated by examples of various reality shows that prove the point.

Organization

An exemplification essay begins with an introductory paragraph that leads to and ends with the thesis statement, or general point the essay will illustrate. The body of the essay features a number of paragraphs that will provide detailed examples, each of which depict some aspect of your thesis and together establish, or prove, your point.

Shaping Paragraphs

Standard paragraphs are the bricks that build your essay. They are a convenient way to lead the reader through your essay and a handy way to help you organize your writing. The following is Paragraphs 101:

1. Each paragraph focuses on a single point or subject.
   a. It has a topic sentence, which is the main point of the para graph, usually located near the beginning of the paragraph.
   b. The rest of the sentences are what you write about that main point: the details and examples.
   c. The last sentence of the paragraph drives the point home.

   d. When you start writing about a different point or subject or shift your attention, even slightly, it's time to make a new paragraph.

2. Keep your paragraphs coherent by:

   a. Connecting each paragraph to your thesis

   b. Carrying over the same idea from sentence to sentence

   c. Repeating key words in several sentences

   d. Repeating synonymous words in several sentences

   e. Using transition words to link ideas from different sentences

3. Keep the paragraph flowing smoothly by using transitions to link them together. You can make a transition by:

   a. Repeating a word or phrase from a previous sentence or para graph

   b. Continuing a thought from an earlier paragraph

   c. Use transitional words, such as *but, however, therefore, indeed, of course.*

4. The topic (which is introduced by the topic sentence) should be discussed fully and adequately.

5. Always keep the same point of view and verb tense throughout your paragraphs.

Simplicity

William Zinsser

Clutter is the disease of American writing. We are a society strangling in unnecessary words, circular constructions, pompous frills and meaningless jargon.

Who can understand the clotted language of everyday American commerce: the memo, the corporation report, the business letter, the notice from the bank explaining its latest "simplified" statement? What member of an insurance or medical plan can decipher the brochure explaining his costs and benefits? What father or mother can put together a child's toy from the instructions on the box? Our national tendency is to inflate and thereby sound important. The airline pilot who announces that he is presently anticipating experiencing considerable precipitation wouldn't think of saying it may rain. The sentence is too simple—there must be something wrong with it.

But the secret of good writing is to strip every sentence to its cleanest components. Every word that serves no function, every long word that could be a short word, every adverb that carries the same meaning that's already in the verb, every passive construction that leaves the reader unsure of who is doing what—these are the thousand and one adulterants that weaken the strength of a sentence. And they usually occur in proportion to education and rank.

During the 1960s the president of my university wrote a letter to mollify the alumni after a spell of campus unrest. "You are probably aware," he began, "that we have been experiencing very considerable potentially explosive expressions of dissatisfaction on issues only partially related." He meant that the students had been hassling them about different things. I was far more upset by the president's English than by the students' potentially explosive expressions of dissatisfaction. I would have preferred the presidential approach taken by Franklin D. Roosevelt when he tried to convert into English his own government's memos, such as this blackout order of 1942:

> Such preparations shall be made as will completely obscure all Federal buildings and non-Federal buildings occupied by the Federal government during an air raid for any period of time from visibility by reason of internal or external illumination.

"Tell them," Roosevelt said, "that in buildings where they have to keep the work going to put something across the windows."

Simplify, simplify. Thoreau said it, as we are so often reminded, and no American writer more consistently practiced what he preached. Open *Walden* to any page and you will find a man saying in a plain and orderly way what is on his mind:

> I went to the woods because I wished to live deliberately, to front only the essential facts of life, and see if I could not learn what it had to teach, and not, when I came to die, discover that I had not lived.

How can the rest of us achieve such enviable freedom from clutter? The answer is to clear our heads of clutter. Clear thinking becomes clear writing; one can't exist without the other. It's impossible for a muddy thinker to write good English. He may get away with it for a paragraph or two, but soon the reader will be lost, and there's no sin so grave, for the reader will not easily be lured back.

Who is this elusive creature, the reader? The reader is someone with an attention span of about 30 seconds—a person assailed by many forces competing for attention. At one time those forces were relatively few: newspapers, magazines, radio, spouse, children, pets. Today they also include a galaxy of electronic devices for receiving entertainment and information—television, VCRs, DVDs, CDs, video games, the Internet, e-mail, cell phones, BlackBerries, iPods—as well as a fitness program, a pool, a lawn and that most potent of competitors, sleep. The man or woman snoozing in a chair with a magazine or a book is a person who was being given too much unnecessary trouble by the writer.

It won't do to say that the reader is too dumb or too lazy to keep pace with the train of thought. If the reader is lost, it's usually because the writer hasn't been careful enough. That carelessness can take any number of forms. Perhaps a sentence is so excessively cluttered that the reader, hacking through the verbiage, simply doesn't know what it means.

Perhaps a sentence has been so shoddily constructed that the reader could read it in several ways. Perhaps the writer has switched pronouns in midsentence, or has switched tenses, so the reader loses track of who is talking or when the action took place. Perhaps Sentence B is not a logical sequel to Sentence A; the writer, in whose head the connection is clear, hasn't bothered to provide the missing link. Perhaps the writer has used a word incorrectly by not taking the trouble to look it up.

Faced with such obstacles, readers are at first tenacious. They blame themselves—they obviously missed something, and they go back over the mystifying sentence, or over the whole paragraph, piecing it out like an ancient rune, making guesses and moving on. But they won't do that for long. The writer is making them work too hard, and they will look for one who is better at the craft.

Writers must therefore constantly ask: what am I trying to say? Surprisingly often they don't know. Then they must look at what they have written and ask: have I said it? Is it clear to someone encountering the subject for the first time? If it's not, some fuzz has worked its way into the machinery. The clear writer is someone clearheaded enough to see this stuff for what it is: fuzz.

I don't mean that some people are born clearheaded and are therefore natural writers, whereas others are naturally fuzzy and will never write well. Thinking clearly is a conscious act that writers must force on themselves, as if they were working on any other project that requires logic: making a shopping list or doing an algebra problem. Good writing doesn't come naturally, though most people seem to think it does. Professional writers are constantly bearded by people who say they'd like to "try a little writing sometime"—meaning when they retire from their real profession, like insurance or real estate, which is hard. Or they say, "I could write a book about that." I doubt it.

Writing is hard work. A clear sentence is no accident. Very few sentences come out right the first time, or even the third time. Remember this in moments of despair. If you find that writing is hard, it's because it *is* hard.

Clutter

William Zinsser

Fighting clutter is like fighting weeds—the writer is always slightly behind. New varieties sprout overnight, and by noon they are part of American speech. Consider what President Nixon's aide John Dean accomplished in just one day of testimony on television during the Watergate hearings. The next day everyone in America was saying "at this point in time" instead of "now."

Consider all the prepositions that are draped onto verbs that don't need any help. We no longer head committees. We head them up. We don't face problems anymore. We face up to them when we can free up a few minutes. A small detail, you may say— not worth bothering about. It *is* worth bothering about. Writing improves in direct ratio to the number of things we can keep out of it that shouldn't be there. "Up" in "free up" shouldn't be there. Examine every word you put on paper. You'll find a surprising number that don't serve any purpose.

Take the adjective "personal," as in "a personal friend of mine," "his personal feeling" or "her personal physician." It's typical of hundreds of words that can be eliminated. The personal friend has come into the language to distinguish him or her from the business friend, thereby debasing both language and friendship. Someone's feeling *is* that person's personal feeling—that's what "his" means. As for the personal physician, that's the man or woman summoned to the dressing room of a stricken actress so she won't have to be treated by the impersonal physician assigned to the theater. Someday I'd like to see that person identified as "her doctor." Physicians are physicians, friends are friends. The rest is clutter.

Clutter is the laborious phrase that has pushed out the short word that means the same thing. Even before John Dean, people and businesses had stopped saying "now." They were saying "currently" ("all our operators are currently assisting other customers"), or "at the present time," or "presently" (which means "soon"). Yet the idea can always be expressed by "now" to mean the immediate moment ("Now I can see him"), or by "today" to mean the historical present ("Today prices are high"), or simply by the verb "to be" ("It is raining"). There's no need to say, "At the present time we are experiencing precipitation."

"Experiencing" is one of the worst clutterers. Even your dentist will ask if you are experiencing any pain. If he had his own kid in the chair he would say, "Does it hurt?" He would, in short, be himself. By using a more pompous phrase in his professional rôle he not only sounds more important; he blunts the painful edge of truth. It's the language of the flight attendant demonstrating the oxygen mask that will drop down if the plane should run out of air. "In the unlikely possibility that the aircraft should experience such an eventuality," she begins—a phrase so oxygen-depriving in itself that we are prepared for any disaster.

Clutter is the ponderous euphemism that turns a slum into a depressed socioeconomic area, garbage collectors into waste-disposal personnel and the town dump into the volume reduction unit. I think of Bill Mauldin's cartoon of two hoboes riding a freight car. One of them says, "I started as a simple bum, but now I'm hard-core unemployed." Clutter is political correctness gone amok. I saw an ad for a boys' camp designed to provide "individual attention for the minimally exceptional."

Clutter is the official language used by corporations to hide their mistakes. When the Digital Equipment Corporation eliminated 3,000 jobs its statement didn't mention layoffs; those were "involuntary methodologies." When an Air Force missile crashed, it "impacted with the ground prematurely." When General Motors had a plant shutdown, that was a "volume-related production-schedule adjustment." Companies that go belly-up have "a negative cash-flow position."

Clutter is the language of the Pentagon calling an invasion a "reinforced protective reaction strike" and justifying its vast budgets on the need for "counterforce deterrence." As George Orwell pointed out in "Politics and the English Language," an essay written in 1946 but often cited during the wars in Cambodia, Vietnam and Iraq, "political speech and writing are largely the defense of the indefensible. . . . Thus political language has to consist largely of euphemism, question-begging and sheer cloudy vagueness." Orwell's warning that clutter is not just a nuisance but a deadly tool has come true in the recent decades of American military adventurism. It was during George W. Bush's presidency that "civilian casualties" in Iraq became "collateral damage."

Verbal camouflage reached new heights during General Alexander Haig's tenure as President Reagan's secretary of state. Before Haig nobody had thought of saying "at this juncture of maturization" to mean "now." He told the American people that terrorism could be fought with "meaningful sanctionary teeth" and that intermediate nuclear missiles were "at the vortex of cruciality." As for any worries that the public might harbor, his message was "leave it to Al," though what he actually said was: "We must push this to a lower decibel of public fixation. I don't think there's much of a learning curve to be achieved in this area of content."

I could go on quoting examples from various fields—every profession has its growing arsenal of jargon to throw dust in the eyes of the populace. But the list would be tedious. The point of raising it now is to serve notice that clutter is the enemy. Beware, then, of the long word that's no better than the short word: "assistance" (help), "numerous" (many), "facilitate" (ease), "individual" (man or woman), "remainder" (rest), "initial" (first), "implement" (do), "sufficient" (enough), "attempt" (try), "referred to as" (called) and hundreds more. Beware of all the slippery new fad words: paradigm and parameter, prioritize and potentialize. They are all weeds that will smother what you write. Don't dialogue with someone you can talk to. Don't interface with anybody.

Just as insidious are all the word clusters with which we explain how we propose to go about our explaining: "I might add," "It should be pointed out," "It is interesting to note." If you might add, add it. If it should be pointed out, point it out. If it is interesting to note, *make* it interesting; are we not all stupefied by what follows when someone says, "This will interest you"? Don't inflate what needs no inflating: "with the possible exception of" (except), "due to the fact that" (because), "he totally lacked the ability to" (he couldn't), "until such time as" (until), "for the purpose of" (for).

Is there any way to recognize clutter at a glance? Here's a device my students at Yale found helpful. I would put brackets around every component in a piece of writing that wasn't doing useful work. Often just one word got bracketed: the unnecessary preposition appended to a verb ("order up"), or the adverb that carries the same meaning as the verb ("smile happily"), or the adjective that states a known fact ("tall skyscraper"). Often my brackets surrounded the little qualifiers that weaken any sentence they inhabit ("a bit," "sort of"), or phrases like "in a sense," which don't mean anything. Sometimes my brackets surrounded an entire sentence—the one that essentially repeats what the previous sentence said, or that says something readers don't need to know or can figure out for themselves. Most first drafts can be cut by 50 percent without losing any information or losing the author's voice.

My reason for bracketing the students' superfluous words, instead of crossing them out, was to avoid violating their sacred prose. I wanted to leave the sentence intact for them to analyze. I was saying, "I may be wrong, but I think this can be deleted and the meaning won't be affected. But *you* decide. Read the sentence without the bracketed material and see if it works." In the early weeks of the term I handed back papers that were festooned with brackets. Entire paragraphs were bracketed. But soon the students learned to put mental brackets around their own clutter, and by the end of the term their papers were almost clean. Today many of those students are professional writers, and they tell me, "I still see your brackets—they're following me through life."

You can develop the same eye. Look for the clutter in your writing and prune it ruthlessly. Be grateful for everything you can throw away. Reexamine each sentence you put on paper. Is every word doing new work? Can any thought be expressed with more economy? Is anything pompous or pretentious or faddish? Are you hanging on to something useless just because you think it's beautiful?

Simplify, simplify.

Just Walk On By: A Black Man Ponders His Power to Alter Public Space

Brent Staples

My first victim was a woman—white, well dressed, probably in her early twenties. I came upon her late one evening on a deserted street in Hyde Park, a relatively affluent neighborhood in an otherwise mean, impoverished section of Chicago. As I swung onto the avenue behind her, there seemed to be a discreet, uninflammatory distance between us. Not so. She cast back a worried glance. To her, the youngish black man—a broad six feet two inches with a beard and billowing hair, both hands shoved into the pockets of a bulky military jacket—seemed menacingly close. After a few more quick glimpses, she picked up her pace and was soon running in earnest. Within seconds she disappeared into a cross street.

That was more than a decade ago. I was twenty-two years old, a graduate student newly arrived at the University of Chicago. It was in the echo of that terrified woman's footfalls that I first began to know the unwieldy inheritance I'd come into—the ability to alter public space in ugly ways. It was clear that she thought herself the quarry of a mugger, rapist, or worse. Suffering a bout of insomnia, however, I was stalking sleep, not defenseless wayfarers. As a softy who is scarcely able to take a knife to a raw chicken—let alone hold it to a person's throat—I was surprised, embarrassed, and dismayed all at once. Her flight made me feel like an accomplice in tyranny. It also made it clear that I was indistinguishable from the muggers who occasionally seeped into the area from the surrounding ghetto. That first encounter, and those that followed, signified that a vast, unnerving gulf lay between nighttime pedestrians—particularly women—and me. And I soon gathered that being perceived as dangerous is a hazard in itself. I only needed to turn a corner into a dicey situation, or crowd some frightened, armed person in a foyer somewhere, or make an errant move after being pulled over by a policeman. Where fear and weapons meet—and they often do in urban America—there is always the possibility of death.

In that first year, my first away from my hometown, I was to become thoroughly familiar with the language of fear. At dark, shadowy intersections in Chicago, I could cross in front of a car stopped at a traffic light and elicit the *thunk, thunk, thunk, thunk* of the driver—black, white, male, or female—hammering down the door locks. On less traveled streets after dark, I grew accustomed to but never comfortable with people who crossed to the other side of the street rather than pass me. Then there were the standard unpleasantries with police, doormen, bouncers, cab drivers, and others whose business it is to screen out troublesome individuals *before* there is any nastiness.

I moved to New York nearly two years ago and I have remained an avid night walker. In central Manhattan, the near-constant crowd cover minimizes tense one-on-one street encounters. Elsewhere—visiting friends in SoHo, where sidewalks are narrow and tightly spaced buildings shut out the sky—things can get very taut indeed.

Black men have a firm place in New York mugging literature. Norman Podhoretz in his famed (or infamous) 1963 essay, "My Negro Problem—and Ours," recalls growing up in terror of black males; they "were tougher than we were, more ruthless," he writes—and as an adult on the Upper West Side of Manhattan, he continues, he cannot constrain his nervousness when he meets black men on certain streets. Similarly, a decade later, the essayist and novelist Edward Hoagland extols a New York where once "Negro bitterness bore down mainly on other Negroes." Where some see mere panhandlers, Hoagland sees "a mugger who is clearly screwing up his nerve to do more than just *ask* for money." But Hoagland has "the New Yorker's quick-hunch posture for broken-field maneuvering," and the bad guy swerves away.

I often witness that "hunch posture," from women after dark on the warrenlike streets of Brooklyn where I live. They seem to set their faces on neutral and, with their purse straps strung across their chests bandolier style, they forge ahead as though bracing themselves against being tackled. I understand, of course, that the danger they perceive is not a hallucination. Women are particularly vulnerable to street violence, and young black males are drastically overrepresented among the perpetrators of that violence. Yet these truths are no solace against the kind of alienation that comes of being ever the suspect, against being set apart, a fearsome entity with whom pedestrians avoid making eye contact.

It is not altogether clear to me how I reached the ripe old age of twenty-two without being conscious of the lethality nighttime pedestrians attributed to me. Perhaps it was because in Chester, Pennsylvania, the small, angry industrial town where I came of age in the 1960s, I was scarcely noticeable against a backdrop of gang warfare, street knifings, and murders. I grew up one of the good boys, had perhaps a half-dozen fist fights. In retrospect, my shyness of combat has clear sources.

Many things go into the making of a young thug. One of those things is the consummation of the male romance with the power to intimidate. An infant discovers that random flailings send the baby bottle flying out of the crib and crashing to the floor. Delighted, the joyful babe repeats those motions again and again, seeking to duplicate the feat. Just so, I recall the points at which some of my boyhood friends were finally seduced by the perception of themselves as tough guys. When a mark cowered and surrendered his money without resistance, myth and reality merged—and paid off. It is, after all, only manly to embrace the power to frighten and intimidate. We, as men, are not supposed to give an inch of our lane on the highway; we are to seize the fighter's edge in work and in play and even in love; we are to be valiant in the face of hostile forces.

Unfortunately, poor and powerless young men seem to take all this nonsense literally. As a boy, I saw countless tough guys locked away; I have since buried several, too. They were babies, really—a teenage cousin, a brother of twenty-two, a childhood friend in his mid-twenties—all gone down in episodes of bravado played out in the streets. I came to doubt the virtues of intimidation early on. I chose, perhaps even unconsciously, to remain a shadow—timid, but a survivor.

The fearsomeness mistakenly attributed to me in public places often has a perilous flavor. The most frightening of these confusions occurred in the late 1970s and early 1980s when I worked as a journalist in Chicago. One day, rushing into the office of a magazine I was writing for with a deadline story in hand, I was mistaken for a burglar. The office manager called security and, with an ad hoc posse, pursued me through the labyrinthine halls, nearly to my editor's door. I had no way of proving who I was. I could only move briskly toward the company of someone who knew me.

Another time I was on assignment for a local paper and killing time before an interview. I entered a jewelry store on the city's affluent Near North Side. The proprietor excused herself and returned with an enormous red Doberman pinscher straining at the end of a leash. She stood, the dog extended toward me, silent to my questions, her eyes bulging nearly out of her head. I took a cursory look around, nodded, and bade her good night. Relatively speaking, however, I never fared as badly as another black male journalist. He went to nearby Waukegan, Illinois, a couple of summers ago to work on a story about a murderer who was born there. Mistaking the reporter for the killer, police hauled him from his car at gunpoint and but for his press credentials would probably have tried to book him. Such episodes are not uncommon. Black men trade tales like this all the time.

In "My Negro Problem—and Ours," Podhoretz writes that the hatred he feels for blacks makes itself known to him through a variety of avenues—one being his discomfort with that "special brand of paranoid touchiness" to which he says blacks are prone. No doubt he is speaking here of black men. In time, I learned to smother the rage I felt at so often being taken for a criminal. Not to do so would surely have led to madness—via that special "paranoid touchiness" that so annoyed Podhoretz at the time he wrote the essay.

I began to take precautions to make myself less threatening. I move about with care, particularly late in the evening. I give a wide berth to nervous people on subway platforms during the wee hours, particularly when I have exchanged business clothes for jeans. If I happen to be entering a building behind some people who appear skittish, I may walk by, letting them clear the lobby before I return, so as not to seem to be following them. I have been calm and extremely congenial on those rare occasions when I've been pulled over by the police.

And on late-evening constitutionals along streets less traveled by, I employ what has proved to be an excellent tension-reducing measure: I whistle melodies from Beethoven and Vivaldi and the more popular classical composers. Even steely New Yorkers hunching toward nighttime destinations seem to relax, and occasionally they even join in the tune. Virtually everybody seems to sense that a mugger wouldn't be warbling bright, sunny selections from Vivaldi's *Four Seasons*. It is my equivalent of the cowbell that hikers wear when they know they are in bear country.

The Catbird Seat

David J. Birnbaum

I wasn't in a hurry to get back to my hospital room, but I had a lot on my mind. I was adjusting to my new fate, quadriplegia. Besides, I had been waiting at least three minutes for the elevator, which in teenage time is three years. When I heard the ding, I dashed into the car, unintentionally cutting off the handful of other riders.

"What's the big hurry?" a pregnant woman asked. An elderly Asian man chimed in: "Leave the young man alone. He's in a wheelchair!"

That was the first time I felt my new place in society. A few months later, my friend Roy and I were in the back of a ticketholders' line that was clogging 34th Street waiting to see *The Empire Strikes Back* at the Murray Hill cinema. Suddenly an usher appeared and asked us to follow him into the theater. Despite the drizzle, the other patrons didn't seem to mind that we were cutting ahead. I was the only one in line that had a chair to sit in. Yet I didn't have to wait. Thereafter, I began to cut ahead often. Cashing a check at Chase, I'd ignore the velvet ropes and go straight to a teller. Registering for classes at N.Y.U., I cut three lines in one day: department approval, course selection, and, finally, registrar payment. Older people who only a few months earlier would have ignored a teenager with long hair began acting very friendly. Senior citizens still smile at me seventeen years after I crashed my car in Park Slope, breaking my neck, just days before my eighteenth birthday. Are they trying to cheer me up? Maybe they just see me as nonthreatening. They're probably thinking, "This guy is less than half my age, but I can still beat him up."

Soon after leaving the hospital, I realized I could now break rules. I would sneak cans of beer into concerts at Madison Square Garden. At the queue where teenagers are routinely patted down, the guards held up the process for me: "Please step back, we gotta wheelchair coming through!"

When I leave Staples, I tell the security guard that I need the plastic shopping basket to carry my goods to my van. He nods his head trustingly, on the assumption that I'll unload and return it. I have five of these red baskets in my hallway closet. I don't know what I'm going to do with them. I just get a kick driving them home.

Before I left Jamaica last January, I hid a box of Cuban cigars in my canvas case. As I passed through customs at Newark International Airport, a woman in a brown uniform looked at my two large bags suspiciously. Perusing the card I filled out on the plane, she asked, "Nothing to declare?"

"Nothing."

"What's the canvas bag for?"

"It's a portable handicap shower seat," I replied truthfully.

"Oh . . . I'm so sorry. Go ahead."

Cutting the lines at the Department of Motor Vehicles to renew my driver's license, getting out of speeding tickets, and arriving late to work without a reprimand are my "even uppers" for my physical limitations and for the difficulties caused by establishments not complying with the Americans with Disabilities Act. I had to sit behind the last row in a theater, separated from my college friends, only once before I stopped being too proud to accept the senior citizens' discount offered by sympathetic employees. When the purser offered to bump me up into first class on that flight from Jamaica, I didn't say: "No, thank you. I've accepted my disability, I have a successful career and live independently. Please treat me like everyone else." I didn't care whether she was condescending, sympathizing, or patronizing. I was just glad to be in "2B" sipping Chardonnay while I eyed the coach passengers frantically seeking space for their carry-on luggage and duty-free rum.

After sneaking my cigars through customs, I headed upstairs to get a taxi. Three carloads of tired travelers, dragging luggage with and without wheels, were waiting for a single elevator to arrive. I waited like an Olympic sprinter anticipating the starting gun. I began inching my wheelchair forward, but accidentally wheeled over some guy's foot.

"Oww!" he turned around, saw my wheelchair, and then followed nervously with, "Oh, I'm ss . . . sss . . . sorry." He stepped to the side, leaving me perfectly positioned in front of the sliding aluminum doors. The

"L" on the display lighted, the ding went off, the doors opened, and I swiftly pushed my chair forward into the car.

"What's wrong with you?" A well-tanned girl asked me angrily. I looked her in the eye with cockiness, expecting my usual support from others. But it didn't come.

"Have some respect, for God's sake!" she continued, holding the door open for a middle-aged man with dark glasses and a white cane.

There in the elevator, as everyone looked at me in disgust, I learned the pecking order: blind trumps wheelchair; wheelchair trumps pregnant; pregnant trumps old; old trumps whatever is left.

The Ends of the World as We Know Them

Jared Diamond

New Year's weekend traditionally is a time for us to reflect, and to make resolutions based on our reflections. In this fresh year, with the United States seemingly at the height of its power and at the start of a new presidential term, Americans are increasingly concerned and divided about where we are going. How long can America remain ascendant? Where will we stand 10 years from now, or even next year?

Such questions seem especially appropriate this year. History warns us that when once-powerful societies collapse, they tend to do so quickly and unexpectedly. That shouldn't come as much of a surprise: peak power usually means peak population, peak needs, and hence peak vulnerability. What can be learned from history that could help us avoid joining the ranks of those who declined swiftly? We must expect the answers to be complex, because historical reality is complex: while some societies did indeed collapse spectacularly, others have managed to thrive for thousands of years without major reversal.

When it comes to historical collapses, five groups of interacting factors have been especially important: the damage that people have inflicted on their environment; climate change; enemies; changes in friendly trading partners; and the society's political, economic and social responses to these shifts. That's not to say that all five causes play a role in every case. Instead, think of this as a useful checklist of factors that should be examined, but whose relative importance varies from case to case.

For instance, in the collapse of the Polynesian society on Easter Island three centuries ago, environmental problems were dominant, and climate change, enemies and trade were insignificant; however, the latter three factors played big roles in the disappearance of the medieval Norse colonies on Greenland. Let's consider two examples of declines stemming from different mixes of causes: the falls of classic Maya civilization and of Polynesian settlements on the Pitcairn Islands.

Maya Native Americans of the Yucatan Peninsula and adjacent parts of Central America developed the New World's most advanced civilization before Columbus. They were innovators in writing, astronomy, architecture and art. From local origins around 2,500 years ago, Maya societies rose especially after the year A.D. 250, reaching peaks of population and sophistication in the late 8th century.

Thereafter, societies in the most densely populated areas of the southern Yucatan underwent a steep political and cultural collapse: between 760 and 910, kings were overthrown, large areas were abandoned, and at least 90 percent of the population disappeared, leaving cities to become overgrown by jungle. The last known date recorded on a Maya monument by their so-called Long Count calendar corresponds to the year 909. What happened?

A major factor was environmental degradation by people: deforestation, soil erosion and water management problems, all of which resulted in less food. Those problems were exacerbated by droughts, which may have been partly caused by humans themselves through deforestation. Chronic warfare made matters worse, as more and more people fought over less and less land and resources.

Why weren't these problems obvious to the Maya kings, who could surely see their forests vanishing and their hills becoming eroded? Part of the reason was that the kings were able to insulate themselves from problems afflicting the rest of society. By extracting wealth from commoners, they could remain well fed while everyone else was slowly starving.

What's more, the kings were preoccupied with their own power struggles. They had to concentrate on fighting one another and keeping up their images through ostentatious displays of wealth. By insulating themselves in the short run from the problems of society, the elite merely bought themselves the privilege of being among the last to starve.

Whereas Maya societies were undone by problems of their own making, Polynesian societies on Pitcairn and Henderson Islands in the tropical Pacific Ocean were undone largely by other people's mistakes. Pitcairn, the uninhabited island settled in 1790 by the H.M.S. Bounty mutineers, had actually been populated by Polynesians 800 years earlier. That society, which left behind temple platforms, stone and shell tools and huge garbage piles of fish and bird and turtle bones as evidence of its existence, survived for several centuries and then vanished. Why?

In many respects, Pitcairn and Henderson are tropical paradises, rich in some food sources and essential raw materials. Pitcairn is home to Southeast Polynesia's largest quarry of stone suited for making adzes, while Henderson has the region's largest breeding seabird colony and its only nesting beach for sea turtles. Yet the islanders depended on imports from Mangareva Island, hundreds of miles away, for canoes, crops, livestock and oyster shells for making tools.

Unfortunately for the inhabitants of Pitcairn and Henderson, their Mangarevan trading partner collapsed for reasons similar to those underlying the Maya decline: deforestation, erosion and warfare. Deprived of essential imports in a Polynesian equivalent of the 1973 oil crisis, the Pitcairn and Henderson societies declined until everybody had died or fled.

The Maya and the Henderson and Pitcairn Islanders are not alone, of course. Over the centuries, many other societies have declined, collapsed or died out. Famous victims include the Anasazi in the American Southwest, who abandoned their cities in the 12th century because of environmental problems and climate change, and the Greenland Norse, who disappeared in the 15th century because of all five interacting factors on the checklist. There were also the ancient Fertile Crescent societies, the Khmer at Angkor Wat, the Moche society of Peru—the list goes on.

But before we let ourselves get depressed, we should also remember that there is another long list of cultures that have managed to prosper for lengthy periods of time. Societies in Japan, Tonga, Tikopia, the New Guinea Highlands, and Central and Northwest Europe, for example, have all found ways to sustain themselves. What separates the lost cultures from those that survived? Why did the Maya fail and the shogun succeed?

Half of the answer involves environmental differences: geography deals worse cards to some societies than to others. Many of the societies that collapsed had the misfortune to occupy dry, cold or otherwise fragile environments, while many of the long-term survivors enjoyed more robust and fertile surroundings. But it's not the case that a congenial environment guarantees success: some societies (like the Maya) managed to ruin lush environments, while other societies—like the Incas, the Inuit, Icelanders and desert Australian Aborigines—have managed to carry on in some of the earth's most daunting environments.

The other half of the answer involves differences in a society's responses to problems. Ninth-century New Guinea Highland villagers, 16th-century German landowners, and the Tokugawa shoguns of 17th-century Japan all recognized the deforestation spreading around them and solved the problem, either by developing scientific reforestation (Japan and Germany) or by transplanting tree seedlings (New Guinea). Conversely, the Maya, Mangarevans and Easter Islanders failed to address their forestry problems and so collapsed.

Consider Japan. In the 1600's, the country faced its own crisis of deforestation, paradoxically brought on by the peace and prosperity following the Tokugawa shoguns' military triumph that ended 150 years of civil war. The subsequent explosion of Japan's population and economy set off rampant logging for construction of palaces and cities, and for fuel and fertilizer.

The shoguns responded with both negative and positive measures. They reduced wood consumption by turning to light-timbered construction, to fuel-efficient stoves and heaters, and to coal as a source of energy. At the same time, they increased wood production by developing and carefully managing plantation forests. Both the shoguns and the Japanese peasants took a long-term view: the former expected to pass on their power to their children, and the latter expected to pass on their land. In addition, Japan's isolation at the time made it obvious that the country would have to depend on its own resources and couldn't meet its needs by pillaging other countries. Today, despite having the highest human population density of any large developed country, Japan is more than 70 percent forested.

There is a similar story from Iceland. When the island was first settled by the Norse around 870, its light volcanic soils presented colonists with unfamiliar challenges. They proceeded to cut down trees and stock sheep as if they were still in Norway, with its robust soils. Significant erosion ensued, carrying half of Iceland's topsoil into the ocean within a century or two. Icelanders became the poorest people in Europe. But they gradually learned from their mistakes, over time instituting stocking limits on sheep and other strict controls, and establishing an entire government department charged with landscape management. Today, Iceland boasts the sixth-highest per-capita income in the world.

What lessons can we draw from history? The most straightforward: take environmental problems seriously. They destroyed societies in the past, and they are even more likely to do so now. If 6,000 Polynesians with stone tools were able to destroy Mangareva Island, consider what six billion people with metal tools and bulldozers are doing today. Moreover, while the Maya collapse affected just a few neighboring societies in Central America, globalization now means that any society's problems have the potential to affect anyone else. Just think how crises in Somalia, Afghanistan and Iraq have shaped the United States today.

Other lessons involve failures of group decision-making. There are many reasons why past societies made bad decisions, and thereby failed to solve or even to perceive the problems that would eventually destroy them. One reason involves conflicts of interest, whereby one group within a society (for instance, the pig farmers who caused the worst erosion in medieval Greenland and Iceland) can profit by engaging in practices that damage the rest of society. Another is the pursuit of short-term gains at the expense of long-term survival, as when fishermen overfish the stocks on which their livelihoods ultimately depend.

History also teaches us two deeper lessons about what separates successful societies from those heading toward failure. A society contains a built-in blueprint for failure if the elite insulates itself from the consequences of its actions. That's why Maya kings, Norse Greenlanders and Easter Island chiefs made choices that eventually undermined their societies. They themselves did not begin to feel deprived until they had irreversibly destroyed their landscape.

Could this happen in the United States? It's a thought that often occurs to me here in Los Angeles, when I drive by gated communities, guarded by private security patrols, and filled with people who drink bottled water, depend on private pensions, and send their children to private schools. By doing these things, they lose the motivation to support the police force, the municipal water supply, Social Security and public schools. If conditions deteriorate too much for poorer people, gates will not keep the rioters out. Rioters eventually burned the palaces of Maya kings and tore down the statues of Easter Island chiefs; they have also already threatened wealthy districts in Los Angeles twice in recent decades.

In contrast, the elite in 17th-century Japan, as in modern Scandinavia and the Netherlands, could not ignore or insulate themselves from broad societal problems. For instance, the Dutch upper class for hundreds of years has been unable to insulate itself from the Netherlands' water management problems for a simple reason: the rich live in the same drained lands below sea level as the poor. If the dikes and pumps keeping out the sea fail, the well-off Dutch know that they will drown along with everybody else, which is precisely what happened during the floods of 1953.

The other deep lesson involves a willingness to re-examine long-held core values, when conditions change and those values no longer make sense. The medieval Greenland Norse lacked such a willingness: they continued to view themselves as transplanted Norwegian pastoralists, and to despise the Inuit as pagan hunters, even after Norway stopped sending trading ships and the climate had grown too cold for a pastoral existence. They died off as a result, leaving Greenland to the Inuit. On the other hand, the British in the 1950's faced up to the need for a painful reappraisal of their former status as rulers of a world empire set apart from Europe. They are now finding a different avenue to wealth and power, as part of a united Europe.

In this New Year, we Americans have our own painful reappraisals to face. Historically, we viewed the United States as a land of unlimited plenty, and so we practiced unrestrained consumerism, but that's no longer viable in a world of finite resources. We can't continue to deplete our own resources as well as those of much of the rest of the world.

Historically, oceans protected us from external threats; we stepped back from our isolationism only temporarily during the crises of two world wars. Now, technology and global interconnectedness have robbed us of our protection. In recent years, we have responded to foreign threats largely by seeking short-term military solutions at the last minute.

But how long can we keep this up? Though we are the richest nation on earth, there's simply no way we can afford (or muster the troops) to intervene in the dozens of countries where emerging threats lurk—particularly when each intervention these days can cost more than $100 billion and require more than 100,000 troops.

A genuine reappraisal would require us to recognize that it will be far less expensive and far more effective to address the underlying problems of public health, population and environment that ultimately cause threats to us to emerge in poor countries. In the past, we have regarded foreign aid as either charity or as buying support; now, it's an act of self-interest to preserve our own economy and protect American lives.

Do we have cause for hope? Many of my friends are pessimistic when they contemplate the world's growing population and human demands colliding with shrinking resources. But I draw hope from the knowledge that humanity's biggest problems today are ones entirely of our own making. Asteroids hurtling at us beyond our control don't figure high on our list of imminent dangers. To save ourselves, we don't need new technology: we just need the political will to face up to our problems of population and the environment.

I also draw hope from a unique advantage that we enjoy. Unlike any previous society in history, our global society today is the first with the opportunity to learn from the mistakes of societies remote from us in space and in time. When the Maya and Mangarevans were cutting down their trees, there were no historians or archaeologists, no newspapers or television, to warn them of the consequences of their actions. We, on the other hand, have a detailed chronicle of human successes and failures at our disposal. Will we choose to use it?

The Growing Cowardice of Online Anonymity

Richard Bernstein

Anonymous sources are of course among the newspaper reporter's best friends, without whom the cause of informing the public would be severely set back.

But anonymity is also a tremendous aid to the resentful, the scandalous and the cowardly, and the signs are that the tidal wave of anonymous comment made possible by the Internet is getting even bigger.

Or that, at any rate, is the impression that some recent reporting on the rising vogue of college gossip Web sites would indicate.

One site, called JuicyCampus.com, which maintains message boards on fifty-nine university campuses, has been attracting special attention. As a recent article in *Radar* magazine put it, JuicyCampus.com is "a virtual bathroom wall upon which college students across the country scrawl slurs, smears, and secrets, true or otherwise, about their classmates."

In one feature to take one modest example, the site asked for replies to the question: Who are the sluttiest girls at Cornell? As of this week, there were forty-seven postings in response, several of which gave names, apparently real ones.

All of the postings, needless to say, were anonymous, and that would appear to be the main point. It's bad enough to tarnish reputations and to publish insults, but if the people doing so identify themselves, there is at least a possibility of censure and accountability.

But the Internet not only makes the anonymous pejorative possible, it also bestows a certain techno glamour to what ought to be a guilty snicker. "C'mon, give us the juice," JuicyCampus.com says on its home page. "Posts are totally, 100 percent anonymous."

To be sure, there are often good reasons for anonymity: an employee of a corporation who uses a company intranet site to criticize senior management or to expose misbehavior at the top could fear for his job if he had to provide his name. In the news business, anonymous sources are ethically tricky, and the better papers handle them with care. But sources are commonly promised anonymity in exchange for information that would otherwise be kept secret.

But what the Internet and its cult of anonymity do is to provide a blanket sort of immunity for anybody who wants to say anything about anybody else, and it would be difficult in this sense to think of a more morally deformed exploitation of the concept of free speech.

An illustration, admittedly personal: Some time ago, I complained to Amazon.com about reviews posted on its site that offered what I felt were viciously negative and factually incorrect views of a book I had written.

Anybody of course is entitled to say what he or she wants about a book, including one written by me. It's the anonymity that Amazon grants to its reader-reviewers that I objected to, on the grounds that anybody who wants to say something nasty about somebody else's work ought to have the little bit of bravery needed to say it under his or her name.

When I wrote an e-mail to that effect to Jeffrey Bezos, Amazon's head and founder, I received a reply from Amazon's customer relations department saying that it allowed anonymous reviews as a way to encourage discussion. My reply was that, under the guise of encouraging free expression and unhindered debate, Amazon was really encouraging cowardice instead.

At the time I earned my living as a book critic for the *New York Times*, which, needless to say, did not allow me to hide behind a shield of anonymity in my own reviews. If I did have negative opinions about a book—and I often did—I could be held responsible if, in fact, my opinion was unjustified or unfair, or if I was avenging myself against someone who had once written negatively about me.

Amazon's reader reviews are an old story. What is more recent is the Internet's encouragement not just of scandalous and malignant personal commentary but of racist remarks of the sort that have for years been branded outside the scope of acceptable discourse.

Reading JuicyCampus.com, for example, I found this remark, anonymous of course: 'Are there any black guys who aren't dumb jocks?"

There was much worse stuff along these lines, unprintable here even if only to illustrate how the grant of anonymity can lead to the regression of public discourse. It almost makes one nostalgic for the days when people who uttered racist slurs were all too happy to identify themselves.

Concerned about the effect of JuicyCampus.com, prosecutors in New Jersey have lately been investigating the site for consumer fraud—on the grounds that it promises in its terms and conditions that no offensive content will be allowed on the site even while it conspicuously provides no enforcement of that promise.

In fact, to get JuicyCampus on the grounds of consumer fraud would be a bit like the feds getting the gangster Al Capone on tax evasion. But the law does make it very hard to hold Web sites legally accountable, even for libelous opinions. This is because the U.S. government's Communications Decency Act grants immunity to Web site operators for false or slanderous information they publish when that information has been provided by third parties.

In other words, the law would seem to contain its own sort of catch-22: the Web site itself can't be held legally responsible for defamatory statements, but neither can anybody else, since the defamatory opinion was expressed anonymously.

There have been other illustrations of the use of anonymity in recent years of questionable moral value. One was the decision of the publisher Random House a few years ago to publish the novel *Primary Colors,* the best-selling satire of Bill Clinton, by "Anonymous." It was a brilliant marketing ploy, the suggestion being that the author was an administration insider who could be harmed if his identity were known.

In fact, as it turned out, the book was written by Joe Klein, a very talented and worthy political journalist but one whose well-being did not require that his identity remain secret.

But that was in the days when there was a certain assumption that people who were anonymous needed to be so for some reason. Now that the Internet has made anonymity almost standard, it's unlikely that anybody would make that assumption anymore.

Homeless

Anna Quindlen

Her name was Ann, and we met in the Port Authority Bus Terminal several Januarys ago. I was doing a story on homeless people. She said I was wasting my time talking to her; she was just passing through, although she'd been passing through for more than two weeks. To prove to me that this was true, she rummaged through a tote bag and a manila envelope and finally unfolded a sheet of typing paper and brought out her photographs.

They were not pictures of family, or friends, or even a dog or cat, its eyes brown-red in the flashbulb's light. They were pictures of a house. It was like a thousand houses in a hundred towns, not suburb, not city, but somewhere in between, with aluminum siding and a chain-link fence, a narrow driveway running up to a one-car garage and a patch of backyard. The house was yellow. I looked on the back for a date or a name, but neither was there. There was no need for discussion. I knew what she was trying to tell me, for it was something I had often felt. She was not adrift, alone, anonymous, although her bags and her raincoat with the grime shadowing its creases had made me believe she was. She had a house, or at least once upon a time had had one. Inside were curtains, a couch, a stove, potholders. You are where you live. She was somebody.

I've never been very good at looking at the big picture, taking the global view, and I've always been a person with an overactive sense of place, the legacy of an Irish grandfather. So it is natural that the thing that seems most wrong with the world to me right now is that there are so many people with no homes. I'm not simply talking about shelter from the elements, or three square meals a day or a mailing address to which the welfare people can send the check—although I know that all these are important for survival. I'm talking about a home, about precisely those kinds of feelings that have wound up in cross-stitch and French knots on samplers over the years.

Home is where the heart is. There's no place like it. I love my home with a ferocity totally out of proportion to its appearance or location. I love dumb things about it: the hot-water heater, the plastic rack you drain dishes in, the roof over my head, which occasionally leaks. And yet it is precisely those dumb things that make it what it is—a place of certainty, stability, predictability, privacy, for me and for my family. It is where I live. What more can you say about a place than that? That is everything.

Yet it is something that we have been edging away from gradually during my lifetime and the lifetimes of my parents and grandparents. There was a time when where you lived often was where you worked and where you grew the food you ate and even where you were buried. When that era passed, where you lived at least was where your parents had lived and where you would live with your children when you became enfeebled. Then, suddenly, where you lived was where you lived for three years, until you could move on to something else and something else again.

And so we have come to something else again, to children who do not understand what it means to go to their rooms because they have never had a room, to men and women whose fantasy is a wall they can paint a color of their own choosing, to old people reduced to sitting on molded plastic chairs, their skin blue-white in the lights of a bus station, who pull pictures of houses out of their bags. Homes have stopped being homes. Now they are real estate.

People find it curious that those without homes would rather sleep sitting up on benches or huddled in doorways than go to shelters. Certainly some prefer to do so because they are emotionally ill, because they have been locked in before and they are damned if they will be locked in again. Others are afraid of the violence and trouble they may find there. But some seem to want something that is not available in shelters, and they will not compromise, not for a cot, or oatmeal, or a shower with special soap that kills the bugs. "One room," a woman with a baby who was sleeping on her sister's floor, once told me, "painted blue." That was the crux of it; not size or location, but pride of ownership. Painted blue.

This is a difficult problem, and some wise and compassionate people are working hard at it. But in the main I think we work around it, just as we walk around it when it is lying on the sidewalk or sitting in the bus terminal—the problem, that is. It has been customary to take people's pain and lessen our own participation in it by turning it into an issue, not a collection of human beings. We turn an adjective into a noun: the poor, not poor people; the homeless, not Ann or the man who lives in the box or the woman who sleeps on the subway grate.

Sometimes I think we would be better off if we forgot about the broad strokes and concentrated on the details. Here is a woman without a bureau. There is a man with no mirror, no wall to hang it on. They are not the homeless. They are people who have no homes. No drawer that holds the spoons. No window to look out upon the world. My God. That is everything.

Definition

"Home is the place where, when you have to go there, they have to take you in," writes Robert Frost in the poem "The Death of the Hired Man." According to Joseph C. Neal, "Home is where the heart is." The concept of home could have many definitions, depending on a person's point of view or experience. For example, what home means to a nomad in Kyrgyzstan would be different than what it means to a fourth-generation farmer in Vermont.

In the process of forming arguments in writing, definition is an important element. To define the limits of a piece of writing is to control the language in support of a position. To define something is to explain its qualities and characteristics, but not necessarily *all of* its qualities and characteristics. Writers use definition to show those aspects of a thing that they want to communicate to the reader. Gloria Naylor's essay in this section is a perfect example of how she controlled the language to support her position on "What Is Poverty?" The focus of a definition essay could be something concrete, such as a motorcycle. The focus also could be something more abstract depending on a person's point of view. "Patriotism," for example, is an abstract concept that might have different meanings for different people. "Home" can be a concrete brick-and-mortar dwelling or a place that dwells in the heart or mind.

The Process

Purpose

When writing a definition essay, your purpose is to provide deeper understanding of a term that goes beyond a simple dictionary meaning. You are not only explaining why a term is defined as such but also how the term can be understood from a different perspective—the perspective that you as the reader controls. The writer paints a picture of a subject, but that picture is limited to the characteristics of the subject that the writer wishes the reader to consider. By limiting the scope of the definition, the writer controls how the reader thinks about the subject.

Thesis

The thesis states the limitations of the subject. By prescribing specific aspects of the subject, the writer limits the discussion to only those things essential to define the subject. If the writer is defining a pickup truck, then the aspects of a pickup truck that contribute to the writer's definition will be featured in the thesis: A pickup truck is a versatile, powerful, and effective vehicle for work.

Organization

Definition essays are broken into three elements: the formal definition, the stipulative definition, and the extended definition. The formal definition is usually found in the dictionary, and it gives a subject's general class. For example, a pickup truck is a vehicle (its general class) that can be used to haul material (its subclass). Notice that the movement from general class to subclass narrows the definition of the subject: we go from talking about a vehicle to a special kind of vehicle that hauls material—a pickup truck. Formal definitions give a general picture of a subject, and are good places to begin in a definition essay. Formal definitions bring the reader into the writing so that they may understand what's being discussed, and so the writer may begin to narrow the scope of the definition.

The next step in narrowing the definition is to stipulate, or specify, certain qualities of the subject, the ones the writer wants the reader to focus on. A stipulative definition specifies the meaning of the subject that the writer wants to focus on. If the writer wanted to focus on diesel powered pickup trucks, stipulating its fuel source and engine type—diesel—narrows the topic further. This technique serves the dual purpose of focusing the writing specifically, and limiting the scope of the discussion for the reader. The formal definition and the stipulative definition are found in the introduction of the essay.

An extended definition is the long piece that becomes the definition essay. Its purpose is to fully explore the qualities and characteristics of the subject that the writer has narrowed through stipulation. The extended definition comprises the elements of the subject that will give it its final form. For example, in the definition essay about diesel powered pickup trucks, the writer might create an extended definition by beginning with a formal definition, narrowing by stipulating, and extending by adding in the key elements that will establish the definition: diesel pickup trucks are powerful, they are versatile, and they are economical. Those three elements become the extended definition, and they form the body of the essay.

When revising the definition essay, it's important to make sure that the subject is defined adequately and narrowly enough, without lapses or generalities that contradict each other. One can't write about the economic benefits of diesel powered pickup trucks and then add that diesel fuel can be more expensive than gasoline.

The World of Doublespeak

William Lutz

There are no potholes in the streets of Tucson, Arizona, just "pavement deficiencies." The Reagan Administration didn't propose any new taxes, just "revenue enhancement" through new "user's fees." Those aren't bums on the street, just "non-goal oriented members of society." There are no more poor people, just "fiscal underachievers." There was no robbery of an automatic teller machine, just an "unauthorized withdrawal." The patient didn't die because of medical malpractice, it was just a "diagnostic misadventure of a high magnitude." The U.S. Army doesn't kill the enemy anymore, it just "services the target." And the doublespeak goes on.

Doublespeak is language that pretends to communicate but really doesn't. It is language that makes the bad seem good, the negative appear positive, the unpleasant appear attractive or at least tolerable. Doublespeak is language that avoids or shifts responsibility, language that is at variance with its real or purported meaning. It is language that conceals or prevents thought; rather than extending thought, doublespeak limits it.

Doublespeak is not a matter of subjects and verbs agreeing; it is a matter of words and facts agreeing. Basic to doublespeak is incongruity, the incongruity between what is said or left unsaid, and what really is. It is the incongruity between the word and the referent, between seem and be, between the essential function of language—communication—and what doublespeak does—mislead, distort, deceive, inflate, circumvent, obfuscate.

How to Spot Doublespeak

How can you spot doublespeak? Most of the time you will recognize doublespeak when you see or hear it. But, if you have any doubts, you can identify doublespeak just by answering these questions: Who is saying what to whom, under what conditions and circumstances, with what intent, and with what results? Answering these questions will usually help you identify as doublespeak language that appears to be legitimate or that at first glance doesn't even appear to be doublespeak.

First Kind of Doublespeak

There are at least four kinds of doublespeak. The first is the euphemism, an inoffensive or positive word or phrase used to avoid a harsh, unpleasant, or distasteful reality. But a euphemism can also be a tactful word or phrase which avoids directly mentioning a painful reality, or it can be an expression used out of concern for the feelings of someone else, or to avoid directly discussing a topic subject to a social or cultural taboo.

When you use a euphemism because of your sensitivity for someone's feelings or out of concern for a recognized social or cultural taboo, it is not doublespeak. For example, you express your condolences that someone has "passed away" because you do not want to say to a grieving person, "I'm sorry your father is dead." When you use the euphemism "passed away," no one is misled. Moreover, the euphemism functions here not just to protect the feelings of another person, but to communicate also your concern for that person's feelings during a period of mourning. When you excuse yourself to go to the "restroom," or you mention that someone is "sleeping with" or "involved with" someone else, you do not mislead anyone about your meaning, but you do respect the social taboos about discussing bodily functions and sex in direct terms. You also indicate your sensitivity to the feelings of your audience, which is usually considered a mark of courtesy and good manners.

However, when a euphemism is used to mislead or deceive, it becomes doublespeak. For example, in 1984 the U.S. State Department announced that it would no longer use the word "killing" in its annual report on the status of human rights in countries around the world. Instead, it would use the phrase "unlawful or arbitrary deprivation of life," which the department claimed was more accurate. Its real purpose for using this phrase was simply to avoid discussing the embarrassing situation of government-sanctioned killings in countries that are supported by the United States and have been certified by the United States as respecting the human rights of their citizens. This use of a euphemism constitutes doublespeak, since it is designed to mislead, to cover up the unpleasant. Its real intent is at variance with its apparent intent. It is language designed to alter our perception of reality.

The Pentagon, too, avoids discussing unpleasant realities when it refers to bombs and artillery shells that fall on civilian targets as "incontinent ordnance." And in 1977 the Pentagon tried to slip funding for the neutron bomb unnoticed into an appropriations bill by calling it a "radiation enhancement device."

Second Kind of Doublespeak

A second kind of doublespeak is jargon, the specialized language of a trade, profession, or similar group, such as that used by doctors, lawyers, engineers, educators, or car mechanics. Jargon can serve an important and useful function. Within a group, jargon functions as a kind of verbal shorthand that allows members of the group to communicate with each other clearly, efficiently, and quickly. Indeed, it is a mark of membership in the group to be able to use and understand the group's jargon.

But jargon, like the euphemism, can also be doublespeak. It can be—and often is—pretentious, obscure, and esoteric terminology used to give an air of profundity, authority, and prestige to speakers and their subject matter. Jargon as doublespeak often makes the simple appear complex, the ordinary profound, the obvious insightful. In this sense it is used not to express but impress. With such doublespeak, the act of smelling something becomes "organoleptic analysis," glass becomes "fused silicate," a crack in a metal support beam becomes a "discontinuity," conservative economic policies become "distributionally conservative notions."

Lawyers, for example, speak of an "involuntary conversion" of property when discussing the loss or destruction of property through theft, accident, or condemnation. If your house burns down or if your car is stolen, you have suffered an involuntary conversion of your property. When used by lawyers in a legal situation, such jargon is a legitimate use of language, since lawyers can be expected to understand the term.

However, when a member of a specialized group uses its jargon to communicate with a person outside the group, and uses it knowing that the nonmember does not understand such language, then there is doublespeak. For example, on May 9, 1978, a National Airlines 727 airplane crashed while attempting to land at the Pensacola, Florida, airport. Three of the fifty-two passengers aboard the airplane were killed. As a result of the crash, National made an after-tax insurance benefit of $1.7 million, or an extra 18¢ a share dividend for its stockholders. Now National Airlines had two problems: It did not want to talk about one of its airplanes crashing, and it had to account for the $1.7 million when it issued its annual report to its stockholders. National solved the problem by inserting a footnote in its annual report which explained that the $1.7 million income was due to "the involuntary conversion of a 727." National thus acknowledged the crash of its airplane and the subsequent profit it made from the crash, without once mentioning the accident or the deaths. However, because airline officials knew that most stockholders in the company, and indeed most of the general public, were not familiar with legal jargon, the use of such jargon constituted doublespeak.

Third Kind of Doublespeak

A third kind of doublespeak is gobbledygook or bureaucratese. Basically, such doublespeak is simply a matter of piling on words, of overwhelming the audience with words, the bigger the words and the longer the sentences the better. Alan Greenspan, then chair of President Nixon's Council of Economic Advisors, was quoted in *The Philadelphia Inquirer* in 1974 as having testified before a Senate committee that "It is a tricky problem to find the particular calibration in timing that would be appropriate to stem the acceleration in risk premiums created by falling incomes without prematurely aborting the decline in the inflation-generated risk premiums."

Nor has Mr. Greenspan's language changed since then. Speaking to the meeting of the Economic Club of New York in 1988, Mr. Greenspan, now Federal Reserve chair, said, "I guess I should warn you, if I turn out to be particularly clear, you've probably misunderstood what I've said." Mr. Greenspan's doublespeak doesn't seem to have held back his career.

Sometimes gobbledygook may sound impressive, but when the quote is later examined in print it doesn't even make sense. During the 1988 presidential campaign, vice-presidential candidate Senator Dan Quayle explained the need for a strategic-defense initiative by saying, "Why wouldn't an enhanced deterrent, a more stable peace, a better prospect to denying the ones who enter conflict in the first place to have a reduction of offensive systems and an introduction to defense capability? I believe this is the route the country will eventually go."

The investigation into the Challenger disaster in 1986 revealed the doublespeak of gobbledygook and bureaucratese used by too many involved in the shuttle program. When Jesse Moore, NASA's associate administrator, was asked if the performance of the shuttle program had improved with each launch or if it had remained the same, he answered, "I think our performance in terms of the liftoff performance and in terms of the orbital performance, we knew more about the envelope we were operating under, and we have been pretty accurately staying in that. And so I would say the performance has not by design drastically improved. I think we have been able to characterize the performance more as a function of our launch experience as opposed to it improving as a function of time." While this language may appear to be jargon, a close look will reveal that it is really just gobbledygook laced with jargon. But you really have to wonder if Mr. Moore had any idea what he was saying.

Fourth Kind of Doublespeak

The fourth kind of doublespeak is inflated language that is designed to make the ordinary seem extraordinary; to make everyday things seem impressive; to give an air of importance to people, situations, or things that would not normally be considered important; to make the simple seem complex. Often this kind of doublespeak isn't hard to spot, and it is usually pretty funny. While car mechanics may be called "automotive internists," elevator operators members of the "vertical transportation corps," used cars "pre-owned" or "experienced cars," and black-and-white television sets described as having "non-multicolor capability," you really aren't misled all that much by such language.

However, you may have trouble figuring out that, when Chrysler "initiates a career alternative enhancement program," it is really laying off five thousand workers; or that "negative patient-care outcome" means the patient died; or that "rapid oxidation" means a fire in a nuclear power plant.

The doublespeak of inflated language can have serious consequences. In Pentagon doublespeak, "pre-emptive counterattack" means that American forces attacked first; "engaged the enemy on all sides" means American troops were ambushed; "backloading of augmentation personnel" means a retreat by American troops. In the doublespeak of the military, the 1983 invasion of Grenada was conducted not by the U.S. Army, Navy, Air Force, and Marines, but by the "Caribbean Peace Keeping Forces." But then, according to the Pentagon, it wasn't an invasion, it was a "predawn vertical insertion.". . .

The Dangers of Doublespeak

Doublespeak is not the product of carelessness or sloppy thinking. Indeed, most doublespeak is the product of clear thinking and is carefully designed and constructed to appear to communicate when in fact it doesn't. It is language designed not to lead but mislead. It is language designed to distort reality and corrupt thought. . . . In the world created by doublespeak, if it's not a tax increase, but rather "revenue enhancement" or "tax base broadening," how can you complain about higher taxes? If it's not acid rain, but rather "poorly buffered precipitation," how can you worry about all those dead trees? If that isn't the Mafia in Atlantic City, but just "members of a career-offender cartel," why worry about the influence of organized crime in the city? If Supreme Court Justice William Rehnquist wasn't addicted to the pain-killing drug his doctor prescribed, but instead it was just that the drug had "established an interrelationship with the body, such that if the drug is removed precipitously, there is a reaction," you needn't question that his decisions might have been influenced by his drug addiction. If it's not a Titan II nuclear-armed intercontinental ballistic missile with a warhead 630 times more powerful than the atomic bomb dropped on Hiroshima, but instead, according to Air Force Colonel Frank Horton, it's just a "very large, potentially disruptive reentry system," why be concerned about the threat of nuclear destruction? Why worry about the neutron bomb escalating the arms race if it's just a "radiation enhancement weapon"? If it's not an invasion, but a "rescue mission" or a "predawn vertical insertion," you won't need to think about any violations of U.S. or international law.

Doublespeak has become so common in everyday living that many people fail to notice it. Even worse, when they do notice doublespeak being used on them, they don't react, they don't protest. Do you protest when you are asked to check your packages at the desk "for your convenience," when it's not for your convenience at all but for someone else's? You see advertisements for "genuine imitation leather," "virgin vinyl," or "real counterfeit diamonds," but do you question the language or the supposed quality of the product? Do you question politicians who don't speak of slums or ghettos but of the "inner city" or "substandard housing" where the "disadvantaged" live and thus avoid talking about the poor who have to live in filthy, poorly heated, ramshackle apartments or houses? Aren't you amazed that patients don't die in the hospital anymore, it's just "negative patient-care outcome"?

Doublespeak such as that noted earlier that defines cab drivers as "urban transportation specialists," elevator operators as members of the "vertical transportation corps," and automobile mechanics as "automotive internists" can be considered humorous and relatively harmless. However, when a fire in a nuclear reactor building is called "rapid oxidation," an explosion in a nuclear power plant is called an "energetic disassembly," the illegal overthrow of a legitimate government is termed "destabilizing a government," and lies are seen as "inoperative statements," we are hearing doublespeak that attempts to avoid responsibility and make the bad seem good, the negative appear positive, something unpleasant appear attractive; and which seems to communicate but doesn't. It is language designed to alter our perception of reality and corrupt our thinking. Such language does not provide us with the tools we need to develop, advance, and preserve our culture and our civilization. Such language breeds suspicion, cynicism, distrust, and, ultimately, hostility.

Doublespeak is insidious because it can infect and eventually destroy the function of language, which is communication between people and social groups. This corruption of the function of language can have serious and far-reaching consequences. We live in a country that depends upon an informed electorate to make decisions in selecting candidates for office and deciding issues of public policy. The use of doublespeak can become so pervasive that it becomes the coin of the political realm, with speakers and listeners convinced that they really understand such language. After a while we may really believe that politicians don't lie but only "misspeak," that illegal acts are merely "inappropriate actions," that fraud and criminal conspiracy are just "miscertification." President Jimmy Carter in April of 1980 could call the aborted raid to free the American hostages in Teheran an "incomplete success" and really believe that he had made a statement that clearly communicated with the American public. So, too, could President Ronald Reagan say in 1985 that "ultimately our security and our hopes for success at the arms reduction talks hinge on the determination that we show here to continue our program to rebuild and refortify our defenses" and really believe that greatly increasing the amount of money spent building new weapons would lead to a reduction in the number of weapons in the world. If we really believe that we understand such language and that such language communicates and promotes clear thought, then the world of *1984*, with its control of reality through language, is upon us.

The "M-Word": Why It Matters to Me

Andrew Sullivan

What's in a name?

Perhaps the best answer is a memory.

As a child, I had no idea what homosexuality was. I grew up in a traditional home—Catholic, conservative, middle class. Life was relatively simple: education, work, family. I was brought up to aim high in life, even though my parents hadn't gone to college. But one thing was instilled in me. What matters is not how far you go in life, how much money you make, how big a name you make for yourself. What really matters is family, and the love you have for one another. The most important day of your life was not graduation from college or your first day at work or a raise or even your first house. The most important day of your life was when you got married. It was on that day that all your friends and all your family got together to celebrate the most important thing in life: your happiness, your ability to make a new home, to form a new but connected family, to find love that puts everything else into perspective.

But as I grew older, I found that this was somehow not available to me. I didn't feel the things for girls that my peers did. All the emotions and social rituals and bonding of teenage heterosexual life eluded me. I didn't know why. No one explained it. My emotional bonds to other boys were one-sided; each time I felt myself falling in love, they sensed it, pushed it away. I didn't and couldn't blame them. I got along fine with my buds in a nonemotional context; but something was awry, something not right. I came to know almost instinctively that I would never be a part of my family the way my siblings one day might be. The love I had inside me was unmentionable, anathema—even, in the words of the Church I attended every Sunday, evil. I remember writing in my teenage journal one day: "I'm a professional human being. But what do I do in my private life?"

So, like many gay men of my generation, I retreated. I never discussed my real life. I couldn't date girls and so immersed myself in schoolwork, in the debate team, school plays, anything to give me an excuse not to confront reality. When I looked toward the years ahead, I couldn't see a future. There was just a void. Was I going to be alone my whole life? Would I ever have a "most important day" in my life? It seemed impossible, a negation, an undoing. To be a full part of my family I had to somehow not be me. So like many gay teens, I withdrew, became neurotic, depressed, at times close to suicidal. I shut myself in my room with my books, night after night, while my peers developed the skills needed to form real relationships, and loves. In wounded pride, I even voiced a rejection of family and marriage. It was the only way I could explain my isolation.

It took years for me to realize that I was gay, years later to tell others, and more time yet to form any kind of stable emotional bond with another man. Because my sexuality had emerged in solitude—and without any link to the idea of an actual relationship—it was hard later to reconnect sex to love and self-esteem. It still is. But I persevered, each relationship slowly growing longer than the last, learning in my twenties and thirties what my straight friends found out in their teens. But even then, my parents and friends never asked the question they would have asked automatically if I were straight: So when are you going to get married? When is your relationship going to be public? When will we be able to celebrate it and affirm it and support it? In fact, no one—no one—has yet asked me that question.

When people talk about "gay marriage," they miss the point. This isn't about gay marriage. It's about marriage. It's about family. It's about love. It isn't about religion. It's about civil marriage licenses—available to atheists as well as believers. These family values are not options for a happy and stable life. They are necessities. Putting gay relationships in some other category—civil unions, domestic partnerships, civil partnerships, whatever—may alleviate real human needs, but, by their very euphemism, by their very separateness, they actually build a wall between gay people and their own families. They put back the barrier many of us have spent a lifetime trying to erase.

It's too late for me to undo my own past. But I want above everything else to remember a young kid out there who may even be reading this now. I want to let him know that he doesn't have to choose between himself and his family anymore. I want him to know that his love has dignity, that he does indeed have a future as a full and equal part of the human race. Only marriage will do that. Only marriage can bring him home.

Meanings of a Word

Gloria Naylor

Language is the subject. It is the written form with which I've managed to keep the wolf away from the door and, in diaries, to keep my sanity. In spite of this, I consider the written word inferior to the spoken, and much of the frustration experienced by novelists is the awareness that whatever we manage to capture in even the most transcendent passages falls far short of the richness of life. Dialogue achieves its power in the dynamics of a fleeting moment of sight, sound, smell and touch.

I'm not going to enter the debate here about whether it is language that shapes reality or vice versa. That battle is doomed to be waged whenever we seek intermittent reprieve from the chicken and egg dispute. I will simply take the position that the spoken word, like the written word, amounts to a nonsensical arrangement of sounds or letters without a consensus that assigns "meaning." And building from the meanings of what we hear, we order reality. Words themselves are innocuous; it is the consensus that gives them true power.

I remember the first time I heard the word nigger. In my third-grade class, our math tests were being passed down the rows, and as I handed the papers to a little boy in back of me, I remarked that once again he had received a much lower mark than I did. He snatched his test from me and spit out that word. Had he called me a nymphomaniac or a necrophiliac, I couldn't have been more puzzled. I didn't know what a nigger was, but I knew that whatever it meant, it was something he shouldn't have called me. This was verified when I raised my hand, and in a loud voice repeated what he had said and watched the teacher scold him for using a "bad" word. I was later to go home and ask the inevitable question that every black parent must face—"Mommy, what does 'nigger' mean?"

And what exactly did it mean? Thinking back, I realize that this could not have been the first time the word was used in my presence. I was part of a large extended family that had migrated from the rural South after World War II and formed a close-knit network that gravitated around my maternal grandparents. Their ground-floor apartment in one of the buildings they owned in Harlem was a weekend mecca for my immediate family, along with countless aunts, uncles and cousins who brought along assorted friends. It was a bustling and open house with assorted neighbors and tenants popping in and out to exchange bits of gossip, pick up an old quarrel or referee the ongoing checkers game in which my grandmother cheated shamelessly. They were all there to let down their hair and put up their feet after a week of labor in the factories, laundries and shipyards of New York.

Amid the clamor, which could reach deafening proportions—two or three conversations going on simultaneously, punctuated by the sound of a baby's crying somewhere in the back rooms or out on the street—there was still a rigid set of rules about what was said and how. Older children were sent out of the living room when it was time to get into the juicy details about "you-know-who" up on the third floor who had gone and gotten herself "p-r-e-g-n-a-n-t!" But my parents, knowing that I could spell well beyond my years, always demanded that I follow the others out to play. Beyond sexual misconduct and death, everything else was considered harmless for our young ears. And so among the anecdotes of the triumphs and disappointments in the various workings of their lives, the word nigger was used in my presence, but it was set within contexts and inflections that caused it to register in my mind as something else.

In the singular, the word was always applied to a man who had distinguished himself in some situation that brought their approval for his strength, intelligence or drive:

"Did Johnny really do that?"

"I'm telling you, that nigger pulled in $6,000 of overtime last year. Said he got enough for a down payment on a house."

When used with a possessive adjective by a woman—"my nigger"—it became a term of endearment for husband or boyfriend. But it could be more than just a term applied to a man. In their mouths it became the pure essence of manhood—a disembodied force that channeled their past history of struggle and present survival against the odds into a victorious statement of being: "Yeah, that old foreman found out quick enough—you don't mess with a nigger."

In the plural, it became a description of some group within the community that had overstepped the bounds of decency as my family defined it: Parents who neglected their children, a drunken couple who fought in public, people who simply refused to look for work, those with excessively dirty mouths or unkempt households were all "trifling niggers." This particular circle could forgive hard times, unemployment, the occasional bout of depression—they had gone through all of that themselves—but the unforgivable sin was lack of self-respect.

A woman could never be a "nigger" in the singular, with its connotation of confirming worth. The noun "girl" was its closest equivalent in that sense, but only when used in direct address and regardless of the gender doing the addressing. "Girl" was a token of respect for a woman. The one-syllable word was drawn out to sound like three in recognition of the extra ounce of wit, nerve or daring that the woman had shown in the situation under discussion.

"G-i-r-l, stop. You mean you said that to his face?"

But if the word was used in a third-person reference or shortened so that it almost snapped out of the mouth, it always involved some element of communal disapproval. And age became an important factor in these exchanges. It was only between individuals of the same generation, or from an older person to a younger (but never the other way around), that "girl" would be considered a compliment.

I don't agree with the argument that use of the word nigger at this social stratum of the black community was an internalization of racism. The dynamics were the exact opposite: the people in my grandmother's living room took a word that whites used to signify worthlessness or degradation and rendered it impotent. Gathering there together, they transformed "nigger" to signify the varied and complex human beings they knew themselves to be. If the word was to disappear totally from the mouths of even the most racist of white society, no one in that room was naive enough to believe it would disappear from white minds. Meeting the word head on, they proved it had absolutely nothing to do with the way they were determined to live their lives.

So there must have been dozens of times that the word "nigger" was spoken in front of me before I reached the third grade. But I didn't "hear" it until it was said by a small pair of lips that had already learned it could be a way to humiliate me. That was the word I went home and asked my mother about. And since she knew that I had to grow up in America, she took me in her lap and explained.

What Is Poverty?

Jo Goodwin Parker

You ask me what is poverty? Listen to me. Here I am, dirty, smelly, and with no "proper" underwear on and with the stench of my rotting teeth near you. I will tell you. Listen to me. Listen without pity. I cannot use your pity. Listen with understanding. Put yourself in my dirty, worn out, ill-fitting shoes, and hear me.

Poverty is getting up every morning from a dirt-and illness-stained mattress. The sheets have long since been used for diapers. Poverty is living in a smell that never leaves. This is a smell of urine, sour milk, and spoiling food sometimes joined with the strong smell of long-cooked onions. Onions are cheap. If you have smelled this smell, you did not know how it came. It is the smell of the outdoor privy. It is the smell of young children who cannot walk the long dark way in the night. It is the smell of the mattresses where years of "accidents" have happened. It is the smell of the milk which has gone sour because the refrigerator long has not worked, and it costs money to get it fixed. It is the smell of rotting garbage. I could bury it, but where is the shovel? Shovels cost money.

Poverty is being tired. I have always been tired. They told me at the hospital when the last baby came that I had chronic anemia caused from poor diet, a bad case of worms, and that I needed a corrective operation. I listened politely—the poor are always polite. The poor always listen. They don't say that there is no money for iron pills, or better food, or worm medicine. The idea of an operation is frightening and costs so much that, if I had dared, I would have laughed. Who takes care of my children? Recovery from an operation takes a long time. I have three children. When I left them with "Granny" the last time I had a job, I came home to find the baby covered with fly specks, and a diaper that had not been changed since I left. When the dried diaper came off, bits of my baby's flesh came with it. My other child was playing with a sharp bit of broken glass, and my oldest was playing alone at the edge of a lake. I made twenty-two dollars a week, and a good nursery school costs twenty dollars a week for three children. I quit my job.

Poverty is dirt. You can say in your clean clothes coming from your clean house, "Anybody can be clean." Let me explain about housekeeping with no money For breakfast I give my children grits with no oleo or corn-bread without eggs and oleo. This does not use up many dishes. What dishes there are, I wash in cold water and with no soap. Even the cheapest soap has to be saved for the baby's diapers. Look at my hands, so cracked and red. Once I saved for two months to buy a jar of Vaseline for my hands and the baby's diaper rash. When I had saved enough, I went to buy it and the price had gone up two cents. The baby and I suffered on. I have to decide every day if I can bear to put my cracked sore hands into the cold water and strong soap. But you ask, why not hot water? Fuel costs money. If you have a wood fire it costs money. If you burn electricity, it costs money. Hot water is a luxury. I do not have luxuries. I know you will be surprised when I tell you how young I am. I look so much older. My back has been bent over the wash tubs every day for so long. I cannot remember when I ever did anything else. Every night I wash every stitch my school age child has on and just hope her clothes will be dry by morning.

Poverty is staying up all night on cold nights to watch the fire knowing one spark on the newspaper covering the walls means your sleeping child dies in flames. In summer, poverty is watching gnats and flies devour your baby's tears when he cries. The screens are torn and you pay so little rent you know they will never be fixed. Poverty means insects in your food, in your nose, in your eyes, and crawling over you when you sleep. Poverty is hoping it never rains because diapers won't dry when it rains and soon you are using newspapers. Poverty is seeing your children forever with runny noses. Paper handkerchiefs cost money and all your rags you need for other things. Even more costly are antihistamines. Poverty is cooking without food and cleaning without soap.

Poverty is asking for help. Have you ever had to ask for help, knowing your children will suffer unless you get it? Think about asking for a loan from a relative, if this is the only way you can imagine asking for help. I will tell you how it feels. You find out where the office is that you are supposed to visit. You circle that block four or five times. Thinking of your children, you go in. Everyone is very busy. Finally, someone comes out and you tell her that you need help. That never is the person you need to see. You go see another person, and after spilling the whole shame of your poverty all over the desk between you, you find that this isn't the right office after all—you must repeat the whole process, and it never is any easier at the next place.

You have asked for help, and after all it has a cost. You are again told to wait. You are told why, but you don't really hear because of the red cloud of shame and the rising cloud of despair.

Poverty is remembering. It is remembering quitting school in junior: high because "nice" children had been so cruel about my clothes and my smell. The attendance officer came. My mother told him I was pregnant. I wasn't, but she thought that I could get a job and help out. I had jobs off and on, but never long enough to learn anything. Mostly I remember being married. I was so young then. I am still young. For a time, we had all the things you have. There was a little house in another town, with hot water and everything. Then my husband lost his job. There was unemployment insurance for a while and what few jobs I could get. Soon, all our nice things were repossessed and we moved back here. I was pregnant then. This house didn't look so bad when we first moved in. Every week it gets worse. Nothing is ever fixed. We now had no money. There were a few odd jobs for my husband, but everything went for food then, as it does now. I don't know how we lived through three years and three babies, but we did. I'll tell you something, after the last baby I destroyed my marriage. It had been a good one, but could you keep on bringing children in this dirt? Did you ever think how much it costs for any kind of birth control? I knew my husband was leaving the day he left, but there were no goodbys between us. I hope he has been able to climb out of this mess somewhere. He never could hope with us to drag him down.

That's when I asked for help. When I got it, you know how much it was? It was, and is, seventy-eight dollars a month for the four of us; that is all I ever can get. Now you know why there is no soap, no needles and thread, no hot water, no aspirin, no worm medicine, no hand cream, no shampoo. None of these things forever and ever and ever. So that you can see clearly, I pay twenty dollars a month rent, and most of the rest goes for food. For grits and cornmeal, and rice and milk and beans. I try my best to use only the minimum electricity. If I use more, there is that much less for food.

Poverty is looking into a black future. Your children won't play with my boys. They will turn to other boys who steal to get what they want. I can already see them behind the bars of their prison instead of behind the bars of my poverty. Or they will turn to the freedom of alcohol or drugs, and find themselves enslaved. And my daughter? At best, there is for her a life like mine.

But you say to me, there are schools. Yes, there are schools. My children have no extra books, no magazines, no extra pencils, or crayons, or paper and most important of all, they do not have health. They have worms, they have infections, they have pinkeye all summer. They do not sleep well on the floor, or with me in my one bed. They do not suffer from hunger, my seventy-eight dollars keeps us alive, but they do suffer from malnutrition. Oh yes, I do remember what I was taught about health in school. It doesn't do much good. In some places there is a surplus commodities program. Not here. The county said it cost too much. There is a school lunch program. But I have two children who will already be damaged by the time they get to school.

But, you say to me, there are health clinics. Yes, there are health clinics and they are in the towns. I live out here eight miles from town. I can walk that far (even if it is sixteen miles both ways), but can my little children? My neighbor will take me when he goes; but he expects to get paid, *one way or another*. I bet you know my neighbor. He is that large man who spends his time at the gas station, the barbershop, and the corner store complaining about the government spending money on the immoral mothers of illegitimate children.

Poverty is an acid that drips on pride until all pride is worn away. Poverty is a chisel that chips on honor until honor is worn away. Some of you say that you would do *something* in my situation, and maybe you would, for the first week or the first month, but for year after year after year?

Even the poor can dream. A dream of a time when there is money. Money for the right kinds of food, for worm medicine, for iron pills, for toothbrushes, for hand cream, for a hammer and nails and a bit of screening, for a shovel, for a bit of paint, for some sheeting, for needles and thread. Money to pay *in money* for a trip to town. And, oh, money for hot water and money for soap. A dream of when asking for help does not eat away the last bit of pride. When the office you visit is as nice as the offices of other governmental agencies, when there are enough workers to help you quickly, when workers do not quit in defeat and despair. When you have to tell your story to only one person, and that person can send you for other help and you don't have to prove your poverty over and over and over again.

I have come out of my despair to tell you this. Remember I did not come from another place or another time. Others like me are all around you. Look at us with an angry heart, anger that will help you help me. Anger that will let you tell of me. The poor are always silent. Can you be silent too?

I Want a Wife

Judy Brady

I belong to that classification of people known as wives. I am A Wife. And, not altogether incidentally, I am a mother.

Not too long ago a male friend of mine appeared on the scene fresh from a recent divorce. He had one child, who is, of course, with his ex-wife. He is looking for another wife. As I thought about him while I was ironing one evening, it suddenly occurred to me that I, too, would like to have a wife. Why do I want a wife?

I would like to go back to school so that I can become economically independent, support myself, and, if need be, support those dependent upon me. I want a wife who will work and send me to school. And while I am going to school I want a wife to take care of my children. I want a wife to keep track of the children's doctor and dentist appointments. And to keep track of mine, too. I want a wife to make sure my children eat properly and are kept clean. I want a wife who will wash the children's clothes and keep them mended. I want a wife who is a good nurturant attendant to my children, who arranges for their schooling, makes sure that they have an adequate social life with their peers, takes them to the park, the zoo, etc. I want a wife who takes care of the children when they are sick, a wife who arranges to be around when the children need special care, because, of course, I cannot miss classes at school. My wife must arrange to lose time at work and not lose the job. It may mean a small cut in my wife's income from time to time, but I guess I can tolerate that. Needless to say, my wife will arrange and pay for the care of the children while my wife is working.

I want a wife who will take care of *my* physical needs. I want a wife who will keep my house clean. A wife who will pick up after my children, a wife who will pick up after me. I want a wife who will keep my clothes clean, ironed, mended, replaced when need be, and who will see to it that my personal things are kept in their proper place so that I can find what I need the minute I need it. I want a wife who cooks the meals, a wife who is a good cook. I want a wife who will plan the menus, do the necessary grocery shopping, prepare the meals, serve them pleasantly, and then do the cleaning up while I do my studying. I want a wife who will care for me when I am sick and sympathize with my pain and loss of time from school. I want a wife to go along when our family takes a vacation so that someone can continue to care for me and my children when I need a rest and change of scene.

I want a wife who will not bother me with rambling complaints about a wife's duties. But I want a wife who will listen to me when I feel the need to explain a rather difficult point I have come across in my course of studies. And I want a wife who will type my papers for me when I have written them.

I want a wife who will take care of the details of my social life. When my wife and I are invited out by my friends, I want a wife who will take care of the babysitting arrangements. When I meet people at school that I like and want to entertain, I want a wife who will have the house clean, will prepare a special meal, serve it to me and my friends, and not interrupt when I talk about things that interest me and my friends. I want a wife who will have arranged that the children are fed and ready for bed before my guests arrive so that the children do not bother us. I want a wife who takes care of the needs of my guests so that they feel comfortable, who makes sure that they have an ashtray, that they are passed the hors d'oeuvres, that they are offered a second helping of the food, that their wine glasses are replenished when necessary, that their coffee is served to them as they like it. And I want a wife who knows that sometimes I need a night out by myself.

I want a wife who is sensitive to my sexual needs, a wife who makes love passionately and eagerly when I feel like it, a wife who makes sure that I am satisfied. And, of course, I want a wife who will not demand sexual attention when I am not in the mood for it. I want a wife who assumes the complete responsibility for birth control, because I do not want more children. I want a wife who will remain sexually faithful to me so that I do not have to clutter up my intellectual life with jealousies. And I want a wife who understands that *my* sexual needs may entail more than strict adherence to monogamy. I must, after all, be able to relate to people as fully as possible.

If, by chance, I find another person more suitable as a wife than the wife I already have, I want the liberty to replace my present wife with another one. Naturally, I will expect a fresh new life; my wife will take the children and be solely responsible for them so that I am left free.

When I am through with school and have a job, I want my wife to quit working and remain at home so that my wife can more fully and completely take care of a wife's duties.

My God, who *wouldn't* want a wife?

Process Analysis

Writing helps us explore what we think through analysis. One of the most familiar forms of analysis is process analysis. It is the step-by-step explanation of how to do something that we find most commonly in how-to articles, directions, or recipes, to name a few. It breaks a process down to its simplest components so the reader can replicate it. This is called a directive process analysis.

Process analysis can also explain how things happen or might have happened. How the Grand Canyon was formed or how the universe was created would be examples of this. Clearly, these are things that could not be replicated by reading the article; the reader would, however, gain an understanding of the stages of how something came to be. This form is called an informative process analysis.

Process analysis also can be used creatively, or imaginatively. When scientists describe the long-term effects of global warming, they are imagining, based on scientific evidence and correlations, what might happen.

Which form you use will depend on your purpose.

The benefit of learning process analysis goes beyond the dual purposes of this rhetorical mode. By consciously analyzing the steps or stages of process, the writer learns the importance of presenting the reader with all necessary information to make the connections. This is true for all rhetorical modes.

The Process

Purpose and Thesis

It is important to consider your purpose beyond whether you are describing a process your reader can replicate or explain a process your reader will find informative or fascinating. What is it about the process that is important, or why is it significant to tell? An example is Jessica Mitford's informative process analysis "The Embalming of Mr. Jones." Her purpose is not only to describe the process of embalming but also to make readers aware of a process that undertakers keep from them and which they might not want if they knew about it. The same is true for Malcolm X's "My First Conk." His description of the torturous process of chemically straightened hair goes beyond the point of a status symbol and what people will do to conform; his purpose is to point out how a conk is really a symbol of degradation for blacks.

The thesis statements for both of these essays make their purpose clear beyond their subject.

> A close look at what does actually take place may explain in large measure the undertaker's intractable reticience concerning a procedure that has become his major *raison d'être.* Is it possible he fears that public information about embalming might lead patrons to wonder if they really want this service?
>
> –Jessica Mitford, "The Embalming of Mr. Jones"

> This was my first really big step toward self-degradation: when I endured all of that pain, literally burning my flesh to have it look like a white man's hair, I had joined that multitude of Negro men and women in America who are brainwashed into believing that the black people are *inferior*—and white people *superior*—that they will even violate and mutilate their God-created bodies to try to look *pretty* by white standards.
>
> –Malcolm X, "My First Conk"

Although both these essays are informative process analysis, the same holds true for directive process analysis. If you are writing an essay explaining how to build a stone wall, for example, you want to make your thesis statement more pointed than presenting your subject and essential steps. You want to convey your reason for writing about your subject. For instance,

Building a stone wall may be labor intensive and require some skill; with practice, patience, and the directions that follow, anyone can create a thing of beauty using one of the basic elements of nature.

Organization

The analysis in a process analysis takes place before you start writing. It is important to think your process through, breaking it down to it simplest steps or stages, examining the order of the steps, determining what materials are needed and when, and noting if any preliminary preparations are necessary. The key to an effective process analysis is maintaining clear chronological order and including all necessary information. The overall format is similar to any essay:

- A process essay begins with an introduction to your subject, an overview of the process, a description of needed materials or preliminary steps, and your thesis statement.
- The body paragraphs focus on each step or stage of the process in chronological order. Make sure each step is explained completely, including any smaller steps that might comprise it. Define any terms that are not commonly known or represent technical jargon. It may be necessary to explain the reason for each step or how it connects with the other steps.
- Conclude with the end result or with a reflection on the significance or usefulness of the process.

On Dumpster Diving

Lars Eighner

Long before I began Dumpster diving I was impressed with Dumpsters, enough so that I wrote the Merriam-Webster research service to discover what I could about the word *Dumpster*. I learned from them that it is a proprietary word belonging to the Dempsey Dumpster company. Since then I have dutifully capitalized the word, although it was lowercased in almost all the citations Merriam-Webster photocopied for me. Dempsey's word is too apt. I have never heard these things called anything but Dumpsters. I do not know anyone who knows the generic name for these objects. From time to time I have heard a wino or hobo give some corrupted credit to the original and call them Dipsy Dumpsters.

I began Dumpster diving about a year before I became homeless.

I prefer the word *scavenging* and use the word *scrounging* when I mean to be obscure. I have heard people, evidently meaning to be polite, use the word *foraging*, but I prefer to reserve that word for gathering nuts and berries and such, which I do also according to the season and the opportunity. *Dumpster diving* seems to me to be a little too cute and, in my case, inaccurate because I lack the athletic ability to lower myself into the Dumpsters as the true divers do, much to their increased profit.

I like the frankness of the word *scavenging*, which I can hardly think of without picturing a big black snail on an aquarium wall. I live from the refuse of others. I am a scavenger. I think it a sound and honorable niche, although if I could I would naturally prefer to live the comfortable consumer life, perhaps—and only perhaps—as a slightly less wasteful consumer, owing to what I have learned as a scavenger.

While Lizbeth and I were still living in the shack on Avenue B as my savings ran out, I put almost all my sporadic income into rent. The necessities of daily life I began to extract from Dumpsters. Yes, we ate from them. Except for jeans, all my clothes came from Dumpsters. Boom boxes, candles, bedding, toilet paper, a virgin male love doll, medicine, books, a typewriter, dishes, furnishings, and change, sometimes amounting to many dollars—I acquired many things from Dumpsters.

I have learned much as a scavenger. I mean to put some of what I have learned down here, beginning with the practical art of Dumpster diving and proceeding to the abstract.

What is safe to eat?

After all, the finding of objects is becoming something of an urban art. Even respectable employed people will sometimes find something tempting sticking out of a Dumpster or standing beside one. Quite a number of people, not all of them of the bohemian type, are willing to brag that they found this or that piece of trash. But eating from Dumpsters is what separates the dilettanti from the professionals. Eating safely from the Dumpsters involves three principles: using the senses and common sense to evaluate the condition of the found materials, knowing the Dumpsters of a given area and checking them regularly, and seeking always to answer the question "Why was this discarded?"

Perhaps everyone who has a kitchen and a regular supply of groceries has, at one time or another, made a sandwich and eaten half of it before discovering mold on the bread or got a mouthful of milk before realizing the milk had turned. Nothing of the sort is likely to happen to a Dumpster diver because he is constantly reminded that most food is discarded for a reason. Yet a lot of perfectly good food can be found in Dumpsters.

Canned goods, for example, turn up fairly often in the Dumpsters I frequent. All except the most phobic people will be willing to eat from a can, even if it came from a Dumpster. Canned goods are among the safest foods to be found in Dumpsters but are not utterly foolproof.

Although very rare with modern canning methods, botulism is a possibility. Most other forms of food poisoning seldom do lasting harm to a healthy person, but botulism is almost certainly fatal and often the first symptom is death. Except for carbonated beverages, all canned goods should contain a slight vacuum and suck air when first punctured. Bulging, rusty, and dented cans and cans that spew when punctured should be avoided, especially when the contents are not very acidic or syrupy.

Heat can break down the botulin, but this requires much more cooking than most people do to canned goods. To the extent that botulism occurs at all, of course, it can occur in cans on pantry shelves as well as in cans from Dumpsters. Need I say that home-canned goods are simply too risky to be recommended.

From time to time one of my companions, aware of the source of my provisions, will ask, "Do you think these crackers are really safe to eat?" For some reason it is most often the crackers they ask about.

This question has always made me angry. Of course I would not offer my companion anything I had doubts about. But more than that, I wonder why he cannot evaluate the condition of the crackers for himself. I have no special knowledge and I have been wrong before. Since he knows where the food comes from, it seems to me he ought to assume some of the responsibility for deciding what he will put in his mouth. For myself I have few qualms about dry foods such as crackers, cookies, cereal, chips, and pasta if they are free of visible contaminates and still dry and crisp. Most often such things are found in the original packaging, which is not so much a positive sign as it is the absence of a negative one.

Raw fruits and vegetables with intact skins seem perfectly safe to me, excluding of course the obviously rotten. Many are discarded for minor imperfections that can be pared away. Leafy vegetables, grapes, cauliflower, broccoli, and similar things may be contaminated by liquids and may be impractical to wash.

Candy, especially hard candy, is usually safe if it has not drawn ants. Chocolate is often discarded only because it has become discolored as the cocoa butter de-emulsified. Candying, after all, is one method of food preservation because pathogens do not like very sugary substances.

All of these foods might be found in any Dumpster and can be evaluated with some confidence largely on the basis of appearance. Beyond these are foods that cannot be correctly evaluated without additional information.

I began scavenging by pulling pizzas out of the Dumpster behind a pizza delivery shop. In general, prepared food requires caution, but in this case I knew when the shop closed and went to the Dumpster as soon as the last of the help left.

Such shops often get prank orders; both the orders and the products made to fill them are called *bogus*. Because help seldom stays long at these places, pizzas are often made with the wrong topping, refused on delivery for being cold, or baked incorrectly. The products to be discarded are boxed up because inventory is kept by counting boxes: A boxed pizza can be written off; an unboxed pizza does not exist.

I never placed a bogus order to increase the supply of pizzas and I believe no one else was scavenging in this Dumpster. But the people in the shop became suspicious and began to retain their garbage in the shop overnight. While it lasted I had a steady supply of fresh, sometimes warm pizza. Because I knew the Dumpster I knew the source of the pizza, and because I visited the Dumpster regularly I knew what was fresh and what was yesterday's.

The area I frequent is inhabited by many affluent college students. I am not here by chance; the Dumpsters in this area are very rich. Students throw out many good things, including food. In particular they tend to throw everything out when they move at the end of a semester, before and after breaks, and around midterm, when many of them despair of college. So I find it advantageous to keep an eye on the academic calendar.

Students throw food away around breaks because they do not know whether it has spoiled or will spoil before they return. A typical discard is a half jar of peanut butter. In fact, nonorganic peanut butter does not require refrigeration and is unlikely to spoil in any reasonable time. The student does not know that, and since it is Daddy's money, the student decides not to take a chance. Opened containers require caution and some attention to the question "Why was this discarded?" But in the case of discards from student apartments, the answer may be that the item was thrown out through carelessness, ignorance, or wastefulness. This can sometimes be deduced when the item is found with many others, including some that are obviously perfectly good.

Some students, and others, approach defrosting a freezer by chucking out the whole lot. Not only do the circumstances of such a find tell the story, but also the mass of frozen goods stays cold for a long time and items may be found still frozen or freshly thawed.

Yogurt, cheese, and sour cream are items that are often thrown out while they are still good. Occasionally I find cheese with a spot of mold, which of course I just pare off, and because it is obvious why such a cheese was discarded, I treat it with less suspicion than an apparently perfect cheese found in similar circumstances. Yogurt is often discarded, still sealed, only because the expiration date on the carton had passed.

This is one of my favorite finds because yogurt will keep for several days, even in warm weather.

Students throw out canned goods and staples at the end of semesters and when they give up college at midterm. Drugs, pornography, spirits, and the like are often discarded when parents are expected—Dad's Day, for example. And spirits also turn up after big party weekends, presumably discarded by the newly reformed. Wine and spirits, of course, keep perfectly well even once opened, but the same cannot be said of beer.

My test for carbonated soft drinks is whether they still fizz vigorously. Many juices or other beverages are too acidic or too syrupy to cause much concern, provided they are not visibly contaminated. I have discovered nasty molds in the vegetable juices, even when the product was found under its original seal; I recommend that such products be decanted slowly into a clear glass. Liquids always require some care. One hot day I found a large jug of Pat O'Brien's Hurricane mix. The jug had been opened but was still ice cold. I drank three large glasses before it became apparent to me that someone had added rum to the mix, and not a little rum. I never tasted the rum, and by the time I began to feel the effects I had already ingested a very large quantity of the beverage. Some divers would have considered this a boon, but being suddenly intoxicated in a public place in the early afternoon is not my idea of a good time.

I have heard of people maliciously contaminating discarded food and even handouts, but mostly I have heard of this from people with vivid imaginations who have had no experience with Dumpsters themselves. Just before the pizza shop stopped discarding its garbage at night, jalapenos began showing up on most of the thrown-out pizzas. If indeed this was meant to discourage me, it was a wasted effort because I am a native Texan.

For myself, I avoid game, poultry, pork, and egg-based foods, whether I find them raw or cooked. I seldom have the means to cook what I find, but when I do I avail myself of plentiful supplies of beef, which is often in very good condition. I suppose fish becomes disagreeable before it becomes dangerous. Lizbeth is happy to have any such thing that is past its prime and, in fact, does not recognize fish as food until it is quite strong.

Home leftovers, as opposed to surpluses from restaurants, are very often bad. Evidently, especially among students, there is a common type of personality that carefully wraps up even the smallest leftover and shoves it into the back of the refrigerator for six months or so before discarding it. Characteristic of this type are the reused jars and margarine tubs to which the remains are committed. I avoid ethnic foods I am unfamiliar with. If I do not know what it is supposed to look like when it is good, I cannot be certain I will be able to tell if it is bad.

No matter how careful I am I still get dysentery at least once a month, oftener in warmer weather. I do not want to paint too romantic a picture. Dumpster diving has serious drawbacks as a way of life.

I learned to scavenge gradually, on my own. Since then I have initiated several companions into the trade. I have learned that there is a predictable series of stages a person goes through in learning to scavenge.

At first the new scavenger is filled with disgust and self-loathing. He is ashamed of being seen and may lurk around, trying to duck behind things, or he may try to dive at night. (In fact, most people instinctively look away from a scavenger. By skulking around, the novice calls attention to himself and arouses suspicion. Diving at night is ineffective and needlessly messy.)

Every grain of rice seems to be a maggot. Everything seems to stink. He can wipe the egg yolk off the found can, but he cannot erase from his mind the stigma of eating garbage.

That stage passes with experience. The scavenger finds a pair of running shoes that fit and look and smell brand-new. He finds a pocket calculator in perfect working order. He finds pristine ice cream, still frozen, more than he can eat or keep. He begins to understand: People throw away perfectly good stuff, a lot of perfectly good stuff.

At this stage, Dumpster shyness begins to dissipate. The diver, after all, has the last laugh. He is finding all manner of good things that are his for the taking. Those who disparage his profession are the fools, not he.

He may begin to hang on to some perfectly good things for which he has neither a use nor a market. Then he begins to take note of the things that are not perfectly good but are nearly so. He mates a Walkman with broken earphones and one that is missing a battery cover. He picks up things that he can repair.

At this stage he may become lost and never recover. Dumpsters are full of things of some potential value to someone and also of things that never have much intrinsic value but are interesting. All the Dumpster divers I have known come to the point of trying to acquire everything they touch. Why not take it, they reason, since it is all free? This is, of course, hopeless. Most divers come to realize that they must restrict themselves to items of relatively immediate utility. But in some cases the diver simply cannot control himself. I have met several of these pack-rat types. Their ideas of the values of various pieces of junk verge on the psychotic. Every bit of glass may be a diamond, they think, and all that glisters, gold.

I tend to gain weight when I am scavenging. Partly this is because I always find far more pizza and doughnuts than water-packed tuna, nonfat yogurt, and fresh vegetables. Also I have not developed much faith in the reliability of Dumpsters as a food source, although it has been proven to me many times. I tend to eat as if I have no idea where my next meal is coming from. But mostly I just hate to see food go to waste and so I eat much more than I should. Something like this drives the obsession to collect junk.

As for collecting objects, I usually restrict myself to collecting one kind of small object at a time, such as pocket calculators, sunglasses, or campaign buttons. To live on the street I must anticipate my needs to a certain extent: I must pick up and save warm bedding I find in August because it will not be found in Dumpsters in November. As I have no access to health care, I often hoard essential drugs, such as antibiotics and antihistamines. (This course can be recommended only to those with some grounding in pharmacology. Antibiotics, for example, even when indicated are worse than useless if taken in insufficient amounts.) But even if I had a home with extensive storage space, I could not save everything that might be valuable in some contingency.

I have proprietary feelings about my Dumpsters. As I have mentioned, it is no accident that I scavenge from ones where good finds are common. But my limited experience with Dumpsters in other areas suggests to me that even in poorer areas, Dumpsters, if attended with sufficient diligence, can be made to yield a livelihood. The rich students discard perfectly good kiwi fruit; poorer people discard perfectly good apples. Slacks and Polo shirts are found in one place; jeans and T-shirts in the other. The population of competitors rather than the affluence of the dumpers most affects the feasibility of survival by scavenging. The large number of competitors is what puts me off the idea of trying to scavenge in places like Los Angeles.

Curiously, I do not mind my direct competition, other scavengers, so much as I hate the can scroungers.

People scrounge cans because they have to have a little cash. I have tried scrounging cans with an able-bodied companion. Afoot a can scrounger simply cannot make more than a few dollars in a day. One can extract the necessities of life from the Dumpsters directly with far less effort than would be required to accumulate the equivalent value in cans. (These observations may not hold in places with container redemption laws.)

Can scroungers, then, are people who must have small amounts of cash. These are drug addicts and winos, mostly the latter because the amounts of cash are so small. Spirits and drugs do, like all other commodities, turn up in Dumpsters and the scavenger will from time to time have a half bottle of a rather good wine with his dinner. But the wino cannot survive on these occasional finds; he must have his daily dose to stave off the DTs. All the cans he can carry will buy about three bottles of Wild Irish Rose.

I do not begrudge them the cans, but can scroungers tend to tear up the Dumpsters, mixing the contents and littering the area. They become so specialized that they can see only cans. They earn my contempt by passing up change, canned goods, and readily hockable items.

There are precious few courtesies among scavengers. But it is common practice to set aside surplus items: pairs of shoes, clothing, canned goods, and such. A true scavenger hates to see good stuff go to waste, and what he cannot use he leaves in good condition in plain sight.

Can scroungers lay waste to everything in their path and will stir one of a pair of good shoes to the bottom of a Dumpster, to be lost or ruined in the muck. Can scroungers will even go through individual garbage cans, something I have never seen a scavenger do.

Individual garbage cans are set out on the public easement only on garbage days. On the other days going through them requires trespassing close to a dwelling. Going through individual garbage cans without scattering litter is almost impossible. Litter is likely to reduce the public's tolerance of scavenging. Individual cans are simply not as productive as Dumpsters; people in houses and duplexes do not move so often and for some reason do not tend to discard as much useful material. Moreover, the time required to go through one garbage can that serves one household is not much less than the time required to go through a Dumpster that contains the refuse of twenty apartments.

But my strongest reservation about going through individual garbage cans is that this seems to me a very personal kind of invasion to which I would object if I were a householder. Although many things in Dumpsters are obviously meant never to come to light, a Dumpster is somehow less personal.

I avoid trying to draw conclusions about the people who dump in the Dumpsters I frequent. I think it would be unethical to do so, although I know many people will find the idea of scavenger ethics too funny for words.

Dumpsters contain bank statements, correspondence, and other documents, just as anyone might expect. But there are also less obvious sources of information. Pill bottles, for example. The labels bear the name of the patient, the name of the doctor, and the name of the drug. AIDS drugs and antipsychotic medicines, to name but two groups, are specific and are seldom prescribed for any other disorders. The plastic compacts for birth-control pills usually have complete label information.

Despite all of this sensitive information, I have had only one apartment resident object to my going through the Dumpster. In that case it turned out the resident was a university athlete who was taking bets and who was afraid I would turn up his wager slips.

Occasionally a find tells a story. I once found a small paper bag containing some unused condoms, several partial tubes of flavored sexual lubricants, a partially used compact of birth-control pills, and the torn pieces of a picture of a young man. Clearly she was through with him and planning to give up sex altogether.

Dumpster things are often sad—abandoned teddy bears, shredded wedding books, despaired-of sales kits. I find many pets lying in state in Dumpsters. Although I hope to get off the streets so that Lizbeth can have a long and comfortable old age, I know this hope is not very realistic. So I suppose when her time comes she too will go into a Dumpster. I will have no better place for her. And after all, it is fitting, since for most of her life her livelihood has come from the Dumpster. When she finds something I think is safe that has been spilled from a Dumpster, I let her have it. She already knows the route around the best ones. I like to think that if she survives me she will have a chance of evading the dog catcher and of finding her sustenance on the route.

Silly vanities also come to rest in the Dumpsters. I am a rather accomplished needleworker. I get a lot of material from the Dumpsters. Evidently sorority girls, hoping to impress someone, perhaps themselves, with their mastery of a womanly art, buy a lot of embroider-by-number kits, work a few stitches horribly, and eventually discard the whole mess. I pull out their stitches, turn the canvas over, and work an original design. Do not think I refrain from chuckling as I make gifts from these kits.

I find diaries and journals. I have often thought of compiling a book of literary found objects. And perhaps I will one day. But what I find is hopelessly commonplace and bad without being, even unconsciously, camp. College students also discard their papers. I am horrified to discover the kind of paper that now merits an A in an undergraduate course. I am grateful, however, for the number of good books and magazines the students throw out.

In the area I know best I have never discovered vermin in the Dumpster, but there are two kinds of kitty surprise. One is alley cats whom I meet as they leap, claws first, out of Dumpsters. This is especially thrilling when I have Lizbeth in tow. The other kind of kitty surprise is a plastic garbage bag filled with some ponderous, amorphous mass. This always proves to be used cat litter.

City bees harvest doughnut glaze and this makes the Dumpster at the doughnut shop more interesting. My faith in the instinctive wisdom of animals is always shaken whenever I see Lizbeth attempt to catch a bee in her mouth, which she does whenever bees are present. Evidently some birds find Dumpsters profitable, for birdie surprise is almost as common as kitty surprise of the first kind. In hunting season all kinds of small game turn up in Dumpsters, some of it, sadly, not entirely dead. Curiously, summer and winter, maggots are uncommon.

The worst of the living and near-living hazards of the Dumpsters are the fire ants. The food they claim is not much of a loss, but they are vicious and aggressive. It is very easy to brush against some surface of the Dumpster and pick up half a dozen or more fire ants, usually in some sensitive area such as the underarm. One advantage of bringing Lizbeth along as I make Dumpster rounds is that, for obvious reasons, she is very alert to ground-based fire ants. When Lizbeth recognizes a fire-ant infestation around our feet, she does the Dance of the Zillion Fire Ants. I have learned not to ignore this warning from Lizbeth, whether I perceive the tiny ants or not, but to remove ourselves at Lizbeth's first *pas de bouree*. All the more so because the ants are the worst in the summer months when I wear flip-flops if I have them. (Perhaps someone will misunderstand this. Lizbeth does the Dance of the Zillion Fire Ants when she recognizes more fire ants than she cares to eat, not when she is being bitten. Since I have learned to react promptly, she does not get bitten at all. It is the isolated patrol of fire ants that falls in Lizbeth's range that deserves pity. She finds them quite tasty.)

By far the best way to go through a Dumpster is to lower yourself into it. Most of the good stuff tends to settle at the bottom because it is usually weightier than the rubbish. My more athletic companions have often demonstrated to me that they can extract much good material from a Dumpster I have already been over.

To those psychologically or physically unprepared to enter a Dumpster, I recommend a stout stick, preferably with some barb or hook at one end. The hook can be used to grab plastic garbage bags. When I find canned goods or other objects loose at the bottom of a Dumpster, I lower a bag into it, roll the desired object into the bag, and then hoist the bag out—a procedure more easily described than executed. Much Dumpster diving is a matter of experience for which nothing will do except practice.

Dumpster diving is outdoor work, often surprisingly pleasant. It is not entirely predictable; things of interest turn up every day and some days there are finds of great value. I am always very pleased when I can turn up exactly the thing I most wanted to find. Yet in spite of the element of chance, scavenging more than most other pursuits tends to yield returns in some proportion to the effort and intelligence brought to bear. It is very sweet to turn up a few dollars in change from a Dumpster that has just been gone over by a wino.

The land is now covered with cities. The cities are full of Dumpsters. If a member of the canine race is ever able to know what it is doing, then Lizbeth knows that when we go around to the Dumpsters, we are hunting. I think of scavenging as a modern form of self-reliance. In any event, after having survived nearly ten years of government service, where everything is geared to the lowest common denominator, I find it refreshing to have work that rewards initiative and effort. Certainly I would be happy to have a sinecure again, but I am no longer heartbroken that I left one.

I find from the experience of scavenging two rather deep lessons. The first is to take what you can use and let the rest go by. I have come to think that there is no value in the abstract. A thing I cannot use or make useful, perhaps by trading, has no value however rare or fine it may be. I mean useful in some broad sense—some art I would find useful and some otherwise.

I was shocked to realize that some things are not worth acquiring, but now I think it is so. Some material things are white elephants that eat up the possessor's substance. The second lesson is the transience of material being. This has not quite converted me to a dualist, but it has made some headway in that direction. I do not suppose that ideas are immortal, but certainly mental things are longer lived than other material things.

Once I was the sort of person who invests objects with sentimental value. Now I no longer have those objects, but I have the sentiments yet.

Many times in our travels I have lost everything but the clothes I was wearing and Lizbeth. The things I find in Dumpsters, the love letters and rag dolls of so many lives, remind me of this lesson. Now I hardly pick up a thing without envisioning the time I will cast it aside. This I think is a healthy state of mind. Almost everything I have now has already been cast out at least once, proving that what I own is valueless to someone.

Anyway, I find my desire to grab for the gaudy bauble has been largely sated. I think this is an attitude I share with the very wealthy—we both know there is plenty more where what we have came from. Between us are the rat-race millions who nightly scavenge the cable channels looking for they know not what.

I am sorry for them.

My First Conk

Malcolm X

Shorty soon decided that my hair was finally long enough to be conked. He had promised to school me in how to beat the barbershop's three and four-dollar price by making up congolene, and then conking ourselves.

I took the little list of ingredients he had printed out for me, and went to a grocery store, where I got a can of Red Devil lye, two eggs, and two medium-sized white potatoes. Then at a drugstore near the poolroom, I asked for a large jar of vaseline, a large bar of soap, a large-toothed comb and a fine-toothed comb, one of those rubber hoses with a metal spray-head, a rubber apron and a pair of gloves.

"Going to lay on that first conk?" the drugstore man asked me. I proudly told him, grinning, "Right!"

Shorty paid six dollars a week for a room in his cousin's shabby apartment. His cousin wasn't at home. "It's like the pad's mine, he spends so much time with his woman," Shorty said. "Now, you watch me—"

He peeled the potatoes and thin-sliced them into a quart-sized Mason fruit jar, then started stirring them with a wooden spoon as he gradually poured in a little over half the can of lye. "Never use a metal spoon; the lye will turn it black," he told me.

A jelly-like, starchy-looking glop resulted from the lye and potatoes, and Shorty broke in the two eggs, stirring real fast—his own conk and dark face bent down close. The congolene turned pale-yellowish. "Feel the jar," Shorty said. I cupped my hand against the outside, and snatched it away. "Damn right, it's hot, that's the lye," he said. "So you know it's going to burn when I comb it in—it burns *bad.* But the longer you can stand it, the straighter the hair."

He made me sit down, and he tied the string of the new rubber apron tightly around my neck, and combed up my bush of hair. Then, from the big vaseline jar, he took a handful and massaged it hard all through my hair and into the scalp. He also thickly vaselined my neck, ears and forehead. "When I get to washing out your head, be sure to tell me anywhere you feel any little stinging," Shorty warned me, washing his hands, then pulling on the rubber gloves, and tying on his own rubber apron. "You always got to remember that any congolene left in burns a sore into your head."

The congolene just felt warm when Shorty started combing it in. But then my head caught fire.

I gritted my teeth and tried to pull the sides of the kitchen table together. The comb felt as if it was raking my skin off.

My eyes watered, my nose was running. I couldn't stand it any longer; I bolted to the washbasin. I was cursing Shorty with every name I could think of when he got the spray going and started soap-lathering my head.

He lathered and spray-rinsed, lathered and spray-rinsed, maybe ten or twelve times, each time gradually closing the hot-water faucet, until the rinse was cold, and that helped some.

"You feel any stinging spots?"

"No." I managed to say. My knees were trembling.

"Sit back down, then. I think we got it all out okay."

The flame came back as Shorty, with a thick towel, started drying my head, rubbing hard. "*Easy, man, easy!*" I kept shouting.

"The first time's always worst. You get used to it better before long. You took it real good, homeboy. You got a good conk."

When Shorty let me stand up and see in the mirror, my hair hung down in limp, damp strings. My scalp still flamed, but not as badly; I could bear it. He draped the towel around my shoulders, over my rubber apron, and began again vaselining my hair.

I could feel him combing, straight back, first the big comb, then the fine-tooth one.

Then, he was using a razor, very delicately, on the back of my neck. Then, finally, shaping the sideburns.

My first view in the mirror blotted out the hurting. I'd seen some pretty conks, but when it's the first time, on your *own* head, the transformation, after the lifetime of kinks, is staggering.

The mirror reflected Shorty behind me. We both were grinning and sweating. And on top of my head was this thick, smooth sheen of shining red hair—real red—as straight as any white man's.

How ridiculous I was! Stupid enough to stand there simply lost in admiration of my hair now looking "white," reflected in the mirror in Shorty's room. I vowed that I'd never again be without a conk, and I never was for many years.

This was my first really big step toward self-degradation: when I endured all of that pain, literally burning my flesh to have it look like white man's hair. I had joined that multitude of Negro men and women in America who are brainwashed into believing that the black people are "inferior"—and white people "superior"—that they will even violate and mutilate their God-created bodies to try to look "pretty" by white standards.

Look around today, in every small town and big city, from two-bit catfish and soda-pop joints into the "integrated" lobby of the Waldorf-Astoria, and you'll see conks on black men. And you'll see black women wearing these green and pink and purple and red and platinum-blonde wigs. They're all more ridiculous than a slapstick comedy. It makes you wonder if the Negro has completely lost his sense of identity, lost touch with himself.

You'll see the conk worn by many, many so-called "upper class" Negroes, and, as much as I hate to say it about them, on all too many Negro entertainers. One of the reasons that I've especially admired some of them, like Lionel Hampton and Sidney Poitier, among others, is that they have kept their natural hair and fought to the top. I admire any Negro man who has never had himself conked, or who has had the sense to get rid of it—as I finally did.

I don't know which kind of self-defacing conk is the greater shame—the one you'll see on the heads of the black so-called "middle class" and "upper class," who ought to know better, or the one you'll see on the heads of the poorest, most downtrodden, ignorant black men. I mean the legal-minimum-wage ghetto-dwelling kind of Negro, as I was when I got my first one. It's generally among these poor fools that you'll see a black kerchief over the man's head, like Aunt Jemima; he's trying to make his conk last longer, between trips to the barbershop. Only for special occasions is this kerchief-protected conk exposed—to show off how "sharp" and "hip" its owner is. The ironic thing is that I have never heard any woman, white or black, express any admiration for a conk. Of course, any white woman with a black man isn't thinking about his hair. But I don't see how on earth a black woman with any race pride could walk down the street with any black man wearing a conk—the emblem of his shame that he is black.

To my own shame, when I say all of this, I'm talking first of all about myself—because you can't show me any Negro who ever conked more faithfully than I did. I'm speaking from personal experience when I say of any black man who conks today, or any white-wigged black woman, that if they gave the brains in their heads just half as much attention as they do their hair, they would be a thousand times better off.

Writing Drafts

Richard Marius

Finally the moment comes when you sit down to begin your first draft. It is always a good idea at the start to list the points you want to cover. A list is not as elaborate as a formal outline. In writing your first list, don't bother to set items down in the order of importance. List your main points and trust your mind to organize them. You will probably make one list, study it, make another, study it, and perhaps make another. You can organize each list more completely than the last. This preliminary process may save you hours of starting and stopping.

Write with your list outline in front of you. Once you begin to write, commit yourself to the task at hand. Do not get up until you have written for an hour. Write your thoughts quickly. Let one sentence give you an idea to develop in the next. Organization, grammar, spelling, and even clarity of sentences are not nearly as important as getting the first draft together. No matter how desperate you feel, keep going.

Always keep your mind open to new ideas that pop into your head as you write. Let your list outline help you, but don't become a slave to it. Writers often start an essay with one topic in mind only to discover that another pushes the first one aside as they work. Ideas you had not even thought of before you began to write may pile onto your paper, and five or six pages into your first draft you may realize that you are going to write about something you did not imagine when you started.

If such a revelation comes, be grateful and accept it. But don't immediately tear up or erase your draft and start all over again. Make yourself keep on writing, developing these new ideas as they come. If you suddenly start all over again, you may break the train of thought that has given you the new topic. Let your thoughts follow your new thesis, sailing on that tack until the wind changes.

When you have said everything you can say in this draft, print it out if you are working on a computer. Get up from your desk and go sit in a chair somewhere else to read it without correcting anything. Then put it aside, preferably overnight. If possible, read your rough draft just before you go to sleep. Many psychological tests have shown that our minds organize and create while we sleep if we pack them full before bedtime. Study a draft just before sleep, and you may discover new ideas in the morning.

Be willing to make radical changes in your second draft. If your thesis changed while you were writing your first draft, you will base your second draft on this new subject. Even if your thesis has not changed, you may need to shift paragraphs around, eliminate paragraphs, or add new ones. Inexperienced writers often suppose that revising a paper means changing only a word or two or adding a sentence or two. This kind of editing is part of the writing process, but it is not the most important part. The most important part of rewriting is a willingness to turn the paper upside down, to shake out of it those ideas that interest you most, to set them in a form where they will interest the reader, too.

I mentioned earlier that some writers cut up their first drafts with a pair of scissors. They toss some paragraphs into the trash; others they paste up with rubber cement in the order that seems most logical and coherent. Afterward they type the whole thing through again, smoothing out the transitions, adding new material, getting new ideas as they work. The translation of the first draft into the second nearly always involves radical cutting and shifting around. Now and then you may firmly fix the order of your thoughts in your first draft, but I find that the order of my essays is seldom established until the second draft.

With the advent of computers the shifting around of parts of the essays has become easy. We can cut and paste electronically with a few strokes of the keyboard. We can also make back-up copies of our earlier drafts so we can go back to them if we wish. But as I said earlier, computers do not remove from us the necessity to think hard about revising. Always be firm enough with yourself to cut out thoughts or stories that have nothing to do with your thesis, even if they are interesting. Cutting is the supreme test of a writer. You may create a smashing paragraph or sentence only to discover later that it does not help you make your point. You may develop six or seven examples to illustrate a point and discover you need only one.

Now and then you may digress a little. If you digress too often or too far, readers will not follow you unless your facts, your thoughts, and your style are so compelling that they are somehow driven to follow you. Not many writers can pull such digressions off, and most editors will cut out the digressions even when they are interesting. In our hurried and harried time, most readers get impatient with the rambling scenic route. They want to take the most direct way to their destination. To appeal to most of them, you must cut things that do not apply to your main argument.

In your third draft, you can sharpen sentences, add information here and there, cut some things, and attend to other details to heighten the force of your writing. In the third draft, writing becomes a lot of fun (for most of us). By then you have usually decided what you want to say. You can now play a bit, finding just the right word, choosing just the right sentence form, compressing here, expanding there.

I find it helpful to put a printed draft down beside my keyboard and type the whole thing through again as a final draft, letting all the words run through my mind and fingers one more time rather than merely deleting and inserting on the computer screen. I wrote four drafts of the first edition of this book; I have preserved the final draft of that edition on computer diskettes. But I am writing this draft by propping the first edition up here beside me and typing it all over again. By comparing the first draft and the second draft, one can see how many changes I have made, most of them unforeseen until I sat down here to work.

I have outlined here my own writing process. It works for me. You must find the process that works for you. It may be different from mine. A friend tells me that his writing process consists of writing a sentence, agonizing over it, walking around the room, thinking, sitting down, and writing the next sentence. He does not revise very much. I think it unnecessarily painful to bleed out prose that way, but he bleeds out enough to write what he needs to write. Several of my friends tell me they cannot compose at a typewriter; they must first write with a pencil on a yellow pad. These are the people most likely to cut up their drafts with scissors and paste them together in a different form. They also tend to be older. Most young writers are learning to compose at a keyboard, and they cannot imagine another way to write. Neither can I—though on occasion yet I go back to my pencil for pages at a time.

The main thing is to keep at it. B. F. Skinner has pointed out that if you write only fifty words a night, you will produce a good-sized book every two or three years. That's not a bad record for any writer. William Faulkner outlined the plot of his Nobel Prize-winning novel *A Fable* on a wall inside his house near Oxford, Mississippi. You can see it there to this day. Once he got the outline on the wall, he sat down with his typewriter and wrote, following the outline to the end. If writing an outline on a kitchen wall does the trick for you, do it. You can always repaint the wall if you must.

Think of writing as a process making its way toward a product—sometimes painfully. Don't imagine you must know everything you are going to say before you begin. Don't demean yourself and insult your readers by letting your first draft be your final draft. Don't imagine that writing is easy or that you can do it without spending time on it. And don't let anything stand in your way of doing it. Let your house get messy. Leave your magazines unread and your mail unanswered. Put off getting up for a drink of water or a cup of tea. (Never mix alcohol with your writing; true, lots of writers have become alcoholics, but it has not helped their writing.) Don't make a telephone call. Don't straighten up your desk. Sit down and write. And write, and write, and write.

Behind the Formaldehyde Curtain

Jessica Mitford

The drama begins to unfold with the arrival of the corpse at the mortuary.

Alas, poor Yorick! How surprised he would be to see how his counterpart of today is whisked off to a funeral parlor and is in short order sprayed, sliced, pierced, pickled, trussed, trimmed, creamed, waxed, painted, rouged, and neatly dressed—transformed from a common corpse into a Beautiful Memory Picture. This process is known in the trade as embalming and restorative art, and is so universally employed in the United States and Canada that the funeral director does it routinely, without consulting corpse or kin. He regards as eccentric those few who are hardy enough to suggest that it might be dispensed with. Yet no law requires embalming, no religious doctrine commends it, nor is it dictated by considerations of health, sanitation, or even of personal daintiness. In no part of the world but in Northern America is it widely used. The purpose of embalming is to make the corpse presentable for viewing in a suitably costly container; and here too the funeral director routinely, without first consulting the family, prepares the body for public display.

Is all this legal? The processes to which a dead body may be subjected are after all to some extent circumscribed by law. In most states, for instance, the signature of next of kin must be obtained before an autopsy may be performed, before the deceased may be cremated, before the body may be turned over to a medical school for research purposes; or such provision must be made in the decedent's will. In the case of embalming, no such permission is required nor is it ever sought. A textbook, *The Principles and Practices of Embalming*, comments on this: "There is some question regarding the legality of much that is done within the preparation room." The author points out that it would be most unusual for a responsible member of a bereaved family to instruct the mortician, in so many words, to "embalm" the body of a deceased relative. The very term *embalming* is so seldom used that the mortician must rely upon custom in the matter. The author concludes that unless the family specifies otherwise, the act of entrusting the body to the care of a funeral establishment carries with it an implied permission to go ahead and embalm.

Embalming is indeed a most extraordinary procedure, and one must wonder at the docility of Americans who each year pay hundreds of millions of dollars for its perpetuation, blissfully ignorant of what it is all about, what is done, how it is done. Not one in ten thousand has any idea of what actually takes place. Books on the subject are extremely hard to come by. They are not to be found in most libraries or bookshops.

In an era when huge television audiences watch surgical operations in the comfort of their living rooms, when, thanks to the animated cartoon, the geography of the digestive system has become familiar territory even to the nursery school set, in a land where the satisfaction of curiosity about almost all matters is a national pastime, the secrecy surrounding embalming can, surely, hardly be attributed to the inherent gruesomeness of the subject. Custom in this regard has within this century suffered a complete reversal. In the early days of American embalming, when it was performed in the home of the deceased, it was almost mandatory for some relative to stay by the embalmer's side and witness the procedure. Today, family members who might wish to be in attendance would certainly be dissuaded by the funeral director. All others, except apprentices, are excluded by law from the preparation room.

A close look at what does actually take place may explain in large measure the undertaker's intractable reticence concerning a procedure that has become his major *raison d'etre.* Is it possible he fears that public information about embalming might lead patrons to wonder if they really want this service? If the funeral men are loath to discuss the subject outside the trade, the reader may, understandably, be equally loath to go on reading at this point. For those who have the stomach for it, let us part the formaldehyde curtain. . . .

The body is first laid out in the undertaker's morgue—or rather, Mr. Jones is reposing in the preparation room—to be readied to bid the world farewell.

The preparation room in any of the better funeral establishments has the tiled and sterile look of a surgery, and indeed the embalmer-restorative artist who does his chores there is beginning to adopt the term *dermasurgeon* (appropriately corrupted by some mortician-writers as "demi-surgeon") to describe his calling. His equipment, consisting of scalpels, scissors, augers, forceps, clamps, needles, pumps, tubes, bowls, and basins, is crudely imitative of the surgeon's, as is his technique, acquired in a nine- or twelve-month post-high-school course in an embalming school. He is supplied by an advanced chemical industry with a bewildering array of fluids, sprays, pastes, oils, powders, creams, to fix or soften tissue, shrink or distend it as needed, dry it here, restore the moisture there. There are cosmetics, waxes, and paints to fill and cover features, even plaster of Paris to replace entire limbs. There are ingenious aids to prop and stabilize the cadaver: a Vari-Pose Head Rest, the Edwards Arm and Hand Positioner, the Repose Block (to support the shoulders during the embalming), and the Throop Foot Positioner, which resembles an old-fashioned stocks.

Mr. John H. Eckels, president of the Eckels College of Mortuary Science, thus describes the first part of the embalming procedure: "In the hands of a skilled practitioner, this work may be done in a comparatively short time and without mutilating the body other than by slight incision—so slight that it scarcely would cause serious inconvenience if made upon a living person. It is necessary to remove the blood, and doing this not only helps in the disinfecting, but removes the principal cause of disfigurements due to discoloration."

Another textbook discusses the all-important time element: "The earlier this is done, the better, for every hour that elapses between death and embalming will add to the problems and complications encountered. . . ." Just how soon should one get going on the embalming? The author tells us, "On the basis of such scanty information made available to this profession through its rudimentary and haphazard system of technical research, we must conclude that the best results are to be obtained if the subject is embalmed before life is completely extinct— that is, before cellular death has occurred. In the average case, this would mean within an hour after somatic death." For those who feel that there is something a little rudimentary, not to say haphazard, about this advice, a comforting thought is offered by another writer. Speaking of fears entertained in early days of premature burial, he points out, "One of the effects of embalming by chemical injection, however, has been to dispel fears of live burial." How true; once the blood is removed, chances of live burial are indeed remote.

To return to Mr. Jones, the blood is drained out through the veins and replaced by embalming fluid pumped in through the arteries. As noted in *The Principles and Practices of Embalming,* "every operator has a favorite injection and drainage point—a fact which becomes a handicap only if he fails or refuses to forsake his favorites when conditions demand it."

Typical favorites are the carotid artery, femoral artery, jugular vein, subclavian vein. There are various choices of embalming fluid. If Flextone is used, it will produce a "mild, flexible rigidity. The skin retains a velvety softness, the tissues are rubbery and pliable. Ideal for women and children." It may be blended with B. and G. Products Company's Lyf-Lyk tint, which is guaranteed to reproduce "nature's own skin texture . . . the velvety appearance of living tissue." Suntone comes in three separate tints: Suntan; Special Cosmetic Tint, a pink shade "especially indicated for female subjects"; and Regular Cosmetic Tint, moderately pink.

About three to six gallons of a dyed and perfumed solution of formaldehyde, glycerin, borax, phenol, alcohol, and water is soon circulating through Mr. Jones, whose mouth has been sewn together with a "needle directed upward between the upper lip and gum and brought out through the left nostril," with the corners raised slightly "for a more pleasant expression." If he should be bucktoothed, his teeth are cleaned with Bon Ami and coated with colorless nail polish. His eyes, meanwhile, are closed with flesh-tinted eye caps and eye cement.

The next step is to have at Mr. Jones with a thing called a trocar. This is a long, hollow needle attached to a tube. It is jabbed into the abdomen, poked around the entrails and chest cavity, the contents of which are pumped out and replaced with "cavity fluid." This done, and the hole in the abdomen sewn up, Mr. Jones's face is heavily creamed (to protect the skin from burns which may be caused by leakage of the chemicals), and he is covered with a sheet and left unmolested for a while. But not for long—there is more, much more, in store for him. He has been embalmed, but not yet restored, and the best time to start the restorative work is eight to ten hours after embalming, when the tissues have become firm and dry.

The object of all this attention to the corpse, it must be remembered, is to make it presentable for viewing in an attitude of healthy repose. "Our customs require the presentation of our dead in the semblance of normality . . . unmarred by the ravages of illness, disease, or mutilation," says Mr. J. Sheridan Mayer in his *Restorative Art*. This is rather a large order since few people die in the full bloom of health, unravaged by illness and unmarked by some disfigurement. The funeral industry is equal to the challenge: "In some cases the gruesome appearance of a mutilated or disease-ridden subject may be quite discouraging. The task of restoration may seem impossible and shake the confidence of the embalmer. This is the time for intestinal fortitude and determination. Once the formative work is begun and affected tissues are cleaned or removed, all doubts of success vanish. It is surprising and gratifying to discover the results which may be obtained."

The embalmer, having allowed an appropriate interval to elapse, returns to the attack, but now he brings into play the skill and equipment of sculptor and cosmetician. Is a hand missing? Casting one in plaster of Paris is a simple matter. "For replacement purposes, only a cast of the back of the hand is necessary; this is within the ability of the average operator and is quite adequate." If a lip or two, a nose, or an ear should be missing, the embalmer has at hand a variety of restorative waxes with which to model replacements. Pores and skin texture are simulated by stippling with a little brush, and over this cosmetics are laid on. Head off? Decapitation cases are rather routinely handled. Ragged edges are trimmed, and head joined to torso with a series of splints, wires, and sutures. It is a good idea to have a little something at the neck—a scarf or a high collar—when time for viewing comes. Swollen mouth? Cut out tissue as needed from inside the lips. If too much is removed, the surface contour can easily be restored by padding with cotton. Swollen necks and cheeks are reduced by removing tissue through vertical incisions made down each side of the neck. "When the deceased is casketed, the pillow will hide the suture incisions . . . as an extra precaution against leakage, the suture may be painted with liquid sealer."

The opposite condition is more likely to present itself—that of emaciation. His hypodermic syringe now loaded with massage cream, the embalmer seeks out and fills the hollowed and sunken areas by injection. In this procedure the backs of the hands and fingers and the under-chin area should not be neglected.

Positioning the lips is a problem that recurrently challenges the ingenuity of the embalmer. Closed too tightly, they tend to give a stern, even disapproving expression. Ideally, embalmers feel, the lips should give the impression of being ever so slightly parted, the upper lip protruding slightly for a more youthful appearance. This takes some engineering, however, as the lips tend to drift apart. Lip drift can sometimes be remedied by pushing one or two straight pins through the inner margin of the lower lip and then inserting them between the two front upper teeth. If Mr. Jones happens to have no teeth, the pins can just as easily be anchored in his Armstrong Face Former and Denture Re-placer. Another method to maintain lip closure is to dislocate the lower jaw, which is then held in its new position by a wire run through holes which have been drilled through the upper and lower jaws at the midline. As the French are fond of saying, *il faut souffrir pour être belle.*

If Mr. Jones has died of jaundice, the embalming fluid will very likely turn him green. Does this deter the embalmer? Not if he has intestinal fortitude. Masking pastes and cosmetics are heavily laid on, burial garments and casket interiors are color-correlated with particular care, and Jones is displayed beneath rose-colored lights. Friends will say "How *well* he looks." Death by carbon monoxide, on the other hand, can be rather a good thing from the embalmer's viewpoint: "One advantage is the fact that this type of discoloration is an exaggerated form of a natural pink coloration." This is nice because the healthy glow is already present and needs but little attention.

The patching and filling completed, Mr. Jones is now shaved, washed, and dressed. Cream-based cosmetic, available in pink, flesh, suntan, brunette, and blond, is applied to his hands and face, his hair is shampooed and combed (and, in the case of Mrs. Jones, set), his hands manicured. For the horny-handed son of toil special care must be taken; cream should be applied to remove ingrained grime, and the nails cleaned. "If he were not in the habit of having them manicured in life, trimming and shaping is advised for better appearance—never questioned by kin."

Jones is now ready for casketing (this is the present participle of the verb "to casket"). In this operation his right shoulder should be depressed slightly "to turn the body a bit to the right and soften the appearance of lying flat on the back." Positioning the hands is a matter of importance, and special rubber positioning blocks may be used. The hands should be cupped slightly for a more lifelike, relaxed appearance. Proper placement of the body requires a delicate sense of balance. It should lie as high as possible in the casket, yet not so high that the lid, when lowered, will hit the nose. On the other hand, we are cautioned, placing the body too low "creates the impression that the body is in a box."

Jones is next wheeled into the appointed slumber room where a few last touches may be added—his favorite pipe placed in his hand or, if he was a great reader, a book propped into position. (In the case of little Master Jones a Teddy bear may be clutched.) Here he will hold open house for a few days, visiting hours 10 a.m. to 9 p.m.

All now being in readiness, the funeral director calls a staff conference to make sure that each assistant knows his precise duties. Mr. Wilber Kriege writes: "This makes your staff feel that they are a part of the team, with a definite assignment that must be properly carried out if the whole plan is to succeed. You never heard of a football coach who failed to talk to his entire team before they go on the field. They have drilled on the plays they are to execute for hours and days, and yet the successful coach knows the importance of making even the bench-warming third-string substitute feel that he is important if the game is to be won." The winning of *this* game is predicated upon glass-smooth handling of the logistics. The funeral director has notified the pallbearers whose names were furnished by the family, has arranged for the presence of clergyman, organist, and soloist, has provided transportation for everybody, has organized and listed the flowers sent by friends. In *Psychology of Funeral Service* Mr. Edward A. Martin points out, "He may not always do as much as the family thinks he is doing, but it is his helpful guidance that they appreciate in knowing they are proceeding as they should. The important thing is how well his services can be used to make the family believe they are giving unlimited expression to their own sentiment."

The religious service may be held in a church or in the chapel of the funeral home; the funeral director vastly prefers the latter arrangement, for not only is it more convenient for him but it affords him the opportunity to show off his beautiful facilities to the gathered mourners. After the clergyman has had his say, the mourners queue up to file past the casket for a last look at the deceased. The family is *never* asked whether they want an open-casket ceremony; in the absence of their instruction to the contrary, this is taken for granted. Consequently well over 90 per cent of all American funerals feature the open casket—a custom unknown in other parts of the world. Foreigners are astonished by it. An English woman living in San Francisco described her reaction in a letter to the writer:

> I myself have attended only one funeral here—that of an elderly fellow worker of mine. After the service I could not understand why everyone was walking towards the coffin (sorry, I mean casket), but thought I had better follow the crowd. It shook me rigid to get there and find the casket open and poor old Oscar lying there in his brown tweed suit, wearing a suntan makeup and just the wrong shade of lipstick. If I had not been extremely fond of the old boy, I have a horrible feeling that I might have giggled. Then and there I decided that I could never face another American funeral—even dead.

The casket (which has been resting throughout the service on a Classic Beauty Ultra Metal Casket Bier) is now transferred by a hydraulically operated device called Porto-Lift to a balloon-tired, Glide Easy casket carriage which will wheel it to yet another conveyance, the Cadillac Funeral Coach. This may be lavender, cream, light green—anything but black. Interiors, of course, are color-correlated, "for the man who cannot stop short of perfection."

At graveside, the casket is lowered into the earth. This office, once the prerogative of friends of the deceased, is now performed by a patented mechanical lowering device. A "Lifetime Green" artificial grass mat is at the ready to conceal the sere earth, and overhead, to conceal the sky, is a portable Steril Chapel Tent ("resists the intense heat and humidity of summer and the terrific storms of winter . . . available in Silver Gray, Rose, or Evergreen"). Now is the time for the ritual scattering of earth over the coffin, as the solemn words "earth to earth, ashes to ashes, dust to dust" are pronounced by the officiating cleric. This can today be accomplished "with a mere flick of the wrist with the Gordon Leak-Proof Earth Dispenser. No grasping of a handful of dirt, no soiled fingers. Simple, dignified, beautiful, reverent! The modern way!" The Gordon Earth Dispenser (at $5) is of nickel-plated brass construction. It is not only "attractive to the eye and long wearing"; it is also "one of the 'tools' for building better public relations" if presented as "an appropriate non-commercial gift" to the clergyman. It is shaped something like a saltshaker.

Untouched by human hand, the coffin and the earth are now united.

It is in the function of directing the participants through this maze of gadgetry that the funeral director has assigned to himself his relatively new role of "grief therapist." He has relieved the family of every detail, he has revamped the corpse to look like a living doll, he has arranged for it to nap for a few days in a slumber room, he has put on a well-oiled performance in which the concept of *death* has played no part whatsoever—unless it was inconsiderately mentioned by the clergyman who conducted the religious service. He has done everything in his power to make the funeral a real pleasure for everybody concerned. He and his team have given their all to score an upset victory over death.

Cause and Effect

If process analyzes how something happens, cause and effect analyzes why. For example: If someone asked the question, "What happens when I ring the doorbell," you could immediately think "process"—how the doorbell works. But with cause and effect, the question is not what physically happens when the doorbell is pressed. The question is why did the person press the button and what will happen because of it.

What would the effect be on the people inside if the doorbell ringer was the repossession man?

Or, the mother-in-law?

A traveling salesman?

Person from Publisher's Clearinghouse?

You use cause and effect to figure out reasons and results, either to explain events or to argue for one version of them.

You try to answer the questions:

- Why did something happen?
- What followed as a result?
- What might be the consequences?

It examines the causes and describes the effects. It links situations and events together in time, with causes preceding effects.

Here is another example of cause and effect:

What caused Rosa Parks to refuse to move to the back of the bus back in 1955? Despite the popular thoughts about why, Rosa was tired after a long day's work. She had plain had it.

What was the effect, or result, of her actions?

- The immediate result was that she was arrested.
- The long-term effect was that the incident contributed to the start of the civil rights movement.

This kind of analysis is one way for the mind to discover order in events that otherwise may seem senseless or obscure.

The Process

Purpose and Thesis

A cause and effect essay can focus on finding the causes, e.g., the causes of obesity in children. Or on describing effects, e.g., the effects of raising the drinking age to 21. Or both, e.g., the causes of the drug addiction and its immediate and long-term effects.

Sometimes there are numerous causes and many different effects. A cause and effect essay does more than list causes or effects. It requires you to judge various factors to assess their relative significance and their connection to each other.

The hardest part may be figuring out what caused what. Sometimes one event will trigger another like a chain reaction—it's called a causal chain. One event does precede another in time, and you have to pay attention to the chronology.

The thesis statement for a cause and effect essay identifies the relationships among the specific causes and effects you will discuss. It should tell three things:

1. the points you plan to consider;
2. the position you will take;
3. whether emphasis is on causes, effects, or both.

Organization

The complexity of a cause and effect essay makes it challenging for the writer; however, careful planning and creating a clear outline can make the task easier. Three main aspects of cause and effect are important to understand as you being to analyze your subject: main and contributory causes, immediate and remote causes, and causal chains.

Main and Contributory Causes

The main cause is the one that is most significant and the contributory causes are less important, though they play a role in the effect. Sometimes the main cause is obvious; sometimes it is not. For example, in 1955, thirteen inches of rain fell over four days in Connecticut and the surrounding area. The result was that in one town, all bridges but one were destroyed by the rivers that surged over their banks. Although the thirteen inches of rain could be perceived as the main cause of the damage, the actual primary cause was two hurricanes four days apart only two months earlier. The water-soaked ground weakened by the hurricanes gave way under the deluge of rain two months later.

Immediate and Remote Causes

An immediate cause is obviously the one that directly precedes an event, and a remote cause is something that happened further back in time. Using the same example of the flood in Connecticut, we can see that the thirteen inches was the immediate cause of the flood and the resulting damage. The twin hurricanes of two months earlier were remote causes.

Causal Chain

Sometimes the result of one action is the cause of another, which in turn causes another action, and so on. Where causal chains exist, it is important to write the sequence of events. The challenge, however, is not to fall into the trap of post hoc reasoning. Post hoc reasoning is the wrong assumption that just because one event preceded another, the first event caused another. Sometimes, this is true; sometimes, it is not.

Once you have determined the cause-and-effect relationships that exist about your subject, you can determine the organizational structure of your essay. You have a number of options:

- Chronological—presenting the cause and effects as they occurred.
- Order the causes in order of significance. List the main causes first, or list the contributory causes first. In the same vein, list the immediate first or vice versa.
- Present the causes only.

- Present the effects only.
- Present first the causes then the effects or vice versa.

Regardless of what organization you choose for your paper, be sure that your thesis statement indicates what you will focus on, consider all possible causes and effects, and avoid post hoc reasoning.

The Closing of the American Book

Andrew Solomon

A survey released on Thursday reports that reading for pleasure is way down in America among every group—old and young, wealthy and poor, educated and uneducated, men and women, Hispanic, black and white. The survey, by the National Endowment for the Arts, also indicates that people who read for pleasure are many times more likely than those who don't to visit museums and attend musical performances, almost three times as likely to perform volunteer and charity work, and almost twice as likely to attend sporting events. Readers, in other words, are active, while nonreaders—more than half the population—have settled into apathy. There is a basic social divide between those for whom life is an accrual of fresh experience and knowledge, and those for whom maturity is a process of mental atrophy. The shift toward the latter category is frightening.

Reading is not an active expression like writing, but it is not a passive experience either. It requires effort, concentration, attention. In exchange, it offers the stimulus to and the fruit of thought and feeling. Kafka said, "A book must be an ice ax to break the seas frozen inside our soul." The metaphoric quality of writing—the fact that so much can be expressed through the rearrangement of 26 shapes on a piece of paper—is as exciting as the idea of a complete genetic code made up of four bases: man's work on a par with nature's. Discerning the patterns of those arrangements is the essence of civilization.

The electronic media, on the other hand, tend to be torpid. Despite the existence of good television, fine writing on the Internet, and video games that test logic, the electronic media by and large invite inert reception. One selects channels, but then the information comes out preprocessed. Most people use television as a means of turning their minds off, not on. Many readers watch television without peril; but for those for whom television replaces reading, the consequences are far-reaching.

My last book was about depression, and the question I am most frequently asked is why depression is on the rise. I talk about the loneliness that comes of spending the day with a TV or a computer or video screen. Conversely, literary reading is an entry into dialogue; a book can be a friend, talking not at you, but to you. That the rates of depression should be going up as the rates of reading are going down is no happenstance. Meanwhile, there is some persuasive evidence that escalating levels of Alzheimer's disease reflect a lack of active engagement of adult minds. While the disease appears to be determined in large part by heredity and environmental stimulants, it seems that those who continue learning may be less likely to develop Alzheimer's.

So the crisis in reading is a crisis in national health.

I will never forget seeing, as a high school student on my first trip to East Berlin, the plaza where Hitler and Goebbels had burned books from the university library. Those bonfires were predicated on the idea that texts could undermine armies. Soviet repression of literature followed the same principle.

The Nazis were right in believing that one of the most powerful weapons in a war of ideas is books. And for better or worse, the United States is now in such a war. Without books, we cannot succeed in our current struggle against absolutism and terrorism. The retreat from civic to virtual life is a retreat from engaged democracy, from the principles that we say we want to share with the rest of the world. You are what you read. If you read nothing, then your mind withers, and your ideals lose their vitality and sway.

So the crisis in reading is a crisis in national politics.

It is important to acknowledge that the falling-off of reading has to do not only with the incursion of anti-intellectualism, but also with a flawed intellectualism. The ascendancy of poststructuralism in the 1980's coincided with the beginning of the catastrophic downturn in reading; deconstructionism's suggestion that all text is equal in its meanings and the denigration of the canon led to the devaluation of literature. The role of literature is to illuminate, to strengthen, to explain why some aspect of life is moving or beautiful or terrible or sad or important or insignificant for people who might otherwise not understand so much or so well. Reading is experience, but it also enriches other experience.

Even more immediate than the crises in health and politics brought on by the decline of reading is the crisis in national education. We have one of the most literate societies in history. What is the point of having a population that can read, but doesn't? We need to teach people not only how, but also why to read. The struggle is not to make people read more, but to make them want to read more.

While there is much work do be done in the public schools, society at large also has a job. We need to make reading, which is in its essence a solitary endeavor, a social one as well, to encourage that great thrill of finding kinship in shared experiences of books. We must weave reading back into the very fabric of the culture, and make it a mainstay of community.

Reading is harder than watching television or playing video games. I think of the Epicurean mandate to exchange easier for more difficult pleasures, predicated on the understanding that those more difficult pleasures are more rewarding. I think of Walter Pater's declaration: "The service of philosophy, of speculative culture, towards the human spirit is to rouse, to startle it to a life of sharp and eager observation. . . . The poetic passion, the desire of beauty, the love of art for its own sake, has most; for art comes to you professing frankly to give nothing but the highest quality to your moments as they pass." Surely that is something all Americans would want, if we only understood how readily we might achieve it, how well worth the effort it is.

Why Don't We Complain?

William F. Buckley Jr.

It was the very last coach and the only empty seat on the entire train, so there was no turning back. The problem was to breathe. Outside the temperature was below freezing. Inside the railroad car the temperature must have been about 85 degrees. I took off my overcoat and a few minutes later my jacket, and noticed that the car was flecked with the white shirts of the passengers. I soon found my hand moving to loosen my tie. From one end of the car to the other, as we rattled through Westchester County, we sweated; but we did not moan.

I watched the train conductor appear at the head of the car. "Tickets, all tickets, please!" In a more virile age, I thought the passengers would seize the conductor and strap him down on a seat over the radiator to share the fate of his patrons. He shuffled down the aisle, picking up tickets, punching commutation cards. *No one addressed a word to him.* He approached my seat, and I drew a deep breath of resolution. "Conductor," I began with a considerable edge to my voice. Instantly the doleful eyes of my seatmate turned tiredly from his newspaper to fix me with a resentful stare: what question could be so important as to justify my sibilant intrusion into his stupor? I was shaken by those eyes. I am incapable of making a discreet fuss, so I mumbled a question about what time we were due in Stamford (I didn't even ask whether it would be before or after dehydration could be expected to set in), got my reply, and went back to my newspaper and to wiping my brow.

The conductor had nonchalantly walked down the gauntlet of eighty sweating American freemen, and not one of them had asked him to explain why the passengers in that car had been consigned to suffer. There is nothing to be done when the temperature *outdoors* is 85 degrees, and indoors the air conditioner has broken down; obviously when that happens there is nothing to do, except perhaps curse the day that one was born. But when the temperature outdoors is below freezing, it takes a positive act of will on somebody's part to set the temperature *indoors* at 85. Somewhere a valve was turned too far, a furnace overstocked, a thermostat maladjusted: something that could easily be remedied by turning off the heat and allowing the great outdoors to come indoors. All this is so obvious. What is not obvious is what has happened to the American people.

It isn't just the commuters, whom we have come to visualize as a supine breed who have got on to the trick of suspending their sensory faculties twice a day while they submit to the creeping dissolution of the railroad industry. It isn't just they who have given up trying to rectify irrational vexations. It is the American people everywhere.

A few weeks ago at a large movie theatre I turned to my wife and said, "The picture is out of focus." "Be quiet," she answered. I obeyed. But a few minutes later I raised the point again, with mounting impatience. "It will be all right in a minute," she said apprehensively. (She would rather lose her eyesight than be around when I make one of my infrequent scenes.) I waited. It was *just* out of focus—not glaringly out, but out. My vision is 20-20, and I assume that is the vision, adjusted, of most people in the movie house. So, after hectoring my wife throughout the first reel, I finally prevailed upon her to admit that it *was* off, and very annoying. We then settled down, coming to rest on the presumption that: a) someone connected with the management of the theater must soon notice the blur and make the correction; or b) that someone seated near the rear of the house would make the complaint in behalf of those of us up front; or c) that—any minute now—the entire house would explode into catcalls and foot stamping, calling dramatic attention to the irksome distortion.

What happened was nothing. The movie ended, as it had begun, *just* out of focus, and we trooped out, we stretched our faces in a variety of contortions to accustom the eye to the shock of normal focus.

I think it is safe to say that everybody suffered on that occasion. And I think it is safe to assume that everyone was expecting someone else to take the initiative in going back to speak to the manager. And it is probably true even that if we had supposed the movie would run right through the blurred image, someone surely would have summoned up the purposive indignation to get up out of his seat and file his complaint.

But notice that no one did. And the reason no one did is because we are all increasingly anxious in America to be unobtrusive, we are reluctant to make our voices heard, hesitant about claiming our rights; we are afraid that our cause is unjust, or that if it is not unjust, that it is ambiguous; or if not even that, that it is too trivial to justify the horrors of a confrontation with Authority; we will sit in an oven or endure a racking headache before undertaking a head-on, I'm-here-to-tell-you complaint. That tendency to passive compliance, to a heedless endurance, is something to keep one's eyes on—in sharp focus.

I myself can occasionally summon the courage to complain, but I cannot, as I have intimated, complain softly. My own instinct is so strong to let the thing ride, to forget about it—to expect that someone will take the matter up, when the grievance is collective, in my behalf—that it is only when the provocation is at a very special key, whose vibrations touch simultaneously a complex of nerves, allergies, and passions, that I catch fire and find the reserves of courage and assertiveness to speak up. When that happens, I get quite carried away. My blood gets hot, my brow wet, I become unbearably and unconscionably sarcastic and bellicose; I am girded for a total showdown.

Why should that be? Why could not I (or anyone else) on that railroad coach have said simply to the conductor, "Sir"—I take that back: that sounds sarcastic—"Conductor, would you be good enough to turn down the heat? I am extremely hot. In fact, I tend to get hot every time the temperature reaches 85 degr—" Strike that last sentence. Just end it with the simple statement that you are extremely hot, and let the conductor infer the cause.

Every New Year's Eve I resolve to do something about the Milquetoast in me and vow to speak up, calmly, for my rights, and for the betterment of our society, on every appropriate occasion. Entering last New Year's Eve I was fortified in my resolve because that morning at breakfast I had had to ask the waitress three times for a glass of milk. She finally brought it—after I had finished my eggs, which is when I don't want it any more. I did not have the manliness to order her to take the milk back, but settled instead for a cowardly sulk, and ostentatiously refused to drink the milk—though I later paid for it—rather than state plainly to the hostess, as I should have, why I had not drunk it, and would not pay for it.

So by the time the New Year ushered out the Old, riding in on my morning's indignation and stimulated by the gastric juices of resolution that flow so faithfully on New Year's Eve, I rendered my vow. Henceforward I would conquer my shyness, my despicable disposition to supineness. I would speak out like a man against the unnecessary annoyances of our time.

Forty-eight hours later, I was standing in line at the ski repair store in Pico Peak, Vermont. All I needed, to get on with my skiing, was the loan, for one minute, of a small screwdriver, to tighten a loose binding. Behind the counter in the workshop were two men. One was industriously engaged in servicing the complicated requirements of a young lady at the head of the line, and obviously he would be tied up for quite a while. The other—"Jiggs," his workmate called him—was a middle-aged man, who sat in a chair puffing a pipe, exchanging small talk with his working partner. My pulse began its telltale acceleration. The minutes ticked on. I stared at the idle shopkeeper, hoping to shame him into action, but he was impervious to my telepathic reproof and continued his small talk with his friend, brazenly insensitive to the nervous demands of six good men who were raring to ski.

Suddenly my New Year's Eve resolution struck me. It was now or never. I broke from my place in line and marched to the counter. I was going to control myself. I dug my nails into my palms. My effort was only partially successful.

"If you are not too busy," I said icily, "would you mind handing me a screwdriver?"

Work stopped and everyone turned his eyes on me, and I experienced that mortification I always feel when I am the center of centripetal shafts of curiosity, resentment, perplexity.

But the worst was yet to come. "I am sorry, sir," said Jiggs deferentially, moving the pipe from his mouth. "I am not supposed to move. I have just had a heart attack." That was the signal for a great whirring noise that descended from heaven. We looked, stricken, out the window, and it appeared as though a cyclone had suddenly focused on the snowy courtyard between the shop and the ski lift. Suddenly a gigantic army helicopter materialized, and hovered down to a landing. Two men jumped out of the plane carrying a stretcher tore into the ski shop, and lifted the shopkeeper onto the stretcher. Jiggs bade his companion goodbye, was whisked out the door, into the plane, up to the heavens, down—we learned—to a near-by army hospital. I looked up manfully—into a score of man-eating eyes. I put the experience down as a reversal.

As I write this, on an airplane, I have run out of paper and need to reach into my briefcase under my legs for more. I cannot do this until my empty lunch tray is removed from my lap. I arrested the stewardess as she passed empty-handed down the aisle on the way to the kitchen to fetch the lunch trays for the passengers up forward who haven't been served yet. "Would you please take my tray?" "Just a *moment*, sir!" she said, and marched on sternly. Shall I tell her that since she is headed for the kitchen *anyway*, it could not delay the feeding of the other passengers by more than two seconds necessary to stash away my empty tray? Or remind her that not fifteen minutes ago she spoke unctuously into the loudspeaker the words undoubtedly devised by the airline's highly paid public relations counselor: "If there is anything I or Miss French can do for you to make your trip more enjoyable, *please* let us—" I have run out of paper.

I think the observable reluctance of the majority of Americans to assert themselves in minor matters is related to our increased sense of helplessness in an age of technology and centralized political and economic power. For generations, Americans who were too hot, or too cold, got up and did something about it. Now we call the plumber, or the electrician, or the furnace man. The habit of looking after our own needs obviously had something to do with the assertiveness that characterized the American family familiar to readers of American literature. With the technification of life goes our direct responsibility for our material environment, and we are conditioned to adopt a position of helplessness not only as regards the broken air conditioner, but as regards the over-heated train. It takes an expert to fix the former, but not the latter; yet these distinctions, as we withdraw into helplessness, tend to fade away.

Our notorious political apathy is a related phenomenon. Every year, whether the Republican or the Democratic Party is in office, more and more power drains away from the individual to feed vast reservoirs in far-off places; and we have less and less say about the shape of events which shape our future. From this alienation of personal power comes the sense of resignation with which we accept the political dispensations of a powerful government whose hold upon us continues to increase.

An editor of a national weekly news magazine told me a few years ago that as few as a dozen letters of protest against an editorial stance of his magazine was enough to convene a plenipotentiary meeting of the board of editors to review policy. "So few people complain, or make their voices heard," he explained to me, "that we assume a dozen letters represent the unarticulated views of thousands of readers." In the past ten years, he said, the volume of mail has noticeably decreased, even though the circulation of his magazine has risen.

When our voices are finally mute, when we have finally suppressed the natural instinct to complain, whether the vexation is trivial or grave, we shall have become automatons, incapable of feeling. When Premier Khrushchev first came to this country late in 1959 he was primed, we are informed, to experience the bitter resentment of the American people against his tyranny, against his persecutions, against the movement which is responsible for the great number of American deaths in Korea, for billions in taxes every year, and for life everlasting on the brink of disaster; but Khrushchev was pleasantly surprised, and reported back to the Russian people that he had been met with overwhelming cordiality (read: apathy), except, to be sure, for "a few fascists who followed me around with their wretched posters, and should be horsewhipped."

I may be crazy, but I say there would have been lots more posters in a society where train temperatures in the dead of winter are not allowed to climb to 85 degrees without complaint.

Losing Private Dwyer

Lawrence Downes

The photo below captures everything that Americans wanted to believe about the Iraq war in the earliest days of the invasion in 2003. Pfc. Joseph Dwyer, an Army medic whose unit was fighting its way up the Euphrates to Baghdad, cradles a wounded boy. The child is half-naked and helpless, but trusting. Private Dwyer's face is strained but calm.

If there are better images of the strength and selflessness of the American soldier, I can't think of any. It is easy to understand why newspapers and magazines around the country ran the photo big, making Private Dwyer an instant hero, back when the war was a triumphal tale of Iraqi liberation.

That story turned bitter years ago, of course. And the mountain of sorrows keeps growing: Mr. Dwyer died last month in North Carolina. He was 31 and very sick. For years he had been in and out of treatment for post-traumatic stress disorder and addiction. He was seized by fearful delusions and fits of violence and rage. His wife left him to save herself and their young daughter. When the police were called to Mr. Dwyer's apartment on June 28, he was alone. They broke down the door and found him dying among pill bottles and cans of cleaning solvent that friends said he sniffed to deaden his pain.

He had been heading for a disastrous end ever since he came home.

Two of his best friends were Angela Minor and Dionne Knapp, fellow medics at Fort Bliss, near El Paso, Texas. For a while, they were part of a small, inseparable group that worked together, ate out, went to movies and called one another by their first names, which is not the military habit.

Joseph was a rock, Ms. Minor said, a guy who would change your oil and check your tires unasked and pick you up by your broken-down car at 3 a.m. Ms. Knapp said he was like an uncle to her son, Justin, who was having trouble in kindergarten and brightened whenever Mr. Dwyer went there to check on him.

Ms. Knapp was called up to Iraq, but Mr. Dwyer insisted on taking her place, because she was a single mom. He had no children at the time, and besides, he had enlisted right after 9/11 just for this. He went and stunned everybody by getting his picture all over the newspapers and TV.

A few months later, he was home. He was shy about his celebrity. He was also skinny and haunted. Ms. Minor said he was afraid. Ms. Knapp said paranoid was more like it.

It didn't help that El Paso looked a lot like Iraq. Once he totaled his car. He said he had seen a box in the road and thought it was a bomb. He couldn't go to the movies anymore: too many people. In restaurants, he sat with his back to the wall.

He said that Iraqis were coming to get him. He would call Angela and Dionne at all hours, to talk vaguely about the "demons" that followed him all day and in his dreams. He became a Baptist, doggedly searching Scripture on his lunch hour—for solace. His friends knew he was also getting high with spray cans bought at computer stores.

"He would call me in the middle of the day," Ms. Minor said. "I'd be like: 'Why are you at Best Buy? Why aren't you at work?' I could tell he'd been drinking and huffing again."

His friends tried an intervention, showing up at his door in October 2005 and demanding his guns and cans of solvent. He refused to give them up.

Hours later, gripped by delusions, he shot up his apartment. He was glad when the SWAT team arrived, Ms. Knapp said, because then he could tell them where the Iraqis were. He was arrested and discharged, and later moved to Pinehurst, North Carolina. His parents tried to get him help, but nothing worked. "He just couldn't get over the war," his mother, Maureen, told a reporter. "Joseph never came home."

It's not clear what therapy and medication could have saved Mr. Dwyer. He admitted lying on a post-deployment questionnaire about what he had seen and suffered because he just wanted to get back to his family. Ms. Minor said he sometimes skipped therapy appointments in El

Paso. One thing that did seem to help, Ms. Knapp and Ms. Minor said, was peer counseling from a fellow veteran, a man who had been ambushed in Iraq and knew about fear and death. But that was too little, too late, and both women say they are frustrated with the military for letting Mr. Dwyer slip away.

Private Dwyer, who survived rocket-propelled grenades and shocking violence, made his way back to his family and friends. But part of him was also stuck forever on a road in Iraq, helpless and terrified, with nobody to carry him to safety.

Words That Wound

Kathleen Vail

Brian Head saw only one way out. On the final day of his life, during economics class, the fifteen-year-old stood up and pointed a semiautomatic handgun at himself. Before he pulled the trigger, he said his last words, "I can't take this anymore."

Brian's father, William Head, has no doubt why his child chose to take his life in front of a classroom full of students five years ago. Brian wanted everyone to know the source of his pain, the suffering he could no longer endure. The Woodstock, GA, teen, overweight with thick glasses, had been systematically abused by school bullies since elementary school. Death was the only relief he could imagine. "Children can't vote or organize, leave or run away," says Head. "They are trapped."

For many students, school is a torture chamber from which there is no escape. Every day, 160,000 children stay home from school because they are afraid of being bullied, according to the National Association of School Psychologists. In a study of junior high school students from small Midwestern towns, nearly 77 percent of the students reported they'd been victims of bullies at school—14 percent saying they'd experienced severe reactions to the abuse. "Bullying is a crime of violence," says June Arnette, associate director of the National School Safety Center. "It's an imbalance of power, sustained over a period of time."

Yet even in the face of this suffering, even after Brian Head's suicide five years ago, even after it was revealed this past spring that a culture of bullying might have played a part in the Columbine High School shootings, bullying remains for the most part unacknowledged, under-reported, and minimized by schools. Adults are unaware of the extent and nature of the problem, says Nancy Mullin-Rindler, associate director of the

Project on Teasing and Bullying in the Elementary Grades at Wellesley College Center for Research for Women. "They underestimate the import. They feel it's a normal part of growing up, that it's character-building."

After his son's death, William Head became a crusader against bullying, founding an effort called Kids Hope to prevent others from suffering as Brian had. Unfortunately, bullying claimed another victim in the small town of Woodstock: thirteen-year-old Josh Belluardo. Last November, on the bus ride home from school, Josh's neighbor, fifteen-year-old Jonathan Miller, taunted him and threw wads of paper at him. He followed Josh off the school bus, hit the younger boy in the back of the head, and kicked him in the stomach. Josh spent the last two days of his life in a coma before dying of his injuries. Miller, it turns out, had been suspended nearly twenty times for offenses such as pushing and taunting other students and cursing at a teacher. He's now serving a life sentence for felony murder while his case is on appeal.

Bullying doesn't have to result in death to be harmful. Bullying and harassment are major distractions from learning, according to the National School Safety Center. Victims' grades suffer, and fear can lead to chronic absenteeism, truancy, or dropping out. Bullies also affect children who aren't victimized: Bystanders feel guilty and helpless for not standing up to the bully. They feel unsafe, unable to take action. They also can be drawn into bullying behavior by peer pressure. "Any time there is a climate of fear, the learning process will be compromised," says Arnette.

A full 70 percent of children believe teachers handle episodes of bullying "poorly," according to a study by John Hoover at the University of North Dakota at Grand Forks. It's no wonder kids are reluctant to tell adults about bullying incidents. "Children feel no one will take them seriously," says Robin Kowalski, professor of psychology at Western Carolina University, Cullowhee, NC, who's done research on teasing behavior.

Martha Rizzo, who lives in a suburb of Cincinnati, calls bullying the "dirty little secret" of her school district. Both her son and daughter were teased in school. Two boys in her son's sixth-grade class began taunting him because he wore sweatpants instead of jeans. They began to intimidate him during class. Once they knocked the pencil out of his hand during a spelling test when the teacher's back was turned. He failed the test. Rizzo made an appointment with the school counselor. The counselor told her he could do nothing about the behavior of the bullies and suggested she get counseling for her son instead. "Schools say they do something, but they don't, and it continues," says Rizzo. "We go in with the same problem over and over again."

Anna Billoit of Louisiana went to her son's middle school teachers when her son, who had asthma and was overweight, was being bullied by his classmates. Some of the teachers made the situation worse, she says. One male teacher suggested to her that the teasing would help her son mature. "His attitude was, 'Suck it up, take it like a man,'" says Billoit.

Much bullying goes on in so-called transition areas where there is little or no adult supervision: hallways, locker rooms, restrooms, cafeterias, playgrounds, buses, and bus stops. When abuse happens away from adult eyes, it's hard to prove that the abuse occurred. Often, though, bullies harass their victims in the open, in full view of teachers and other adults. Some teachers will ignore the behavior, silently condoning. But even when adults try to deal with the problem, they sometimes make things worse for the victim by not handling the situation properly. Confronting bullies in front of their peers only enhances the bullies' prestige and power. And bullies often step up the abuse after being disciplined. "People know it happens, but there's no structured way to deal with it," says Mullin-Rindler. "There's lots of confusion about what to do and what is the best approach."

Societal expectations play a part in adult reactions to childhood bullying. Many teachers and administrators buy into a widespread belief that bullying is a normal part of childhood and that children are better off working out such problems on their own. But this belief sends a dangerous message to children, says Head. Telling victims they must protect themselves from bullies shows children that adults can't and won't protect them. And, he points out, it's an attitude adults would never tolerate themselves. "If you go to work and get slapped on the back of the head, you wouldn't expect your supervisor to say, 'It's your problem—you need to learn to deal with it yourself,'" says Head. "It's a human rights issue."

Ignoring bullying is only part of the problem. Some teachers go further by blaming the victims for their abuse by letting their own dislike for the victimized child show. "There's a lot of secret admiration for the strong kids," says Eileen Faucette of Augusta, GA. Her daughter was teased so badly in the classroom that she was afraid to go to the blackboard or raise her hand to answer a question. The abuse happened in front of the teacher, who did nothing to stop it.

Head also encountered a blame-the-victim attitude toward his son. Brian would get into trouble for fighting at school, but when Head and his wife investigated what happened, they usually found that Brian had been attacked by other students. The school, Head said, wanted to punish Brian along with his attackers. "The school calls it fighting," Head says. "But it's actually assault and battery."

And changes are coming. This past April, five months after Josh Belluardo's death, the Georgia State Legislature passed an anti-bullying law. The law defines bullying as "any willful attempt or threat to inflict injury on another person when accompanied by an apparent present ability to do so" or "any intentional display of force such as would give the victim reason to fear or expect immediate bodily harm." Schools are required to send students to an alternative school if they commit a third act of bullying in a school year. The law also requires school systems to adopt anti-bullying policies and to post the policies in middle and high schools.

Head was consulted by the state representatives who sponsored the bill, but he believes the measure won't go far enough. He urges schools to treat bullying behavior as a violation of the state criminal law against assault, stalking, and threatening and to call police when the law is broken. He knows it's too late for Brian, too late for Josh, too late for the teens who died in Littleton. But he continues to work, to educate and lobby on the devastating effects of bullying so that his son's death will not have been in vain.

"We should come clean and say what we've done in the past is wrong," says Head. "Now we will guarantee we'll protect the rights of students."

Comparison and Contrast

It's time to buy a new car. You've narrowed your options down to two brands and now you need to choose which one is right for you. You line up the specifications side by side and compare cost, fuel economy, cargo space, seating room and capacity, warranties, Bluetooth hands-free phone availability, and other options. Then you check with *Consumer Reports* for return on investment and performance. Once you determine which features are similar and which are different, you make your choice based on your preferences.

As consumers, we are used to comparing and contrasting in order to make decisions about our purchases, whether it is choosing a car brand or comparing the ingredients in name or generic brands. This type of analysis, however, extends to every aspect of our lives. Comparison and contrast can be used to analyze any two different items, ideas, philosophies, persons, lifestyles, works of literature, artistic renderings, political candidates—the list goes on. The method not only helps to determine preferences but also to uncover connections that we did not realize existed. For example, in his essay "Grant and Lee: A Study in Contrasts," author Bruce Catton outlines how the disparate backgrounds and personalities of the two Civil War generals epitomized their cultures, and yet he also reveals that what they had in common was even more significant. This connection between the two men would not come to light had Catton not analyzed the two men side by side. Another great example of an enlightening analysis of similarities and differences is the book *Men Are from Mars, Women Are from Venus*.

The Process

Purpose and Thesis

The key to a comparison and contrast is to keep the analysis to two of a kind: two courses of action, two ideologies, one people, two works of literature, and the like. It is also important that the two subjects have a clear basis for comparison—while they might be dissimilar in a number of ways, they also should enough similar elements so the comparison will make sense. Sometimes it is fun and interesting to examine two seemingly unlike subjects by use of analogy to explain one by example of the other. An example of a common analogy is the comparison of the human eye to a camera.

Your purpose for bringing your two subjects together to compare and constrast is to analyze them both, side by side, either to show their distinctiveness or similarity in ways not typically perceived or to evaluate two possibilities in order to choose between them. The example above of Bruce Catton's essay "Grant and Lee" would represent the first purpose, and the example of shopping for a car would represent the second.

The basis of comparison between your two subjects informs the thesis statement—your claim about your subjects and why. The thesis statement not only presents the subjects but also indicates whether you are evaluating (two cars) or explaining (Grant and Lee). Here are two thesis statements from essays in this section:

> Neat people are lazier and meaner than sloppy people.
>
> --Suzanne Britt, "Neat People vs. Sloppy People"

> The primary difference between men and women is that women can see extremely small quantities of dirt.
>
> --Dave Barry, "Batting Clean Up and Striking Out"

Organization

Two ways to organize a comparison and contrast essay are subject by subject and point by point.

1. **Subject by subject:** In this organization structure you provide all the information about your first subject, then all the information about your second subject. Next, you provide a summary of their similarities and differences, followed by a conclusion that discusses the outcome of your analysis. This structure works best for shorter essays. Your outline might look something like this:

Introduction

Subject A

Point 1

Point 2

Point 3

Subject B

Point 1

Point 2

Point 3

Summary

Conclusion

2. **Point by point:** In this structure, which is best suited for longer essays, you decide what are the main points to be considered about your two subjects and then compare and contrast both subjects one point at a time. In this case, your outline would be structured differently:

Introduction

Point 1

Subject A

Subject B

Point 2

Subject A

Subject B

Point 3

Subject A

Subject B

Conclusion

For example, if you were comparing two political candidates, your points might include such topics as economic initiatives, social concerns, and foreign policy. For each of these points, you would compare and contrast where the candidates stand on these issues and what their record is.

No matter which organizational structure you choose, there must be balance but not symmetry, like a Rorschach ink test. You must discuss the same points for each of your subjects, but you do not need to discuss them with the same number of words or with the exact same balance of similarities and difference for each point. You want to avoid a monotonous structure that is boring or tedious for the reader.

The Banality of Narcissism

Ron Rosenbaum

The class war over cultural diagnosis.

The great schism in American culture, the most deeply rooted civil war, is not the rift between the two major political parties but a battle at the center of our other two-party system, the two parties of societal self-diagnosis: the Party of Narcissism (PON) and the Party of Low Self-Esteem (PLSE).

The PON attributes all ills—personal, political, and cultural—to (a very vaguely defined) "narcissism" and its consequences, which include materialism, celebrity worship, and the rise of the memoir. The PLSE attributes all ills—personal, political, and cultural—to "low self-esteem" and its consequences: materialism, celebrity worship, and the rise of the memoir.

There are problems with both "parties," unfortunately. Using "narcissism" as an all-purpose explainer of personal and cultural ills has become a sophisticated-sounding substitute for saying something meaningful. The word has become almost as banal as "the banality of evil"—using it requires no actual thought. And the low self-esteem explanation—or, more often, exculpation—for misdeeds and misfortunes has become a near-parody of itself, as most New Age "spiritual" guides such as *The Secret* and its new sequel, *The Power*, argue for virtually unlimited (and unearned) self-esteem.

Almost every cultural essay you read these days originates in one or the other worldview. We, as individuals, as a culture, as a nation, as a species, think too much of ourselves (PON) or too little (PLSE). The tide of battle between the PON and PLSE washes endlessly back and forth, but what prompts these observations was the appearance, on Labor Day weekend, in the usually sophisticated *Financial Times*, of a breathless two-page tribute to the explanatory power of "narcissistic personality disorder"—a rubric from the *American Psychiatric Association's Diagnostic and Statistical Manual* that has been around for decades—as if it were a remarkable new discovery about human nature.

The *FT* story did at least have the virtue of making apparent to me the problem that neither party has been able to solve, the crucial "goldilocks question"—how much self-esteem is too much, how much is not enough, and how much is just the right amount.

And who will tell us? If only there were an objective standard that would make esteem levels as easy to measure as blood pressure. Perhaps it's a ratio, whereby O.W. (Objective Worth, whatever that is) is divided by SSW (Subjective Sense of Worth) and a percentage (like body mass!) is established for every individual so that he or she can make an informed decision about whether to seek professional help.

What's more, in the combat of cultural diagnoses, these competing constructs are often poorly defined, even by supposed "scientists." The report from a York University study I saw posted on Facebook about Facebook claimed: "Facebook provides an ideal setting for narcissists to monitor what they look like and how many friends they have. People who constantly check Facebook may be lacking in self-esteem . . ."

So, wait. Narcissists lack self-esteem? I thought they had too much self-esteem. And people with low self-esteem are really narcissists because they get spurious self-esteem according to the number of "friends" they have? Even researchers can't keep these terms straight.

I've tried to follow the yin-yang shifts of this schism over the decades. Of course, it's a dialectic that has persisted for centuries of American history, ever since Cotton Mather called for rooting out pride (aka self-esteem) from the most pious Puritan minds by means of rigorous introspection, only to be followed by Ralph Waldo Emerson, who almost deified the spiritual nobility of the self and the esteem in which it should be held. But the battle has sharpened in recent years to the point of cultural civil war.

For instance, I recall reading Christopher Lasch's scathing critique of what he called "the culture of narcissism" in an early-'80s book of the same title. Lasch's book was, I believe, a reaction to the self-esteem boosting mania described in Tom Wolfe's "Me Decade" portrait of the '70s, and I remember thinking how smart Lasch was. Yes, narcissism, I thought—that's the problem! It boosted my self-esteem that I was able to realize the utter justness of this diagnosis.

Then, in the middle of the '80s, I read a remarkably persuasive critique of Lasch's thesis that changed my thinking completely. It was a somewhat overlooked essay by the late philosopher Robert Solomon, also the author of the much admired study of *The Passions*. In the essay, sadly not available on Google, Solomon portrayed Lasch as indulging in a puritanical witch hunt against the benevolent human desire to lead a more, rather than less, gratified life; to be admired rather than scorned; to develop one's own personality, however idiosyncratic and inappropriately flashy it might seem to the sourpuss Lasch. Solomon painted Lasch as a modern Cotton Mather preaching stultifying dullness rather than individual self-fulfillment and condemning just about any path in life other than becoming a stern, narcissist-hating social critic. In other words, Solomon argued, what's so bad about wanting to enrich one's own experience, enjoy life, and have a good time? Solomon's essay made me think of *Twelfth Night*, with Lasch as the puritanical Malvolio counterpoised to the inebriated but life-affirming Sir Toby Belch, who cries out against Malvolio's strictures, "Dost thou think, because thou art virtuous, there shall be no more cakes and ale?"

Solomon also offered an interesting defense of the "narcissist's" introspection: It's not all pathological self-absorption. At least some of it could be looked upon as cultivating a thoughtful interior life. Shortly after I read Solomon, I read Harvard philosopher Elaine Scarry's wonderfully revelatory and daring riff in *The Body in Pain* about materialism, often demonized by the anti-narcissists as a way of showing off one's special self-worth. One could frown at the values espoused in Madonna's "Material Girl" for instance, but one could also recognize that diamonds can be valued for their beauty as well as their cash value.

Scarry contends that gazing at beautiful works of art or the intricacies of lace, that sort of thing, is an appreciation of the potential of the material world to confront us with the glory of consciousness. The love of material things should not be automatically demonized or disdained as mere "materialism" by the PON.

But then in the '90s, I began to see that, taken too far, the anti-antinarcissist position could put you in the camp of the cult of self-esteem, somewhere on the road to accepting Tony Robbins as your higher power. This was the era of school systems instituting self-esteem-boosting programs for their students. The theory was that dysfunctional later development was derived from an early lack of self-esteem. This decade also saw a new wave of self-help and self-fulfillment preachers and preachments. Oprah!

The embarrassments of the New Age positive-thinking gospel made me glad that, in some respects, I was already an anti-anti-anti-narcissist: I'd begun writing about New Age folly in the '80s, including attacks on phenomena such as the cult of Elisabeth Kübler-Ross and the way her "five stages" of grieving turned death into an uplifting final exercise in self-esteem. I also knocked the way the cancer cure clinics of Tijuana, Mexico, had adopted New Age rhetoric to market their age-old quackery. I had become wary of the PLSE but not quite ready to return to the puritanical strictures of the PON.

Especially now, since there seems to be an elitist rush to ridicule, beat up on, and shoot all the remaining fish in the barrel of positive thinking. There's a certain snobbery here, no? An idea that self-help is too popular with the masses who didn't go to Ivy League schools. Beginning with Barbara Ehrenreich's recently published *Bright-Sided: How the Relentless Promotion of Positive Thinking Has Undermined America.*

In the book, Ehrenreich makes the important point that the fixation on positive thinking as a way to prevent and even cure disease can lead to a malign tendency to blame oneself for getting sick, and she also offers a valuable warning against forsaking medical science for New Age mysticism.

She also rejects the pink baubles of breast-cancer-survivor culture and its "pink sticky sentiment," as she puts it. But I was struck by a tone of disdain for those who went for all the pink baubles. Shouldn't people in dire straits be given some absolution for the lesser aesthetic sensibilities of the comforts they seek and find, however embarrassingly pink?

Then there's "The War on Unhappiness," the lead story in this month's *Harper's*, in which the author tells us that positive psychology evokes "Nuremberg" to him and, in words that could have come from a Cotton Mather sermon, "the concupiscence and the stain" of Adam and Eve. (I could be reading the wrong Bible, but if I remember my *Paradise Lost*, Adam and Eve were not expelled from the Garden for "staining" it (ick) with their concupiscence—God didn't mind them gettin' it on—but because they allowed Lucifer to tempt them to violate a ban that had provoked their curiosity, not their lust. This is a kind of basic error.) Still, here we have positive psychology associated with Hitler and Satan by the Party of Narcissism.

It was then it began to dawn on me that what was going on was not just a conceptual war but a kind of aesthetic class war as well. Ehrenreich seemed to be looking down on the kinds of consolation sought out by those with less refined sensibilities, those who lacked her fierce intellectual honesty. Same with the *Harper's* story, which, after deriding the positive-thinking psychologists for enabling the sin of concupiscence, ends with a turgid quote from Nietzsche, which I'd have to say is a egotist's move, one that says, "I'm better educated in the humanities than you smiley-faced happiness shrinks. Nobody can trump the sophistication of my tragic sense of life. Like Freud and Nietzsche, I'm really self-aware compared with the grinning simpletons of the lower intellectual orders."

One hesitates to call him a narcissist, but there's no low self-esteem there.

In almost every attack on the self-help movement one can detect a subtext of "I wouldn't fall for such pap. I went to an Ivy League school. I'm fabulously complex. Not like the poor souls in the flyover who have to cling to their guns, their god, and their simple-minded positive thinking."

The one contemporary instance in which I think "narcissism" has not been brought to bear when it deserves to be is in the Tea Party and conservative talk radio's fetishization of "American exceptionalism." This is the belief, the virtually religious creed, that America is better than any nation that has ever existed in history, because our Constitution was given to us by God. A bit of narcissism there, I'd say. I like Obama's answer when he was asked whether he believed in American exceptionalism and he said, "I believe in American exceptionalism, just as I suspect that the Brits believe in British exceptionalism and the Greeks believe in Greek exceptionalism."

But perhaps the best exemplar of the resurgence of the PON and the utter emptiness of the narcissism metaphor, the most concentrated, state-of-the-art compendium of the banality of narcissism, the article that convinced me it was time to take a stand against the PON tide, was that long, sedulous, and credulous two-page cover story in the ordinarily acute *Financial Times* weekend "Arts & Leisure" section over Labor Day.

I say "ordinarily acute" *Financial Times* (witness their review of my Shakespeare book; OK, call me a narcissist but one with low self-esteem, too), because this naive essay seemed to be presenting narcissism and Narcissistic Personality Disorder as a new revelation to the world, a fantastically exciting new scientific way of explaining human behavior. Talk about being late to the party.

But in the comprehensiveness of its awe and wonder at the explanatory power of Narcissistic Personality Disorder, as the *Diagnostic and Statistical Manual of Mental Disorders* calls it, the article should serve as a warning to cultural critics about the shaky foundation for their societal metaphors.

Now, I know there are intelligent people who believe in the heuristic utility of NPD, but the pretensions of the DSM to science are sketchy at best, when its real-world usage has more to do with rationalizing billing codes of shrink services. In addition, I believe there are philosophical problems with the definition the DSM gives to such "personality disorders."

A personality disorder, it says, is "[a]n enduring pattern of inner experience and behavior that deviates markedly from the expectation of the individual's culture, is pervasive and inflexible, has an onset in adolescence or early adulthood, is stable over time, and leads to distress or impairment."

Note the deference given to "the expectation of the individual's culture." Thus an abolitionist in the pre-Civil War South would have a "personality disorder." And if he thought he could play a role in changing that culture he would be considered a "narcissist" suffering from the key word in the DSM's definition of Narcissistic Personality Disorder: "grandiosity." Someone like John Brown for instance, not an idealist obsessed with ending the murderous crime of enslavement but according to the "experts" who wrote the DSM definition of NPD, a sick man who would have been better off if he'd had our sophisticated modern shrinks to work on him. Grandiosity: Melville, too. Couldn't it have been a white tuna rather than a white whale? Much healthier! Less grandiose!

Consider the history of NPD. The easily impressed author of the *FT* article tells us NPD was "first diagnosed by the psychoanalyst Heinz Kohut in 1968." The acceptance of a psychoanalytically derived diagnosis at this late date after so much of Freudian theory has been discredited or found to rest on fabrications (if you haven't read Frederick Crews' "Talking Back to Prozac," do yourself a favor) is just the first warning sign of the author's notion of expertise.

The article delivers pronouncements from unnamed "experts," as in: "Today, experts believe disproportionate numbers of pathological narcissists are at work in the most influential reaches of society." Who are these "experts"? Are we really supposed to believe all experts—neuroscientists, say—buy into this antiquated conjectural fabrication? How do we decide who are the "pathological" and who the nonpathological narcissists? Sam Vaknin, the one "expert" most prominently featured, is an ex-criminal securities fraudster now flogging a pop-psych book on narcissism (for which he blames his crime, of course, which will be comforting to those he defrauded) and who tells us that "narcissists gravitate toward professions where they can control people and elicit adulation."

Well, duh. Was Winston Churchill a "pathological narcissist" for thinking he and the RAF could hold off Hitler alone in 1940? Was FDR a narcissist when he said, "We have nothing to fear . . ."? If cinema didn't have narcissists, some of them probably pathological, we'd have no movies, certainly not masterpieces like *The Godfather* or *Chinatown*. Good thing this narcissism disease hasn't migrated from directors to great actors and actresses, who we know are spared the ravages of narcissism, right?

But the most shameful thing about the sedulous credulousness of this story is the way it buys into the use of Narcissistic Personality Disorder as science to exculpate murderers. Thus we get the story of poor Brian Blackwell, who murdered his mother and father with a claw hammer in Merseyside but only did it because of his narcissism, so it's totally understandable. "His lawyers argued that he had NPD, pointing to his fantasy lifestyle (Blackwell claimed to be a professional tennis player)." This farrago of nonsense got him off with a lighter sentence.

So next time you pick up a claw hammer with intent to kill your loved ones, make sure you've previously boasted of beating Roger Federer in three straight sets.

But our *FT* writer swallows this crap whole and goes on to lay some more experts on us: "Experts believe that NPD patients are dysfunctional and immature, and that to compensate for this inner, sick child the narcissist invents a fiction." Voila! The deadly tennis fantasy.

But, wait. "Inner sick child" seems as if it comes from the rhetoric of the Party of Low Self-Esteem. Do we have here a Unified Field Theory of PON and PLSE emerging? LSE causes narcissism. But, then, our *FT* guide tells us no one knows whether it's caused by "an excess of love in infancy" or by childhood abuse. Or both.

It is only several thousand words later that we learn that nobody knows what narcissism is or "where it comes from," whether it's organic, psychogenic, genetic or just made up by a bunch of shrinks who want to medicalize every aspect of human character. But it's really, really scary. And guess what, ladies? It—and its claw hammer!—are coming for you!

Although "experts say" narcissism is more prevalent in men, these days, "with gender models changing, there is no known reason why women won't succumb to this disorder in greater numbers." (Another bad repercussion of feminism, it is implied. Uppity women = more narcissism.)

Meanwhile, the author shows his deep concern for the "victims" of narcissists by quoting a woman who claims to have been married to one and suffered the ravages of it: "It's a huge comfort to know it's NPD," she tells us. "You realize it's not you that's the problem."

So it's really a consolatory mechanism, a way of encapsulating in a word what's wrong with someone you don't like.

No, it's not you that's the problem: It's NPD itself. A construct that can mean anything, is subjective rather than scientific, and is all too often a consolatory mechanism for essayists looking to diagnose American culture.

So please, people, attack positive thinking all you want, take your cheap shots at the lower orders, shoot your fish in a barrel, vaunt your superior complexity and tragic sense of life, but don't think you can demonstrate said complexity by throwing around equally vacant psychobabble about narcissism. It just makes you look, well, like a narcissist.

Neat People vs. Sloppy People

Suzanne Britt

I've finally figured out the difference between neat people and sloppy people. The distinction is, as always, moral. Neat people are lazier and meaner than sloppy people.

Sloppy people, you see, are not really sloppy. Their sloppiness is merely the unfortunate consequence of their extreme moral rectitude. Sloppy people carry in their mind's eye a heavenly vision, a precise plan, that is so stupendous, so perfect, it can't be achieved in this world or the next.

Sloppy people live in Never-Never Land. Someday is their métier. Someday they are planning to alphabetize all their books and set up home catalogs. Someday they will go through their wardrobes and mark certain items for tentative mending and certain items for passing on to relatives of similar shape and size. Someday sloppy people will make family scrapbooks into which they will put newspaper clippings, postcards, locks of hair, and the dried corsage from their senior prom. Someday they will file everything on the surface of their desks, including the cash receipts from coffee purchases at the snack shop. Someday they will sit down and read all the back issues of *The New Yorker*.

For all these noble reasons and more, sloppy people never get neat. They aim too high and wide. They save everything, planning someday to file, order, and straighten out the world. But while these ambitious plans take clearer and clearer shape in their heads, the books spill from the shelves onto the floor, the clothes pile up in the hamper and closet, the family mementos accumulate in every drawer, the surface of the desk is buried under mounds of paper, and the unread magazines threaten to reach the ceiling.

Sloppy people can't bear to part with anything. They give loving attention to every detail. When sloppy people say they're going to tackle the surface of a desk, they really mean it. Not a paper will go unturned; not a rubber band will go unboxed. Four hours or two weeks into the excavation, the desk looks exactly the same, primarily because the sloppy person is meticulously creating new piles of papers with new headings and scrupulously stopping to read all the old book catalogs before he throws them away. A neat person would just bulldoze the desk.

Neat people are bums and clods at heart. They have cavalier attitudes toward possessions, including family heirlooms. Everything is just another dust-catcher to them. If anything collects dust, it's got to go and that's that. Neat people will toy with the idea of throwing the children out of the house just to cut down on the clutter.

Neat people don't care about process. They like results. What they want to do is get the whole thing over with so they can sit down and watch the rasslin' on TV. Neat people operate on two unvarying principles: Never handle any item twice, and throw everything away.

The only thing messy in a neat person's house is the trash can. The minute something comes to a neat person's hand, he will look at it, try to decide if it has immediate use and, finding none, throw it in the trash.

Neat people are especially vicious with mail. They never go through their mail unless they are standing directly over a trash can. If the trash can is beside the mailbox, even better. All ads, catalogs, pleas for charitable contributions, church bulletins, and money-saving coupons go straight into the trash can without being opened. All letters from home, postcards from Europe, bills, and paychecks are opened, immediately responded to, then dropped in the trash can. Neat people keep their receipts only for tax purposes. That's it. No sentimental salvaging of birthday cards or the last letter a dying relative ever wrote. Into the trash it goes.

Neat people place neatness above everything, even economics. They are incredibly wasteful. Neat people throw away several toys every time they walk through the den. I knew a neat person once who threw away a perfectly good dish drainer because it had mold on it. The drainer was too much trouble to wash. And neat people sell their furniture when they move. They will sell a La-Z-Boy recliner while you are reclining in it.

Neat people are no good to borrow from. Neat people buy everything in expensive little single portions. They get their flour and sugar in two-pound bags. They wouldn't consider clipping a coupon, saving a leftover, reusing plastic nondairy whipped cream containers, or rinsing off tin foil and draping it over the unmoldy dish drainer. You can never borrow a neat person's newspaper to see what's playing at the movies. Neat people have the paper all wadded up and in the trash by 7:05 a.m.

Neat people cut a clean swath through the organic as well as the inorganic world. People, animals, and things are all one to them. They are so insensitive. After they've finished with the pantry, the medicine cabinet, and the attic, they will throw out the red geranium (too many leaves), sell the dog (too many fleas), and send the children off to boarding school (too many scuff-marks on the hardwood floors).

Batting Clean-Up and Striking Out

Dave Barry

The primary difference between men and women is that women can see extremely small quantities of dirt. Not when they're babies, of course. Babies of both sexes have a very low awareness of dirt, other than to think it tastes better than food.

But somewhere during the growth process, a hormonal secretion takes place in women that enables them to see dirt that men cannot see, dirt at the level of *molecules,* whereas men don't generally notice it until it forms clumps large enough to support agriculture. This can lead to tragedy, as it did in the ill-fated ancient city of Pompeii, where the residents all got killed when the local volcano erupted and covered them with a layer of ash twenty feet deep. Modern people often ask, "How come, when the ashes started falling, the Pompeii people didn't just *leave*?" The answer is that in Pompeii, it was the custom for the men to do the housework. They never even *noticed* the ash until it had for the most part covered the children. "Hey!" the men said (in Latin). "It's mighty quiet around here!" This is one major historical reason why, to this very day, men tend to do extremely little in the way of useful housework.

What often happens in my specific family unit is that my wife will say to me: "Could you clean Robert's bathroom? It's filthy." So I'll gather up the Standard Male Cleaning Implements, namely a spray bottle of Windex and a wad of paper towels, and I'll go into Robert's bathroom, and it *always looks perfectly fine*. I mean, when I hear the word "filthy" used to describe a bathroom, I think about this bar where I used to hang out called Joe's Sportsman's Lounge, where the men's room had bacteria you could enter in a rodeo.

Nevertheless, because I am a sensitive and caring kind of guy, I "clean" the bathroom, spraying Windex all over everything including the six hundred action figures each sold separately that God forbid Robert should ever take a bath without, and then I wipe it back off with the paper towels, and I go back to whatever activity I had been engaged in, such as doing an important project on the Etch-a-Sketch, and a little while later my wife will say: "I hate to rush you, but could you do Robert's bathroom? It's really *filthy.*" She is in there looking at the very walls I just *Windexed,* and she is seeing dirt! *Everywhere!* And if I tell her I already *cleaned* the bathroom, she gives me this look that she has perfected, the same look she used on me the time I selected Robert's outfit for school and part of it turned out to be pajamas.

The opposite side of the dirt coin, of course, is sports. This is an area where men tend to feel very sensitive and women tend to be extremely callous. I have written about this before and I always get irate letters from women who say they are the heavyweight racquetball champion of some place like Iowa and are sensitive to sports to the point where they could crush my skull like a ripe grape, but I feel these women are the exception.

A more representative woman is my friend Maddy, who once invited some people, including my wife and me, over to her house for an evening of stimulating conversation and jovial companionship, which sounds fine except that this particular evening occurred *during a World Series game.* If you can imagine such a social gaffe.

We sat around the living room and Maddy tried to stimulate a conversation, but we males could not focus our attention on the various suggested topics because we could actually *feel* the World Series television and radio broadcast rays zinging through the air, penetrating right into our bodies, causing our dental fillings to vibrate, and all the while the women were behaving *as though nothing were wrong.* It was exactly like that story by Edgar Allan Poe where the murderer can hear the victim's heart beating louder and louder even though he (the murder victim) is dead, until finally he (the murderer) can't stand it anymore, and he just *has* to watch the World Series on television. That was how we felt.

Maddy's husband made the first move, coming up with an absolutely brilliant means of escape: *He used their baby.* He picked up Justine, their seven-month-old daughter, who was fussing a little, and announced: "What this child needs is to have her bottle and watch the World Series." And just like that he was off to the family room, moving very quickly for a big man holding a baby. A second male escaped by pretending to clear the dessert plates. Soon all four of us were in there, watching the Annual Fall Classic, while the women prattled away about human relationships or something. It turned out to be an extremely pivotal game.

Talk in the Intimate Relationship: His and Hers

Deborah Tannen

Male-female conversation is cross-cultural communication. Culture is simply a network of habits and patterns gleaned from past experience, and women and men have different past experiences. From the time they're born, they're treated differently, talked to differently, and talk differently as a result. Boys and girls grow up in different worlds, even if they grow up in the same house. And as adults they travel in different worlds, reinforcing patterns established in childhood. These cultural differences include different expectations about the role of talk in relationships and how it fulfills that role.

Everyone knows that as a relationship becomes long-term, its terms change. But women and men often differ in how they expect them to change. Many women feel, "After all this time, you should know what I want without my telling you." Many men feel, "After all this time, we should be able to tell each other what we want."

These incongruent expectations capture one of the key differences between men and women. Communication is always a matter of balancing conflicting needs for involvement and independence. Though everyone has both these needs, women often have a relatively greater need for involvement, and men a relatively greater need for independence. Being understood without saying what you mean gives a payoff in involvement, and that is why women value it so highly.

If you want to be understood without saying what you mean explicitly in words, you must convey meaning somewhere else—in how words are spoken, or by metamessages. Thus it stands to reason that women are often more attuned than men to the metamessages of talk. When women surmise meaning in this way, it seems mysterious to men, who call it "women's intuition" (if they think it's right) or "reading things in" (if they think it's wrong). Indeed, it could be wrong, since metamessages are not on record. And even if it is right, there is still the question of scale: How significant are the metamessages that are there?

Metamessages are a form of indirectness. Women are more likely to be indirect, and to try to reach agreement by negotiation. Another way to understand this preference is that negotiation allows a display of solidarity, which women prefer to the display of power (even though the aim may be the same—getting what you want). Unfortunately, power and solidarity are bought with the same currency: Ways of talking intended to create solidarity have the simultaneous effect of framing power differences. When they think they're being nice, women often end up appearing deferential and unsure of themselves or of what they want.

When styles differ, misunderstandings are always rife. As their differing styles create misunderstandings, women and men try to clear them up by talking things out. These pitfalls are compounded in talks between men and women because they have different ways of going about talking things out, and different assumptions about the significance of going about it.

Sylvia and Harry celebrated their fiftieth wedding anniversary at a mountain resort. Some of the guests were at the resort for the whole weekend, others just for the evening of the celebration: A cocktail party followed by a sit-down dinner. The manager of the dining room approached Sylvia during dinner. "Since there's so much food tonight," he said, "and the hotel prepared a fancy dessert and everyone already ate at the cocktail party anyway, how about cutting and serving the anniversary cake at lunch tomorrow?" Sylvia asked the advice of the others at her table. All the men agreed: "Sure, that makes sense. Save the cake for tomorrow." All the women disagreed: "No, the party is tonight. Serve the cake tonight." The men were focusing on the message: The cake as food. The women were thinking of the metamessage: Serving a special cake frames an occasion as a celebration.

Why are women more attuned to metamessages? Because they are more focused on involvement, that is, on relationships among people, and it is through metamessages that relationships among people are established and maintained. If you want to take the temperature and check the vital signs of a relationship, the barometers to check are its metamessages: What is said and how.

Everyone can see these signals, but whether or not we pay attention to them is another matter—a matter of being sensitized. Once you are sensitized, you can't roll your antennae back in; they're stuck in the extended position.

When interpreting meaning, it is possible to pick up signals that weren't intentionally sent out, like an innocent flock of birds on a radar screen. The birds are there—and the signals women pick up are there—but they may not mean what the interpreter thinks they mean. For example, Maryellen looks at Larry and asks, "What's wrong?" because his brow is furrowed. Since he was only thinking about lunch, her expression of concern makes him feel under scrutiny.

The difference in focus on messages and metamessages can give men and women different points of view on almost any comment. Harriet complains to Morton, "Why don't you ask me how my day was?" He replies, "If you have something to tell me, tell me. Why do you have to be invited?" The reason is that she wants the metamessage of interest: Evidence that he cares how her day was, regardless of whether or not she has something to tell.

A lot of trouble is caused between women and men by, of all things, pronouns. Women often feel hurt when their partners use "I" or "me" in a situation in which they would use "we" or "us." When Morton announces, "I think I'll go for a walk," Harriet feels specifically uninvited, though Morton later claims she would have been welcome to join him. She felt locked out by his use of "I" and his omission of an invitation: "Would you like to come?" Metamessages can be seen in what is not said as well as what is said.

It's difficult to straighten out such misunderstandings because each one feels convinced of the logic of his or her position and the illogic—or irresponsibility—of the other's. Harriet knows that she always asks Morton how his day was, and that she'd never announce, "I'm going for a walk," without inviting him to join her. If he talks differently to her, it must be that he feels differently. But Morton wouldn't feel unloved if Harriet didn't ask about his day, and he would feel free to ask, "Can I come along?" if she announced she was taking a walk. So he can't believe she is justified in feeling responses he knows he wouldn't have.

These processes are dramatized with chilling yet absurdly amusing authenticity in Jules Feiffer's play *Grown Ups*. To get a closer look at what happens when men and women focus on different levels of talk in talking things out, let's look at what happens in this play.

Jake criticizes Louise for not responding when their daughter, Edie, called her. His comment leads to a fight even though they're both aware that this one incident is not in itself important.

JAKE: Look, I don't care if it's important or not, when a kid calls its mother the mother should answer.

LOUISE: Now I'm a bad mother.

JAKE: I didn't say that.

LOUISE: It's in your stare.

JAKE: Is that another thing you know? My stare?

Louise ignores Jake's message—the question of whether or not she responded when Edie called—and goes for the metamessage: His implication that she's a bad mother, which Jake insistently disclaims. When Louise explains the signals she's reacting to, Jake not only discounts them but is angered at being held accountable not for what he said but for how he looked—his stare.

As the play goes on, Jake and Louise replay and intensify these patterns:

LOUISE: If I'm such a terrible mother, do you want a divorce?

JAKE: I do not think you're a terrible mother and no, thank you, I do not want a divorce. Why is it that whenever I bring up any difference between us you ask me if I want a divorce?

The more he denies any meaning beyond the message, the more she blows it up, the more adamantly he denies it, and so on:

JAKE: I have brought up one thing that you do with Edie that I don't think you notice that I have noticed for some time but which I have deliberately not brought up before because I had hoped you would notice it for yourself and stop doing it and also—frankly, baby, I have to say this—I knew if I brought it up we'd get into exactly the kind of circular argument we're in right now. And I wanted to avoid it. But I haven't and we're in it, so now, with your permission, I'd like to talk about it.

LOUISE: You don't see how that puts me down?

JAKE: What?

LOUISE: If you think I'm so stupid why do you go on living with me?

JAKE: Dammit! Why can't anything ever be simple around here?!

It can't be simple because Louise and Jake are responding to different levels of communication. As in Bateson's example of the dual-control electric blanket with crossed wires, each one intensifies the energy going to a different aspect of the problem. Jake tries to clarify his point by over-elaborating it, which gives Louise further evidence that he's condescending to her, making it even less likely that she will address his point rather than his condescension.

What pushes Jake and Louise beyond anger to rage is their different perspectives on metamessages. His refusal to admit that his statements have implications and overtones denies her authority over her own feelings. Her attempts to interpret what he didn't say and put the metamessage into the message makes him feel she's putting words into his mouth—denying his authority over his own meaning.

The same thing happens when Louise tells Jake that he is being manipulated by Edie:

LOUISE: Why don't you ever make her come to see you? Why do you always go to her?

JAKE: You want me to play power games with a nine year old? I want her to know I'm interested in her. Someone around here has to show interest in her.

LOUISE: You love her more than I do.

JAKE: I didn't say that.

LOUISE: Yes, you did.

JAKE: You don't know how to listen. You have never learned how to listen. It's as if listening to you is a foreign language.

Again, Louise responds to his implication—this time, that he loves Edie more because he runs when she calls. And yet again, Jake cries literal meaning, denying he meant any more than he said.

Throughout their argument, the point to Louise is her feelings—that Jake makes her feel put down—but to him the point is her actions—that she doesn't always respond when Edie calls:

LOUISE: You talk about what I do to Edie, what do you think you do to me?

JAKE: This is not the time to go into what we do to each other.

Since she will talk only about the metamessage, and he will talk only about the message, neither can get satisfaction from their talk, and they end up where they started—only angrier:

JAKE: That's not the point!

LOUISE: It's my point!

JAKE: It's hopeless!

LOUISE: Then get a divorce.

American conventional wisdom (and many of our parents and English teachers) tell us that meaning is conveyed by words, so men who tend to be literal about words are supported by conventional wisdom. They may not simply deny but actually miss the cues that are sent by how words are spoken. If they sense something about it, they may nonetheless discount what they sense. After all, it wasn't said. Sometimes that's a dodge—a plausible defense rather than a gut feeling. But sometimes it is a sincere conviction. Women are also likely to doubt the reality of what they sense. If they don't doubt it in their guts, they nonetheless may lack the arguments to support their position and thus are reduced to repeating, "You said it. You did so." Knowing that metamessages are a real and fundamental part of communication makes it easier to understand and justify what they feel.

An article in a popular newspaper reports that one of the five most common complaints of wives about their husbands is "He doesn't listen to me anymore." Another is "He doesn't talk to me anymore." Political scientist Andrew Hacker noted that lack of communication, while high on women's lists of reasons for divorce, is much less often mentioned by men. Since couples are parties to the same conversations, why are women more dissatisfied with them than men? Because what they expect is different, as well as what they see as the significance of talk itself.

First, let's consider the complaint "He doesn't talk to me."

One of the most common stereotypes of American men is the strong silent type. Jack Kroll, writing about Henry Fonda on the occasion of his death, used the phrases "quiet power," "abashed silences," "combustible catatonia," and "sense of power held in check." He explained that Fonda's goal was not to let anyone see "the wheels go around," not to let the "machinery" show. According to Kroll, the resulting silence was effective on stage but devastating to Fonda's family.

The image of a silent father is common and is often the model for the lover or husband. But what attracts us can become flypaper to which we are unhappily stuck. Many women find the strong silent type to be a lure as a lover but a lug as a husband. Nancy Schoenberger begins a poem with the lines "It was your silence that hooked me, / so like my father's." Adrienne Rich refers in a poem to the "husband who is frustratingly mute." Despite the initial attraction of such quintessentially male silence, it may begin to feel, to a woman in a long-term relationship, like a brick wall against which she is banging her head.

In addition to these images of male and female behavior—both the result and the cause of them—are differences in how women and men view the role of talk in relationships as well as how talk accomplishes its purpose. These differences have their roots in the settings in which men and women learn to have conversations among their peers, growing up.

Children whose parents have foreign accents don't speak with accents. They learn to talk like their peers. Little girls and little boys learn how to have conversations as they learn how to pronounce words from their playmates. Between the ages of five and fifteen, when children are learning to have conversations, they play mostly with friends of their own sex. So it's not surprising that they learn different ways of having and using conversations.

Anthropologists Daniel Maltz and Ruth Borker point out that boys and girls socialize differently. Little girls tend to play in small groups or, even more common, in pairs. Their social life usually centers around a best friend, and friendships are made, maintained, and broken by talk—especially "secrets." If a little girl tells her friend's secret to another little girl, she may find herself with a new best friend. The secrets themselves may or may not be important, but the fact of telling them is all-important. It's hard for newcomers to get into these tight groups, but anyone who is admitted is treated as an equal. Girls like to play cooperatively; if they can't cooperate, the group breaks up.

Little boys tend to play in larger groups, often outdoors, and they spend more time doing things than talking. It's easy for boys to get into the group, but not everyone is accepted as an equal. Once in the group, boys must jockey for their status in it. One of the most important ways they do this is through talk: Verbal display such as telling stories and jokes, challenging and sidetracking the verbal displays of other boys, and withstanding other boys' challenges in order to maintain their own story—and status. Their talk is often competitive talk about who is best at what.

Feiffer's play is ironically named *Grown Ups* because adult men and women struggling to communicate often sound like children: "You said so!" "I did not!" The reason is that when they grow up, women and men keep the divergent attitudes and habits they learned as children—which they don't recognize as attitudes and habits but simply take for granted as ways of talking.

Women want their partners to be a new and improved version of a best friend. This gives them a soft spot for men who tell them secrets. As Jack Nicholson once advised a guy, in a movie: "Tell her about your troubled childhood—that always gets em." Men expect to do things together and don't feel anything is missing if they don't have heart-to-heart talks all the time.

If they do have heart-to-heart talks, the meaning of those talks may be opposite for men and women. To many women, the relationship is working as long as they can talk things out. To many men, the relationship isn't working out if they have to keep working it over. If she keeps trying to get talks going to save the relationship, and he keeps trying to avoid them because he sees them as weakening it, then each one's efforts to preserve the relationship appear to the other as reckless endangerment.

If talks (of any kind) do get going, men's and women's ideas about how to conduct them may be very different. For example, Dora is feeling comfortable and close to Tom. She settles into a chair after dinner and begins to tell him about a problem at work. She expects him to ask questions to show he's interested; reassure her that he understands and that what she feels is normal; and return the intimacy by telling her a problem of his. Instead, Tom sidetracks her story, cracks jokes about it, questions her interpretation of the problem, and gives her advice about how to solve it and avoid such problems in the future.

All of these responses, natural to men, are unexpected to women, who interpret them in terms of their own habits—negatively. When Tom comments on side issues or cracks jokes, Dora thinks he doesn't care about what she's saying and isn't really listening. If he challenges her reading of what went on, she feels he is criticizing her and telling her she's crazy, when what she wants is to be reassured that she's not. If he tells her how to solve the problem, it makes her feel as if she's the patient to his doctor—a metamessage of condescension, echoing male one-upmanship compared to the female etiquette of equality. Because he doesn't volunteer information about his problems, she feels he's implying he doesn't have any.

His way of responding to her bid for intimacy makes her feel distant from him. She tries harder to regain intimacy the only way she knows how—by revealing more and more about herself. He tries harder by giving more insistent advice. The more problems she exposes, the more incompetent she feels, until they both see her as emotionally draining and problem-ridden. When his efforts to help aren't appreciated, he wonders why she asks for his advice if she doesn't want to take it . . .

When women talk about what seems obviously interesting to them, their conversations often include reports of conversations. Tone of voice, timing, intonation, and wording are all re-created in the telling in order to explain—dramatize, really—the experience that is being reported. If men tell about an incident and give a brief summary instead of re-creating what was said and how, the women often feel that the essence of the experience is being omitted. If the woman asks, "What exactly did he say?," and "How did he say it?," the man probably can't remember. If she continues to press him, he may feel as if he's being grilled.

All these different habits have repercussions when the man and the woman are talking about their relationship. He feels out of his element, even one down. She claims to recall exactly what he said, and what she said, and in what sequence, and she wants him to account for what he said. He can hardly account for it since he has forgotten exactly what was said—if not the whole conversation. She secretly suspects he's only pretending not to remember, and he secretly suspects that she's making up the details.

One woman reported such a problem as being a matter of her boyfriend's poor memory. It is unlikely, however, that his problem was poor memory in general. The question is what types of material each person remembers or forgets.

Frances was sitting at her kitchen table talking to Edward, when the toaster did something funny. Edward began to explain why it did it. Frances tried to pay attention, but very early in his explanation, she realized she was completely lost. She felt very stupid. And indications were that he thought so too.

Later that day they were taking a walk. He was telling her about a difficult situation in his office that involved a complex network of interrelationships among a large number of people. Suddenly he stopped and said, "I'm sure you can't keep track of all these people." "Of course I can," she said, and she retraced his story with all the characters in place, all the details right. He was genuinely impressed. She felt very smart.

How could Frances be both smart and stupid? Did she have a good memory or a bad one? Frances's and Edward's abilities to follow, remember, and recount depended on the subject—and paralleled her parents' abilities to follow and remember. Whenever Frances told her parents about people in her life, her mother could follow with no problem, but her father got lost as soon as she introduced a second character. "Now who was that?" he'd ask. "Your boss?" "No, my boss is Susan. This was my friend." Often he'd still be in the previous story. But whenever she told them about her work, it was her mother who would get lost as soon as she mentioned a second step: "That was your tech report?" "No, I handed my tech report in last month. This was a special project."

Frances's mother and father, like many men and women, had honed their listening and remembering skills in different arenas. Their experience talking to other men and other women gave them practice in following different kinds of talk.

Knowing whether and how we are likely to report events later influences whether and how we pay attention when they happen. As women listen to and take part in conversations, knowing they may talk about them later makes them more likely to pay attention to exactly what is said and how. Since most men aren't in the habit of making such reports, they are less likely to pay much attention at the time. On the other hand, many women aren't in the habit of paying attention to scientific explanations and facts because they don't expect to have to perform in public by reciting them—just as those who aren't in the habit of entertaining others by telling jokes "can't" remember jokes they've heard, even though they listened carefully enough to enjoy them.

So women's conversations with their women friends keep them in training for talking about their relationships with men, but many men come to such conversations with no training at all—and an uncomfortable sense that this really isn't their event.

Most of us place enormous emphasis on the importance of a primary relationship. We regard the ability to maintain such relationships as a sign of mental health—our contemporary metaphor for being a good person.

Yet our expectations of such relationships are nearly—maybe in fact—impossible. When primary relationships are between women and men, male-female differences contribute to the impossibility. We expect partners to be both romantic interests and best friends. Though women and men may have fairly similar expectations for romantic interests, obscuring their differences when relationships begin, they have very different ideas about how to be friends, and these are the differences that mount over time.

In conversations between friends who are not lovers, small misunderstandings can be passed over or diffused by breaks in contact. But in the context of a primary relationship, differences can't be ignored, and the pressure cooker of continued contact keeps both people stewing in the juice of accumulated minor misunderstandings. And stylistic differences are sure to cause misunderstandings—not, ironically, in matters such as sharing values and interests or understanding each other's philosophies of life. These large and significant yet palpable issues can be talked about and agreed on. It is far harder to achieve congruence—and much more surprising and troubling that it is hard—in the simple day-to-day matters of the automatic rhythms and nuances of talk. Nothing in our backgrounds or in the media (the present-day counterpart to religion or grandparents' teachings) prepares us for this failure. If two people share so much in terms of point of view and basic values, how can they continually get into fights about insignificant matters?

If you find yourself in such a situation and you don't know about differences in conversational style, you assume something's wrong with your partner, or you for having chosen your partner. At best, if you are forward thinking and generous minded, you may absolve individuals and blame the relationship. But if you know about differences in conversational style, you can accept that there are differences in habits and assumptions about how to have conversation, show interest, be considerate, and so on. You may not always correctly interpret your partner's intentions, but you will know that if you get a negative impression, it may not be what was intended—and neither are your responses unfounded. If he says he really is interested even though he doesn't seem to be, maybe you should believe what he says and not what you sense.

Sometimes explaining assumptions can help. If a man starts to tell a woman what to do to solve her problem, she may say, "Thanks for the advice but I really don't want to be told what to do. I just want you to listen and say you understand." A man might want to explain, "If I challenge you, it's not to prove you wrong; it's just my way of paying attention to what you're telling me." Both may try either or both to modify their ways of talking and to try to accept what the other does. The important thing is to know that what seem like bad intentions may really be good intentions expressed in a different conversational style. We have to give up our conviction that, as Robin Lakoff put it, "Love means never having to say 'What do you mean?'"

Beauty and the Beast

Dave Barry

If you're a man, at some point a woman will ask you how she looks.

"How do I look?" she'll ask.

You must be careful how you answer this question. The best technique is to form an honest yet sensitive opinion, then collapse on the floor with some kind of fatal seizure. Trust me, this is the easiest way out. Because you will never come up with the right answer.

The problem is that women generally do not think of their looks in the same way that men do. Most men form an opinion of how they look in seventh grade, and they stick to it for the rest of their lives. Some men form the opinion that they are irresistible stud muffins, and they do not change this opinion even when their faces sag and their noses bloat to the size of eggplants and their eyebrows grow together to form what appears to be a giant forehead-dwelling tropical caterpillar.

Most men, I believe, think of themselves as average-looking. Men will think this even if their faces cause heart failure in cattle at a range of three hundred yards. Being average does not bother them; average is fine, for men. This is why men never ask anybody how they look. Their primary form of beauty care is to shave themselves, which is essentially the same form of beauty care that they give to their lawns. If, at the end of his four-minute daily beauty regimen, a man has managed to wipe most of the shaving cream out of his hair and is not bleeding too badly, he feels that he has done all he can, so he stops thinking about his appearance and devotes his mind to more critical issues, such as the Super Bowl.

Women do not look at themselves this way. If I had to express, in three words, what I believe most women think about their appearance those words would be: "not good enough." No matter how attractive a woman may appear to be to others, when she looks at herself in the mirror, she thinks: woof. She thinks that at any moment a municipal animal-control officer is going to throw a net over her and haul her off to the shelter.

Why do women have such low self-esteem? There are many complex psychological and societal reasons, by which I mean Barbie. Girls grow up playing with a doll proportioned such that, if it were a human, it would be seven feet tall and weigh eighty-one pounds, of which fifty-three pounds would be bosoms. This is a difficult appearance standard to live up to, especially when you contrast it with the standard set for little boys by their dolls . . . excuse me, by their action figures. Most of the action figures that my son played with when he was little were hideous-looking. For example, he was very fond of an action figure (part of the He-Man series) called "Buzz-Off," who was part human, part flying insect. Buzz-Off was not a looker. But he was extremely self-confident. You could not imagine Buzz-Off saying to the other action figures: "Do you think these wings make my hips look big?"

But women grow up thinking they need to look like Barbie, which for most women is impossible, although there is a multibillion-dollar beauty industry devoted to convincing women that they must try. I once saw an *Oprah* show wherein supermodel Cindy Crawford dispensed makeup tips to the studio audience. Cindy had all these middle-aged women applying beauty products to their faces; she stressed how important it was to apply them in a certain way, using the tips of their fingers. All the women dutifully did this, even though it was obvious to any sane observer that, no matter how carefully they applied these products, they would never look remotely like Cindy Crawford, who is some kind of genetic mutation.

I'm not saying that men are superior. I'm just saying that you're not going to get a group of middle-aged men to sit in a room and apply cosmetics to themselves under the instruction of Brad Pitt, in hopes of looking more like him. Men would realize that this task was pointless and demeaning. They would find some way to bolster their self-esteem that did not require looking like Brad Pitt. They would say to Brad: "Oh YEAH? Well what do you know about LAWN CARE, pretty boy?"

Of course many women will argue that the reason they become obsessed with trying to look like Cindy Crawford is that men, being as shallow as a drop of spit, WANT women to look that way. To which I have two responses:

1. Hey, just because WE'RE idiots, that does not mean YOU have to be; and

2. Men don't even notice 97 percent of the beauty efforts you make anyway. Take fingernails. The average woman spends 5,000 hours per year worrying about her fingernails; I have never once, in more than forty years of listening to men talk about women, heard a man say, "She has a nice set of fingernails!" Many men would not notice if a woman had upward of four hands.

Anyway, to get back to my original point: If you're a man, and a woman asks you how she looks, you're in big trouble. Obviously, you can't say she looks bad. But you also can't say that she looks great, because she'll think you're lying, because she has spent countless hours, with the help of the multibillion-dollar beauty industry, obsessing about the differences between herself and Cindy Crawford. Also, she suspects that you're not qualified to judge anybody's appearance. This is because you have shaving cream in your hair.

Division and Classification

When you (or iTunes) separate music types into different musical genres, you are dividing what was one general subject—music—into sensible subgroups to make the music fit into categories that can make your music collection better organized and can make the process of finding a particular song or artist easier. Another example would be if you moved and all your glassware was packed in assorted boxes, you then had to make decisions as to how it should be organized. Now you open your kitchen cabinets that hold glassware, and you likely have it separated as to mugs, short glasses, and tall glasses, or some other sensible order. The process of division and classification is common in our everyday life.

The expository style of essays known as division and classification looks to organize and explain subjects or ideas as part of an analytical process.

- *Division* takes a general subject and breaks it into parts and subparts, often in order to explain or justify the parts' crucial importance to the whole. Division essays divide only one category, item, or idea. Although process essays work with parts to create a whole, the goal is to merely describe the steps in the process, where a division essay will describe each part and how it interrelates with the other parts in order to form the whole.
- *Classification* looks to group subjects into categories based on similarities. Classification, like division, is an analytical process, in that it breaks a larger subject into smaller subjects; however, the primary difference is that in classification, the breaking apart is done in order to organize subgroups based on similarities, often with a goal of using the subgroups as a basis of comparison or ranking.

The process of sorting and organizing through division and classification writing can be seen in multiple college courses and in the workplace. In a science course, you may be asked to describe the different parts of a plant in an essay and how those parts work together in keeping the plant alive. In your career as a hospital administrator, you may be asked by the hospital board of directors to create a report on how often nurses have undergone hospital-sponsored trainings in the last year. You decide that the best way to present your report is to categorize the information as to the rankings of the nurses you have: Licensed Practical Nurses (LPNs), Registered Nurses (RNs), and Nurse Practioners (NPs). Division and classification forms of writing are two of the most useful styles of writing due to their applicability in both college and work settings, and they largely function together.

The Process

Purpose

Choosing a topic for your division and classification essay that you not only find of interest, but also one that you feel will lend itself well for classification and / or division, is important. After choosing a topic, spend some time considering your purpose. Is your purpose to inform or to persuade? Knowing your purpose will help you to know how to best sort your topic into sensible subgroups. Also, like all other essays, you need to identify who your reading audience is. Ask yourself, "Is the way in which I've divided a group or an idea, or classified groups based on their similar qualities, the best way to make my essay's purpose clear to my reading audience?"

Thesis

In the following example, Russell Baker, in "The Plot Against the People," states his purpose in his first sentence, which happens to be his thesis statement: "Inanimate objects are classified scientifically into three major categories—those that break down, those that get lost, and those that don't work."

Likely written for a general reading audience, Baker's thesis statement (his purpose statement) identifies his use of classification, but throughout the essay, he also uses division in his use of details that support his purpose in writing. Some of the details in the essay are: how cars always seem to break down in the worst possible places, how keys and gloves and many other items seem to always get lost, and how certain items never really seem to work even when new. Baker combined both classification and then division to support his purpose in writing: to present a humorous view of the frustration most of us feel with inanimate objects we seem to be encumbered with in America and how those objects can seem a subversive plot against us as people.

The thesis you choose should clearly identify the subjects and the process in which you intend to divide or classify. Even though Baker's thesis statement was humorous, he clearly laid out what his principle method of division or classification would be and what his purpose was.

Organization

Prior to writing your paper, there are some pre-writing strategies that will likely help you to decide how to best organize your paper.

- **For division essays:** Brainstorm, list, or think about how your topic can be divided into sensible parts. Once you have done that, create a new list of details that gives information about each part.
- **For classification essays:** Start with the categories (three categories is a common number to explore) that are under your topic "umbrella," and then make a list of details that defines each category.

A division and classification essay, like other essays, needs to have a strong, clear thesis that creates an obvious sense of purpose throughout your essay, plenty of sensory details, description, examples, facts (if needed), comparisons, smooth transitions between paragraphs, and a compelling conclusion. There are, in addition, specific aspects of organizing a division or classification essay to consider.

Several methods of organization can be effectively used within division and classification essays, but some methods work best with one or the other. You will want to choose the method that seems to best suit your purpose.

1. **Division:** Spatial order and order of importance are often the most effective ways to organize division essays. If you are describing the overall messy state of your bedroom, you might move from the floor to the bed and other furniture and then to the ceiling. If you are describing a local "green" group that you belong to with the purpose of informing your readers of its high level of functionality, you will likely describe the factors that you see as most important in its success and later describe the lesser important factors.

2. **Classification:** Spatial order and order of importance can also work well in classification essays, but ranking order is used often. If you were writing about nurses, "nurses" would be your "large" subject. If you were to apply a classification process to the large subject "nurses," you would then look at the sub-groups of nurses mentioned earlier: LPNs, RNs, and NPs. This subgrouping lists nurses from the least-skilled nursing positions to the highest-skilled nursing positions. This ranking process, along with the supporting details you provide, is often used in classification essays as a means to prove or to inform readers of your purpose.

You may want to consider headings and subheadings with these essays, as they can help the reader in his/her understanding of your divisions and classifications, and can help you in your ability to keep specific categories of information set apart and/or in order.

Notes on Punctuation

Lewis Thomas

There are no precise rules about punctuation (Fowler lays out some general advice (as best he can under the complex circumstances of English prose (he points out, for example, that we possess only four stops (the comma, the semicolon, the colon and the period (the question mark and exclamation point are not, strictly speaking, stops; they are indicators of tone (oddly enough, the Greeks employed the semicolon for their question mark (it produces a strange sensation to read a Greek sentence which is a straightforward question: Why weepest thou; (instead of Why weepest thou? (and, of course, there are parentheses (which are surely a kind of punctuation making this whole much more complicated by having to count up the left-handed parentheses in order to be sure of closing with the right number (but if the parentheses were left out, with nothing to work with but the stops, we would have considerably more flexibility in the deploying of layers of meaning than if we tried to separate all the clauses by physical barriers (and in the latter case, while we might have more precision and exactitude for our meaning, we would lose the essential flavor of language, which is its wonderful ambiguity))))))))))))).

The commas are the most useful and usable of all the stops. It is highly important to put them in place as you go along. If you try to come back after doing a paragraph and stick them in the various spots that tempt you you will discover that they tend to swarm like minnows into all sorts of crevices whose existence you hadn't realized and before you know it the whole long sentence becomes immobilized and lashed up squirming in commas. Better to use them sparingly, and with affection, precisely when the need for each one arises, nicely, by itself.

I have grown fond of semicolons in recent years. The semicolon tells you that there is still some question about the preceding full sentence;

something needs to be added; it reminds you sometimes of the Greek usage. It is almost always a greater pleasure to come across a semicolon than a period. The period tells you that that is that; if you didn't get all the meaning you wanted or expected, anyway you got all the writer intended to parcel out and now you have to move along. But with a semicolon there you get a pleasant little feeling of expectancy; there is more to come; read on; it will get clearer.

Colons are a lot less attractive, for several reasons: firstly, they give you the feeling of being rather ordered around, or at least having your nose pointed in a direction you might not be inclined to take if left to yourself, and, secondly, you suspect you're in for one of those sentences that will be labeling the points to be made: firstly, secondly and so forth, with the implication that you haven't sense enough to keep track of a sequence of notions without having them numbered. Also, many writers use this system loosely and incompletely, starting out with number one and number two as though counting off on their fingers but then going on and on without the succession of labels you've been led to expect, leaving you floundering about searching for the ninthly or seventeenthly that ought to be there but isn't.

Exclamation points are the most irritating of all. Look! they say, look at what I just said! How amazing is my thought! It is like being forced to watch someone else's small child jumping up and down crazily in the center of the living room shouting to attract attention. If a sentence really has something of importance to say, something quite remarkable, it doesn't need a mark to point it out. And if it is really, after all, a banal sentence needing more zing, the exclamation point simply emphasizes its banality!

Quotation marks should be used honestly and sparingly, when there is a genuine quotation at hand, and it is necessary to be very rigorous about the words enclosed by the marks. If something is to be quoted, the *exact* words must be used. If part of it must be left out because of space limitations, it is good manners to insert three dots to indicate the omission, but it is unethical to do this if it means connecting two thoughts which the original author did not intend to have tied together. Above all, quotation marks should not be used for ideas that you'd like to disown, things in the air so to speak. Nor should they be put in place around clichés; if you want to use a cliché you must take full responsibility for it yourself and not try to job it off on anon., or on society. The most objectionable misuse of quotation marks, but one which illustrates the dangers of misuse in ordinary prose, is seen in advertising, especially in advertisements for small restaurants, for example "just around the corner," or "a good place to eat." No single, identifiable, citable person ever really said, for the record, "just around the corner," much less "a good place to eat," least likely of all for restaurants of the type that use this type of prose.

The dash is a handy device, informal and essentially playful, telling you that you're about to take off on a different tack but still in some way connected with the present course—only you have to remember that the dash is there, and either put a second dash at the end of the notion to let the reader know that he's back on course, or else end the sentence, as here, with a period.

The greatest danger in punctuation is for poetry. Here it is necessary to be as economical and parsimonious with commas and periods as with the words themselves, and any marks that seem to carry their own subtle meanings, like dashes and little rows of periods, even semicolons and question marks, should be left out altogether rather than inserted to clog up the thing with ambiguity. A single exclamation point in a poem, no matter what else the poem has to say, is enough to destroy the whole work.

The things I like best in T. S. Eliot's poetry, especially in the *Four Quartets,* are the semicolons. You cannot hear them, but they are there, laying out the connections between the images and the ideas. Sometimes you get a glimpse of a semicolon coming, a few lines farther on, and it is like climbing a steep path through woods and seeing a wooden bench just at a bend in the road ahead, a place where you can expect to sit for a moment, catching your breath.

Commas can't do this sort of thing; they can only tell you how the different parts of a complicated thought are to be fitted together, but you can't sit, not even take a breath, just because of a comma,

The Dog Ate My Disk, and Other Tales of Woe

Carolyn Foster Segal

Taped to the door of my office is a cartoon that features a cat explaining to his feline teacher, "The dog ate my homework." It is intended as a gently humorous reminder to my students that I will not accept excuses for late work, and it, like the lengthy warning on my syllabus, has had absolutely no effect. With a show of energy and creativity that would be admirable if applied to the (missing) assignments in question, my students persist, week after week, semester after semester, year after year, in offering excuses about why their work is not ready. Those reasons fall into several broad categories: the family, the best friend, the evils of dorm life, the evils of technology, and the totally bizarre.

The Family

The death of the grandfather/grandmother is, of course, the grandmother of all excuses. What heartless teacher would dare to question a student's grief or veracity? What heartless student would lie, wishing death on a revered family member, just to avoid a deadline? Creative students may win extra extensions (and days off) with a little careful planning and fuller plot development, as in the sequence of "My grandfather/grandmother is sick"; "Now my grandfather/grandmother is in the hospital"; and finally, "We could all see it coming—my grandfather/grandmother is dead."

Another favorite excuse is "the family emergency," which (always) goes like this: "There was an emergency at home, and I had to help my family." It's a lovely sentiment, one that conjures up images of Louisa May Alcott's little women rushing off with baskets of food and copies of

Pilgrim's Progress, but I do not understand why anyone would turn to my most irresponsible students in times of trouble.

The Best Friend

This heartwarming concern for others extends beyond the family to friends, as in, "My best friend was up all night and I had to (a) stay up with her in the dorm, (b) drive her to the hospital, or (c) drive to her college because (1) her boyfriend broke up with her, (2) she was throwing up blood [no one catches a cold anymore; everyone throws up blood], or (3) her grandfather/grandmother died."

At one private university where I worked as an adjunct, I heard an interesting spin that incorporated the motifs of both best friend and dead relative: "My best friend's mother killed herself." One has to admire the cleverness here: A mysterious woman in the prime of her life has allegedly committed suicide, and no professor can prove otherwise! And I admit I was moved, until finally I had to point out to my students that it was amazing how the simple act of my assigning a topic for a paper seemed to drive large numbers of otherwise happy and healthy middle-aged women to their deaths. I was careful to make that point during an off week, during which no deaths were reported.

The Evils of Dorm Life

These stories are usually fairly predictable; almost always feature the evil roommate or hallmate, with my student in the role of the innocent victim; and can be summed up as follows: My roommate, who is a horrible person, likes to party, and I, who am a good person, cannot concentrate on my work when he or she is partying. Variations include stories about the two people next door who were running around and crying loudly last night because (a) one of them had boyfriend/girlfriend problems; (b) one of them was throwing up blood; or (c) someone, somewhere, died. A friend of mine in graduate school had a student who claimed that his roommate attacked him with a hammer. That, in fact, was a true story; it came out in court when the bad roommate was tried for killing his grandfather.

The Evils of Technology

The computer age has revolutionized the student story, inspiring almost as many new excuses as it has Internet businesses. Here are just a few electronically enhanced explanations:

- The computer wouldn't let me save my work.
- The printer wouldn't print.
- The printer wouldn't print this disk.
- The printer wouldn't give me time to proofread.
- The printer made a black line run through all my words, and I know you can't read this, but do you still want it, or wait, here, take my disk. File name? I don't know what you mean.
- I swear I attached it.
- It's my roommate's computer, and she usually helps me, but she had to go to the hospital because she was throwing up blood.
- I did write to the newsgroup, but all my messages came back to me.
- I just found out that all my other newsgroup messages came up under a diferent name. I just want you to know that its really me who wrote all those messages, you can tel which ones our mine because I didnt use the spelcheck! But it was yours truely :) Anyway, just in case you missed those messages or dont belief its my writting. I'll repeat what I sad: I thought the last movie we watched in clas was borring.

The Totally Bizarre

I call the first story "The Pennsylvania Chain Saw Episode." A commuter student called to explain why she had missed my morning class. She had gotten up early so that she would be wide awake for class. Having a bit of extra time, she walked outside to see her neighbor, who was cutting some wood. She called out to him, and he waved back to her with the saw. Wouldn't you know it, the safety catch wasn't on or was broken, and the blade flew right out of the saw and across his lawn and over her fence and across her yard and severed a tendon in her right hand. So she was calling me from the hospital, where she was waiting for surgery. Luckily, she reassured me, she had remembered to bring her paper and a stamped envelope (in a plastic bag, to avoid bloodstains) along with her in the ambulance, and a nurse was mailing everything to me even as we spoke.

That wasn't her first absence. In fact, this student had missed most of the class meetings, and I had already recommended that she withdraw from the course. Now I suggested again that it might be best if she dropped the class. I didn't harp on the absences (what if even some of this story were true?). I did mention that she would need time to recuperate and that making up so much missed work might be difficult. "Oh, no," she said, "I can't drop this course. I had been planning to go on to medical school and become a surgeon, but since I won't be able to operate because of my accident, I'll have to major in English, and this course is more important than ever to me." She did come to the next class, wearing—as evidence of her recent trauma—a bedraggled Ace bandage on her left hand.

You may be thinking that nothing could top that excuse, but in fact I have one more story, provided by the same student, who sent me a letter to explain why her final assignment would be late. While recuperating from her surgery, she had begun corresponding on the Internet with a man who lived in Germany. After a one-week, whirlwind Web romance, they had agreed to meet in Rome, to rendezvous (her phrase) at the papal Easter Mass. Regrettably, the time of her flight made it impossible for her to attend class, but she trusted that I—just this once—would accept late work if the pope wrote a note.

The Ways We Lie

Stephanie Ericsson

The bank called today and I told them my deposit was in the mail, even though I hadn't written a check yet. It'd been a rough day. The baby I'm pregnant with decided to do aerobics on my lungs for two hours, our three-year-old daughter painted the living-room couch with lipstick, the IRS put me on hold for an hour, and I was late to a business meeting because I was tired.

I told my client that traffic had been bad. When my partner came home, his haggard face told me his day hadn't gone any better than mine, so when he asked, "How was your day?" I said, "Oh, fine," knowing that one more straw might break his back. A friend called and wanted to take me to lunch. I said I was busy. Four lies in the course of a day, none of which I felt the least bit guilty about.

We lie. We all do. We exaggerate, we minimize, we avoid confrontation, we spare people's feelings, we conveniently forget, we keep secrets, we justify lying to the big-guy institutions. Like most people, I indulge in small falsehoods and still think of myself as an honest person. Sure I lie, but it doesn't hurt anything. Or does it?

I once tried going a whole week without telling a lie, and it was paralyzing. I discovered that telling the truth all the time is nearly impossible. It means living with some serious consequences: The bank charges me $60 in overdrafts fees, my partner keels over when I tell him about my travails, my client fires me for telling her I didn't feel like being on time, and my friend takes it personally when I say I'm not hungry. There must be some merit to lying.

But if I justify lying, what makes me any different from slick politicians or the corporate robbers who raided the S&L industry? Saying it's okay to lie one way and not another is hedging. I cannot seem to escape the voice deep inside me that tells me: When someone lies, someone loses.

What far-reaching consequences will I, or others, pay as a result of my lie? Will someone's trust be destroyed? Will someone else pay *my* penance because I ducked out? We must consider the *meaning of our actions*. Deception, lies, capital crimes, and misdemeanors all carry meanings. *Webster's* definition of *lie* is specific:

> 1: a false statement or action especially made with the intent to deceive;
> 2: anything that gives or is meant to give a false impression.

A definition like this implies that there are many, many ways to tell a lie. Here are just a few.

The White Lie

A man who won't lie to a woman has very little consideration for her feelings.

—Bergen Evans

The white lie assumes that the truth will cause more damage than a simple, harmless untruth. Telling a friend he looks great when he looks like hell can be based on a decision that the friend needs a compliment more than a frank opinion. But, in effect, it is the liar deciding what is best for the lied to. Ultimately, it is a vote of no confidence. It is an act of subtle arrogance for anyone to decide what is best for someone else.

Yet not all circumstances are quite so cut-and-dried. Take, for instance, the sergeant in Vietnam who knew one of his men was killed in action but listed him as missing so that the man's family would receive indefinite compensation instead of the lump-sum pittance the military gives widows and children. His intent was honorable. Yet for twenty years this family kept their hopes alive, unable to move on to a new life.

Façades

Et tu, Brute?

—Caesar

We all put up façades to one degree or another. When I put on a suit to go to see a client, I feel as though I am putting on another face, obeying the expectation that serious businesspeople wear suits rather than sweatpants. But I'm a writer. Normally, I get up, get the kid off to school, and sit at my computer in my pajamas until four in the afternoon. When

I answer the phone, the caller thinks I'm wearing a suit (though the UPS man knows better).

But façades can be destructive because they are used to seduce others into an illusion. For instance, I recently realized that a former friend was a liar. He presented himself with all the right looks and the right words and offered lots of new consciousness theories, fabulous books to read, and fascinating insights. Then I did some business with him, and the time came for him to pay me. He turned out to be all talk and no walk. I heard a plethora of reasonable excuses, including in-depth descriptions of the big break around the corner. In six months of work, I saw less than a hundred bucks. When I confronted him, he raised both eyebrows and tried to convince me that I'd heard him wrong, that he'd made no commitment to me. A simple investigation into his past revealed a crowded graveyard of disenchanted former friends.

Ignoring the Plain Facts

Well, you must understand that Father Porter is only human.

—A Massachusetts priest

In the '60s, the Catholic Church in Massachusetts began hearing complaints that Father James Porter was sexually molesting children. Rather than relieving him of his duties, the ecclesiastical authorities simply moved him from one parish to another between 1960 and 1967, actually providing him with a fresh supply of unsuspecting families and innocent children to abuse. After treatment in 1967 for pedophilia, he went back to work, this time in Minnesota. The new diocese was aware of Father Porter's obsession with children, but they needed priests and recklessly believed treatment had cured him. More children were abused until he was relieved of his duties a year later. By his own admission, Porter may have abused as many as a hundred children.

Ignoring the facts may not in and of itself be a form of lying, but consider the context of this situation. If a lie is *a false action done with the intent to deceive,* then the Catholic Church's conscious covering for Porter created irreparable consequences. The church became a co-perpetrator with Porter.

Deflecting

When you have no basis for an argument, abuse the plaintiff.

—Cicero

I've discovered that I can keep anyone from seeing the true me by being selectively blatant. I set a precedent of being up-front about intimate issues, but I never bring up the things I truly want to hide; I just let people assume I'm revealing everything. It's an effective way of hiding.

Any good liar knows that the way to perpetuate an untruth is to deflect attention from it. When Clarence Thomas exploded with accusations that the Senate hearings were a "high-tech lynching," he simply switched the focus from a highly charged subject to a radioactive subject. Rather than defending himself, he took the offensive and accused the country of racism. It was a brilliant maneuver. Racism is now politically incorrect in official circles—unlike sexual harassment, which still rewards those who can get away with it.

Some of the most skilled deflectors are passive-aggressive people who, when accused of inappropriate behavior, refuse to respond to the accusations. This you-don't-exist stance infuriates the accuser, who, understandably, screams something obscene out of frustration. The trap is sprung and the act of deflection successful, because now the passive-aggressive person can indignantly say, "Who can talk to someone as unreasonable as you?" The real issue is forgotten and the sins of the original victim become the focus. Feeling guilty of name-calling, the victim is fully tamed and crawls into a hole, ashamed. I have watched this fighting technique work thousands of times in disputes between men and women, and what I've learned is that the real culprit is not necessarily the one who swears the loudest.

Omission

The cruelest lies are often told in silence.

—R. L. Stevenson

Omission involves telling most of the truth minus one or two key facts whose absence changes the story completely. You break a pair of glasses that are guaranteed under normal use and get a new pair, without mentioning that the first pair broke during a rowdy game of basketball. Who hasn't tried something like that? But what about omission of information that could make a difference in how a person lives his or her life?

For instance, one day I found out that rabbinical legends tell of another woman in the Garden of Eden before Eve. I was stunned. The omission of the Sumerian goddess Lilith from Genesis—as well as her demonization by ancient misogynists as an embodiment of female evil—felt like spiritual robbery. I felt like I'd just found out my mother was really my stepmother. To take seriously the tradition that Adam was created out of the same mud as his equal counterpart, Lilith, redefines all of Judeo-Christian history.

Some renegade Catholic feminists introduced me to a view of Lilith that had been suppressed during the many centuries when this strong goddess was seen only as a spirit of evil. Lilith was a proud goddess who defied Adam's need to control her, attempted negotiations, and when this failed, said adios and left the Garden of Eden.

This omission of Lilith from the Bible was a patriarchal strategy to keep women weak. Omitting the strong-woman archetype of Lilith from Western religions and starting the story with Eve the Rib has helped keep Christian and Jewish women believing they were the lesser sex for thousands of years.

Stereotypes and Clichés

Where opinion does not exist, the status quo becomes stereotyped and all originality is discouraged.

—Bertrand Russell

Stereotype and cliché serve a purpose as a form of shorthand. Our need for vast amounts of information in nanoseconds has made the stereotype vital to modern communication. Unfortunately, it often shuts down original thinking, giving those hungry for the truth a candy bar of misinformation instead of a balanced meal. The stereotype explains a situation with just enough truth to seem unquestionable.

All the "isms"—racism, sexism, ageism, et al.—are founded on and fueled by the stereotype and the cliché, which are lies of exaggeration, omission, and ignorance. They are always dangerous. They take a single tree and make it a landscape. They destroy curiosity. They close minds and separate people. The single mother on welfare is assumed to be cheating. Any black male could tell you how much of his identity is obliterated daily by stereotypes. Fat people, ugly people, beautiful people, old people, large-breasted women, short men, the mentally ill, and the homeless all could tell you how much more they are like us than we want to think. I once admitted to a group of people that I had a mouth like a truck driver. Much to my surprise, a man stood up and said, "I'm a truck driver, and I never cuss." Needless to say, I was humbled.

Groupthink

Who is more foolish, the child afraid of the dark, or the man afraid of the light?

—Maurice Freehill

Irving Janis, in *Victims of Group* Think, defines this sort of lie as a psychological phenomenon within decision-making groups in which loyalty to the group has become more important than any other value, with the result that dissent and the appraisal of alternatives are suppressed. If you've ever worked on a committee or in a corporation, you've encountered groupthink. It requires a combination of other forms of lying—ignoring facts, selective memory, omission, and denial, to name a few.

The textbook example of groupthink came on December 7, 1941. From as early as the fall of 1941, the warnings came in, one after another, that Japan was preparing for a massive military operation. The navy command in Hawaii assumed Pearl Harbor was invulnerable—the Japanese weren't stupid enough to attack the United States' most important base. On the other hand, racist stereotypes said the Japanese weren't smart enough to invent a torpedo effective in less than 60 feet of water (the fleet was docked in 30 feet); after all, US technology hadn't been able to do it.

On Friday, December 5, normal weekend leave was granted to all the commanders at Pearl Harbor, even though the Japanese consulate in Hawaii was busy burning papers. Within the tight, good-ole-boy cohesiveness of the US command in Hawaii, the myth of invulnerability stayed well entrenched. No one in the group considered the alternatives. The rest is history.

Out-and-Out Lies

The only form of lying that is beyond reproach is lying for its own sake.

—Oscar Wilde

Of all the ways to lie, I like this one the best, probably because I get tired of trying to figure out the real meanings behind things. At least I can trust the bald-faced lie. I once asked my five-year-old nephew, "Who broke the fence?" (I had seen him do it.) He answered, "The murderers." Who could argue?

At least when this sort of lie is told it can be easily confronted. As the person who is lied to, I know where I stand. The bald-faced lie doesn't toy with my perceptions—it argues with them. It doesn't try to refashion reality, it tries to refute it. *Read my lips. . . .* No sleight of hand. No guessing. If this were the only form of lying, there would be no such things as floating anxiety or the adult-children-of-alcoholics movement.

Dismissal

Pay no attention to that man behind the curtain! I am the Great Oz!

—The Wizard of Oz

Dismissal is perhaps the slipperiest of all lies. Dismissing feelings, perceptions, or even the raw facts of a situation ranks as a kind of lie that can do as much damage to a person as any other kind of lie.

The roots of many mental disorders can be traced back to the dismissal of reality. Imagine that a person is told from the time she is a tot that her perceptions are inaccurate. *"Mommy, I'm scared."* "No you're not, darling." *"I don't like that man next door, he makes me feel icky."* "Johnny, that's a terrible thing to say, of course you like him. You go over there right now and be nice to him."

I've often mused over the idea that madness is actually a sane reaction to an insane world. Psychologist R. D. Laing supports this hypothesis in *Sanity, Madness and the Family,* an account of his investigation into the families of schizophrenics. The common thread that ran through all of the families he studied was a deliberate, staunch dismissal of the patient's perceptions from a very early age. Each of the patients started out with an accurate grasp of reality, which, through meticulous and methodical dismissal, was demolished until the only reality the patient could trust was catatonia.

Dismissal runs the gamut. Mild dismissal can be quite handy for forgiving the foibles of others in our day-to-day lives. Toddlers who have just learned to manipulate their parents' attention sometimes are dismissed out of necessity. Absolute attention from the parents would require so much energy that no one would get to eat dinner. But we must be careful and attentive about how far we take our "necessary" dismissals. Dismissal is a dangerous tool, because it's nothing less than a lie.

Delusion

We lie loudest when we lie to ourselves.

—Eric Hoffer

I could write the book on this one. Delusion, a cousin of dismissal, is the tendency to see excuses as facts. It's a powerful lying tool because it filters out information that contradicts what we want to believe. Alcoholics who believe that the problems in their lives are legitimate reasons for drinking rather than results of the drinking offer the classic example of deluded thinking. Delusion uses the mind's ability to see things in myriad ways to support what it wants to be the truth.

But delusion is also a survival mechanism we all use. If we were to fully contemplate the consequences of our stockpiles of nuclear weapons or global warming, we could hardly function on a day-to-day level. We don't want to incorporate that much reality into our lives because to do so would be paralyzing.

Delusion acts as an adhesive to keep the status quo intact. It shamelessly employs dismissal, omission, and amnesia, among other sorts of lies. Its most cunning defense is that it cannot see itself.

• • •

The liar's punishment [. . .] is that he cannot believe anyone else.

—George Bernard Shaw

These are only a few of the ways we lie. Or are lied to. As I said earlier, it's not easy to entirely eliminate lies from our lives. No matter how pious we may try to be, we will still embellish, hedge, and omit to lubricate the daily machinery of living. But there is a world of difference between telling functional lies and living a lie. Martin Buber once said, "The lie is the spirit committing treason against itself." Our acceptance of lies becomes a cultural cancer that eventually shrouds and reorders reality until moral garbage becomes as invisible to us as water is to a fish.

How much do we tolerate before we become sick and tired of being sick and tired? When will we stand up and declare our *right* to trust? When do we stop accepting that the real truth is in the fine print? Whose lips do we read this year when we vote for president? When will we stop being so reticent about making judgments? When do we stop turning over our personal power and responsibility to liars?

Maybe if I don't tell the bank the check's in the mail I'll be less tolerant of the lies told me every day. A country song I once heard said it all for me: "You've got to stand for something or you'll fall for anything."

Argumentation

Argumentation

Argumentation is about taking a stand on a topic or issue, and, in stating your opinion, you present what you see is the truth. Gaining the skill in writing an effective argumentation has many practical purposes from writing business proposals and reports of findings to letters of complaint to town listers or irresponsible landlords.

In writing an argumentation essay, you are asserting the soundness of your position or belief and presenting evidence that supports your claim in the hope that you will win over skeptical, if not critical readers, or at least get them to consider the possibility. You do this by engaging the readers' **powers of reasoning** by developing a series of statements that lead **logically** to a conclusion.

That does not mean that you cannot make an emotional appeal, but you need to have reasons to back it up. You appeal to reason to show the logic behind your convictions. An argumentation essay is not a rant. There is no bashing of differing opinions. We use what is called Rogerian argument, named after psychologist Carl Rogers:

- You refute the opposition, but there is
    - No confrontation
    - No attacking the opponent
    - Instead, you enter a cooperative relationship with the opponent by acknowledging opposing viewpoints.

Why? To appear reasonable because there are two sides to every opinion. You want to express your view clearly and vigorously but you need to be honest and fair, acknowledging that other people may think differently than you. You don't have to be 100% right.

The Process

There are two steps to an argument essay: (1) Planning and (2) Making your case.

Planning

No matter how passionate you are, you need to think your argument through clearly and present it logically. The basic format for logic we will use is called Toulmin Logic, developed by Professor Stephen E. Toulmin. The steps to thinking an argument through using Toulmin logic are as follows:

- **Choose a topic** in which you have an emotional or intellectual stake and on which you know there are or could be differing opinions or points of view.
- **Make a claim:** Make a well-formed assertion (thesis) that clearly addresses the debatable issue—one that at least some people would disagree with or object to. It should be focused enough so you can prove it in a paper's length. You should be able to reverse your thesis to state the opposite viewpoint. There are various types of claims:
  a. Claims of fact—*Incarcerating criminals does (does not) protect society.*
  b. Claims of value—*Rock music is better than country music*
  c. Claims of policy—*Children over age thirteen should be allowed to vote.*
- **Examine your assertions:** Where does your assertion come from and where does it lead? Ask yourself:
  a. Why am I taking this stand?
  b. What experiences have I had or what principles or values do I have to shape my opinion?
- **Weigh the consequences:** Weigh the pros and cons. What would be the consequences if your assertion came true? For example, what would be the consequences if thirteen-year-olds could vote?
- **Be prepared:** If your position is controversial, you should assume that an informed opposition is looking for holes in your argument.

Making Your Case

- You've got your topic.
- You know where you stand and why.
- You're willing to accept the consequences.
- How are you going to sell your case to the reader?

There are three parts to a typical Toulmin argument: the claim (discussed above), the warrant (otherwise known as the underlying assumptions also described above), and the grounds—the evidence or reasons that explains your claim.

Children over age thirteen should be allowed to vote because . . .

Your thesis should present at least three reasons why you take the stand you do.

> *Cats are better pets than dogs because they are independent, they provide a service by killing mice*

These reasons are supported by evidence in the body of the paper. The evidence includes:

- Facts
- Examples
- Statistics
- Opinions of experts

Your evidence should appeal

- Rationally to your readers' intelligence
- Emotionally to their feelings
- Ethically to show you are to be believed

Criteria for evidence

- ☐ Relevant: It should support your thesis and be pertinent to your argument.
- ☐ Representative: It should represent the full range of opinions about your subject.

- ☐ Sufficient: It should include enough facts, opinions, and exam ples to support your claims and convince the reader.
- ☐ Accurate: Does it ring true or does it make you suspicious?

With the evidence, you must also anticipate the objections. You want to acknowledge them, but you also want to refute them. The balance of pro and con is called dialectic thinking. You want to present the opposition; however, you then want to demolish it point by point.

Your argumentation paper will follow this pattern:

- Present and support your position by making and supporting at least three main points.
- Acknowledge at least two points from the opposition.
- Refute, or counter-argue, the opposition, knocking it flat.
- Conclude by reaffirming your position and hammering your point home.

Letter from a Birmingham Jail

Martin Luther King Jr.

Birmingham City Jail
April 16, 1963

Bishop C. C. J. Carpenter
Bishop Joseph A. Durick
Rabbi Milton L. Grafman
Bishop Paul Hardin
Bishop Nolan B. Harmon
The Reverend George M. Murray
The Reverend Edward V. Ramage
The Reverend Earl Stallings

My dear Fellow Clergymen,

While confined here in Birmingham City jail, I came across your recent statement calling our present activities "unwise and untimely." Seldom, if ever, do I pause to answer criticism of my work and ideas. If I sought to answer all of the criticisms that cross my desk, my secretaries would be engaged in little else in the course of the day and I would have no time for constructive work. But since I feel that you are men of genuine good will and your criticisms are sincerely set forth, I would like to answer your statement in what I hope will be patient and reasonable terms.

I think I should give the reason for my being in Birmingham, since you have been influenced by the argument of "outsiders coming in." I have the honor of serving as president of the Southern Christian Leadership Conference, an organization operating in every Southern state with headquarters in Atlanta, Georgia. We have some eighty-five affiliate organizations all across the South—one being the Alabama

Christian Movement for Human Rights. Whenever necessary and possible we share staff, educational, and financial resources with our affiliates. Several months ago our local affiliate here in Birmingham invited us to be on call to engage in a nonviolent direct action program if such were deemed necessary. We readily consented and when the hour came we lived up to our promises. So I am here, along with several members of my staff, because we were invited here. I am here because I have basic organizational ties here. Beyond this, I am in Birmingham because injustice is here. Just as the eighth century prophets left their little villages and carried their "thus saith the Lord" far beyond the boundaries of their home town, and just as the Apostle Paul left his little village of Tarsus and carried the gospel of Jesus Christ to practically every hamlet and city of the Graeco-Roman world, I too am compelled to carry the gospel of freedom beyond my particular home town. Like Paul, I must constantly respond to the Macedonian call for aid.

Moreover, I am cognizant of the interrelatedness of all communities and states. I cannot sit idly by in Atlanta and not be concerned about what happens in Birmingham. Injustice anywhere is a threat to justice everywhere. We are caught in an inescapable network of mutuality tied in a single garment of destiny. Whatever affects one directly affects all indirectly. Never again can we afford to live with the narrow, provincial "outside agitator" idea. Anyone who lives inside the United States can never be considered an outsider anywhere in this country.

You deplore the demonstrations that are presently taking place in Birmingham. But I am sorry that your statement did not express a similar concern for the conditions that brought the demonstrations into being. I am sure that each of you would want to go beyond the superficial social analyst who looks merely at effects, and does not grapple with underlying causes. I would not hesitate to say that it is unfortunate that so-called demonstrations are taking place in Birmingham at this time, but I would say in more emphatic terms that it is even more unfortunate that the white power structure of this city left the Negro community with no other alternative.

In any nonviolent campaign there are four basic steps: (1) collection of the facts to determine whether injustices are alive; (2) negotiation; (3) self-purification; and (4) direct action. We have gone through all of these steps in Birmingham. There can be no gainsaying of the fact that racial injustice engulfs this community. Birmingham is probably the most thoroughly segregated city in the United States. Its ugly record of police brutality is known in every section of this country. Its unjust treatment of Negroes in the courts is a notorious reality. There have been more unsolved bombings of Negro homes and churches in Birmingham than any city in this nation. These are the hard, brutal, and unbelievable facts. On the basis of these conditions Negro leaders sought to negotiate with the city fathers. But the political leaders consistently refused to engage in good faith negotiation.

Then came the opportunity last September to talk with some of the leaders of the economic community. In these negotiating sessions certain promises were made by the merchants—such as the promise to remove the humiliating racial signs from the stores. On the basis of these promises Rev. Shuttlesworth and the leaders of the Alabama Christian Movement for Human Rights agreed to call a moratorium on any type of demonstrations. As the weeks and months unfolded we realized that we were the victims of a broken promise. The signs remained. As in so many experiences of the past we were confronted with blasted hopes, and the dark shadow of a deep disappointment settled upon us. So we had no alternative except that of preparing for direct action, whereby we would present our very bodies as a means of laying our case before the conscience of the local and national community. We were not unmindful of the difficulties involved. So we decided to go through a process of self-purification. We started having workshops on nonviolence and repeatedly asked ourselves the questions, "Are you able to accept blows without retaliating?" "Are you able to endure the ordeals of jail?"

We decided to set our direct action program around the Easter season, realizing that with the exception of Christmas, this was the largest shopping period of the year. Knowing that a strong economic withdrawal program would be the by-product of direct action, we felt that this was the best time to bring pressure on the merchants for the needed changes. Then it occurred to us that the March election was ahead, and so we speedily decided to postpone action until after election day. When we discovered that Mr. Connor was in the runoff, we decided again to postpone action so that the demonstrations could not be used to cloud the issues. At this time we agreed to begin our nonviolent witness the day after the runoff.

This reveals that we did not move irresponsibly into direct action. We too wanted to see Mr. Connor defeated; so we went through postponement after postponement to aid in this community need. After this we felt that direct action could be delayed no longer.

You may well ask, "Why direct action? Why sit-ins, marches, etc.? Isn't negotiation a better path?" You are exactly right in your call for negotiation. Indeed, this is the purpose of direct action. Nonviolent direct action seeks to create such a crisis and establish such creative tension that a community that has constantly refused to negotiate is forced to confront the issue. It seeks so to dramatize the issue that it can no longer be ignored. I just referred to the creation of tension as a part of the work of the nonviolent resister. This may sound rather shocking. But I must confess that I am not afraid of the word tension. I have earnestly worked and preached against violent tension, but there is a type of constructive nonviolent tension that is necessary for growth. Just as Socrates felt that it was necessary to create a tension in the mind so that individuals could rise from the bondage of myths and half-truths to the unfettered realm of creative analysis and objective appraisal, we must see the need of having nonviolent gadflies to create the kind of tension in society that will help men rise from the dark depths of prejudice and racism to the majestic heights of understanding and brotherhood. So the purpose of the direct action is to create a situation so crisis-packed that it will inevitably open the door to negotiation. We, therefore, concur with you in your call for negotiation. Too long has our beloved Southland been bogged down in the tragic attempt to live in monologue rather than dialogue.

One of the basic points in your statement is that our acts are untimely. Some have asked, "Why didn't you give the new administration time to act?" The only answer that I can give to this inquiry is that the new administration must be prodded about as much as the outgoing one before it acts. We will be sadly mistaken if we feel that the election of Mr. Boutwell will bring the millennium to Birmingham. While Mr. Boutwell is much more articulate and gentle than Mr. Connor, they are both segregationists dedicated to the task of maintaining the status quo. The hope I see in Mr. Boutwell is that he will be reasonable enough to see the futility of massive resistance to desegregation. But he will not see this without pressure from the devotees of civil rights. My friends, I must say to you that we have not made a single gain in civil rights without determined legal and nonviolent pressure. History is the long and tragic story of the fact that privileged groups seldom give up their privileges voluntarily. Individuals may see the moral light and voluntarily give up their unjust posture; but as Reinhold Niebuhr has reminded us, groups are more immoral than individuals.

We know through painful experience that freedom is never voluntarily given by the oppressor; it must be demanded by the oppressed. Frankly I have never yet engaged in a direct action movement that was "well timed," according to the timetable of those who have not suffered unduly from the disease of segregation. For years now I have heard the word "Wait!" It rings in the ear of every Negro with a piercing familiarity.

This "wait" has almost always meant "never." It has been a tranquilizing thalidomide, relieving the emotional stress for a moment, only to give birth to an ill-formed infant of frustration. We must come to see with the distinguished jurist of yesterday that "justice too long delayed is justice denied." We have waited for more than three hundred and forty years for our constitutional and God-given rights. The nations of Asia and Africa are moving with jet-like speed toward the goal of political independence, and we still creep at horse and buggy pace toward the gaining of a cup of coffee at a lunch counter.

I guess it is easy for those who have never felt the stinging darts of segregation to say wait. But when you have seen vicious mobs lynch your mothers and fathers at will and drown your sisters and brothers at whim; when you have seen hate-filled policemen curse, kick, brutalize, and even kill your black brothers and sisters with impunity; when you see the vast majority of your twenty million Negro brothers smothering in an airtight cage of poverty in the midst of an affluent society; when you suddenly find your tongue twisted and your speech stammering as you seek to explain to your six-year-old daughter why she can't go to the public amusement park that has just been advertised on television, and see tears welling up in her little eyes when she is told that Funtown is closed to colored children, and see the depressing clouds of inferiority begin to form in her little mental sky, and see her begin to distort her little personality by unconsciously developing a bitterness toward white people; when you have to concoct an answer for a five-year-old son asking in agonizing pathos: "Daddy, why do white people treat colored people so mean?"; when you take a cross-country drive and find it necessary to sleep night after night in the uncomfortable corners of your automobile because no motel will accept you; when you are humiliated day in and day out by nagging signs reading "white" men and "colored"; when your first name becomes "nigger" and your middle name becomes "boy" (however old you are) and your last name becomes "John," and when your wife and mother are never given the respected title "Mrs."; when you are harried by day and haunted by night by the fact that you are a Negro, living constantly at tip-toe stance never quite knowing what to expect next, and plagued with inner fears and outer resentments; when you are forever fighting a degenerating sense of "nobodiness";—then you will understand why we find it very difficult to wait. There comes a time when the cup of our endurance runs over, and men are no longer willing to be plunged into an abyss of injustice where they experience the bleakness of a corroding despair. I hope, sirs, you can understand our legitimate and unavoidable impatience.

You express a great deal of anxiety over our willingness to break laws. This is certainly a legitimate concern. Since we so diligently urge people to obey the Supreme Court's decision of 1954 outlawing segregation in the public schools, it is rather strange and paradoxical to find us consciously breaking laws. One may well ask, "How can you advocate breaking some laws and obeying others?" The answer is found in the fact that there are two types of laws. There are *just* laws and there are *unjust* laws. I would be the first to advocate obeying just laws. One has not only a legal but moral responsibility to obey just laws. Conversely, one has a moral responsibility to disobey unjust laws. I would agree with Saint Augustine that "An unjust law is no law at all."

Now what is the difference between the two? How does one determine when a law is just or unjust? A just law is a man-made code that squares with the moral law or the law of God. An unjust law is a code that is out of harmony with the moral law. To put it in the terms of Saint Thomas Aquinas, an unjust law is a human law that is not rooted in eternal and natural law. Any law that uplifts human personality is just. Any law that degrades human personality is unjust. All segregation statutes are unjust because segregation distorts the soul and damages the personality. It gives the segregator a false sense of superiority and the segregated a false sense of inferiority. To use the words of Martin Buber, the great Jewish philosopher, segregation substitutes an "I-it" relationship for the "I-thou" relationship, and ends up relegating persons to the status of things. So segregation is not only politically, economically, and sociologically unsound, but it is morally wrong and sinful. Paul Tillich has said that sin is separation. Isn't segregation an existential expression of man's tragic separation, an expression of his awful estrangement, his terrible sinfulness? So I can urge men to obey the 1954 decision of the Supreme Court because it is morally right, and I can urge them to disobey segregation ordinances because they are morally wrong.

Let us turn to a more concrete example of just and unjust laws. An unjust law is a code that a majority inflicts on a minority that is not binding on itself. This is *difference* made legal. On the other hand a just law is a code that a majority compels a minority to follow that it is willing to follow itself. This is *sameness* made legal.

Let me give another explanation. An unjust law is a code inflicted upon a minority which that minority had no part in enacting or creating because they did not have the unhampered right to vote. Who can say the legislature of Alabama which set up the segregation laws was democratically elected? Throughout the State of Alabama all types of conniving methods are used to prevent Negroes from becoming registered voters and there are some counties without a single Negro registered to vote despite the fact that the Negro constitutes a majority of the population. Can any law set up in such a state be considered democratically structured?

These are just a few examples of unjust and just laws. There are some instances when a law is just on its face but unjust in its application. For instance, I was arrested Friday on a charge of parading without a permit. Now there is nothing wrong with an ordinance which requires a permit for a parade, but when the ordinance is used to preserve segregation and to deny citizens the First Amendment privilege of peaceful assembly and peaceful protest, then it becomes unjust.

I hope you can see the distinction I am trying to point out. In no sense do I advocate evading or defying the law as the rabid segregationist would do. This would lead to anarchy. One who breaks an unjust law must do it *openly, lovingly* (not hatefully as the white mothers did in New Orleans when they were seen on television screaming "nigger, nigger, nigger") and with a willingness to accept the penalty. I submit that an individual who breaks a law that conscience tells him is unjust, and willingly accepts the penalty by staying in jail to arouse the conscience of the community over its injustice, is in reality expressing the very highest respect for law.

Of course there is nothing new about this kind of civil disobedience. It was seen sublimely in the refusal of Shadrach, Meshach, and Abednego to obey the unjust laws of Nebuchadnezzar because a higher moral law was involved. It was practiced superbly by the early Christians who were willing to face hungry lions and the excruciating pain of chopping blocks, before submitting to certain very unjust laws of the Roman Empire. To a degree our academic freedom is a reality today because Socrates practiced civil disobedience.

We can never forget that everything Hitler did in Germany was "legal" and everything the Hungarian freedom fighters did in Hungary was "illegal." It was "illegal" to aid and comfort a Jew in Hitler's Germany. But I am sure that, if I had lived in Germany during that time, I would have aided and comforted my Jewish brothers even though it was illegal. If I lived in a communist country today where certain principles dear to the Christian faith are suppressed, I believe I would openly advocate disobeying these antireligious laws.

I must make two honest confessions to you, my Christian and Jewish brothers. First I must confess that over the last few years I have been gravely disappointed with the white moderate. I have almost reached the regrettable conclusion that the Negroes' great stumbling block in the stride toward freedom is not the White Citizens' "Councilor" or the Ku Klux Klanner, but the white moderate who is more devoted to "order" than to justice; who prefers a negative peace which is the absence of tension to a positive peace which is the presence of justice; who constantly says "I agree with you in the goal you seek, but I can't agree with your methods of direct action"; who paternalistically feels that he can set the timetable for another man's freedom; who lives by the myth of time and who constantly advises the Negro to wait until a "more convenient season." Shallow understanding from people of good will is more frustrating than absolute misunderstanding from people of ill will. Lukewarm acceptance is much more bewildering than outright rejection.

I had hoped that the white moderate would understand that law and order exist for the purpose of establishing justice, and that when they fail to do this they become the dangerously structured dams that block the flow of social progress. I had hoped that the white moderate would understand that the present tension in the South is merely a necessary phase of the transition from an obnoxious negative peace, where the Negro passively accepted his unjust plight, to a substance-filled positive peace, where all men will respect the dignity and worth of human personality. Actually, we who engage in nonviolent direct action are not the creators of tension. We merely bring to the surface the hidden tension that is already alive. We bring it out in the open where it can be seen and dealt with. Like a boil that can never be cured as long as it is covered up but must be opened with all its pus-flowing ugliness to the natural medicines of air and light, injustice must likewise be exposed, with all of the tension its exposing creates, to the light of human conscience and the air of national opinion before it can be cured.

In your statement you asserted that our actions, even though peaceful, must be condemned because they precipitate violence. But can this assertion be logically made? Isn't this like condemning the robbed man because his possession of money precipitated the evil act of robbery? Isn't this like condemning Socrates because his unswerving commitment to truth and his philosophical delvings precipitated the misguided popular mind to make him drink the hemlock? Isn't this like condemning Jesus because His unique God consciousness and never-ceasing devotion to His will precipitated the evil act of crucifixion? We must come to see, as federal courts have consistently affirmed, that it is immoral to urge an individual to withdraw his efforts to gain his basic constitutional rights because the quest precipitates violence. Society must protect the robbed and punish the robber.

I had also hoped that the white moderate would reject the myth of time. I received a letter this morning from a white brother in Texas which said: "All Christians know that the colored people will receive equal rights eventually, but is it possible that you are in too great of a religious hurry? It has taken Christianity almost 2000 years to accomplish what it has. The teachings of Christ take time to come to earth." All that is said here grows out of a tragic misconception of time. It is the strangely irrational notion that there is something in the very flow of time that will inevitably cure all ills. Actually time is neutral. It can be used either destructively or constructively. I am coming to feel that the people of ill will have used time much more effectively than the people of good will. We will have to repent in this generation not merely for the vitriolic words and actions of the bad people, but for the appalling silence of the good people. We must come to see that human progress never rolls in on wheels of inevitability. It comes through the tireless efforts and persistent work of men willing to be co-workers with God, and without this hard work time itself becomes an ally of the forces of social stagnation.

We must use time creatively, and forever realize that the time is always ripe to do right. Now is the time to make real the promise of democracy, and transform our pending national elegy into a creative psalm of brotherhood. Now is the time to lift our national policy from the quicksand of racial injustice to the solid rock of human dignity.

You spoke of our activity in Birmingham as extreme. At first I was rather disappointed that fellow clergymen would see my nonviolent efforts as those of the extremist. I started thinking about the fact that I stand in the middle of two opposing forces in the Negro community. One is a force of complacency made up of Negroes who, as a result of long years of oppression, have been so completely drained of self-respect and a sense of "somebodiness" that they have adjusted to segregation, and of a few Negroes in the middle class who, because of a degree of academic and economic security, and because at points they profit by segregation, have unconsciously become insensitive to the problems of the masses. The other force is one of bitterness and hatred and comes perilously close to advocating violence. It is expressed in the various black nationalist groups that are springing up over the nation, the largest and best known being Elijah Muhammad's Muslim movement. This movement is nourished by the contemporary frustration over the continued existence of racial discrimination. It is made up of people who have lost faith in America, who have absolutely repudiated Christianity, and who have concluded that the white man is an incurable "devil." I have tried to stand between these two forces saying that we need not follow the "do-nothingism" of the complacent or the hatred and despair of the black nationalist. There is the more excellent way of love and nonviolent protest. I'm grateful to God that, through the Negro church, the dimension of nonviolence entered our struggle. If this philosophy had not emerged I am convinced that by now many streets of the South would be flowing with floods of blood. And I am further convinced that if our white brothers dismiss us as "rabble rousers" and "outside agitators"—those of us who are working through the channels of nonviolent direct action—and refuse to support our nonviolent efforts, millions of Negroes, out of frustration and despair, will seek solace and security in black nationalist ideologies, a development that will lead inevitably to a frightening racial nightmare.

Oppressed people cannot remain oppressed forever. The urge for freedom will eventually come. This is what has happened to the American Negro. Something within has reminded him of his birthright of freedom; something without has reminded him that he can gain it. Consciously and unconsciously, he has been swept in by what the Germans call the *Zeitgeist*, and with his black brothers of Africa, and his brown and yellow brothers of Asia, South America, and the Caribbean, he is moving with a sense of cosmic urgency toward the promised land of racial justice. Recognizing this vital urge that has engulfed the Negro community, one should readily understand public demonstrations. The Negro has many pent-up resentments and latent frustrations. He has to get them out. So let him march sometime; let him have his prayer pilgrimages to the city hall; understand why he must have sit-ins and freedom rides. If his repressed emotions do not come out in these nonviolent ways, they will come out in ominous expressions of violence. This is not a threat; it is a fact of history. So I have not said to my people, "Get rid of your discontent." But I have tried to say that this normal and healthy discontent can be channeled through the creative outlet of nonviolent direct action. Now this approach is being dismissed as extremist. I must admit that I was initially disappointed in being so categorized.

But as I continued to think about the matter I gradually gained a bit of satisfaction from being considered an extremist. Was not Jesus an extremist in love? "Love your enemies, bless them that curse you, pray for them that despitefully use you." Was not Amos an extremist for justice—"Let justice roll down like waters and righteousness like a mighty stream." Was not Paul an extremist for the gospel of Jesus Christ—"I bear in my body the marks of the Lord Jesus." Was not Martin Luther an extremist—"Here I stand; I can do none other so help me God." Was not John Bunyan an extremist—"I will stay in jail to the end of my days before I make a butchery of my conscience." Was not Abraham Lincoln an extremist—"This nation cannot survive half slave and half free." Was not Thomas Jefferson an extremist—"We hold these truths to be self-evident that all men are created equal." So the question is not whether we will be extremist but what kind of extremist will we be. Will we be extremists for hate or will we be extremists for love? Will we be extremists for the preservation of injustice—or will we be extremists for the cause of justice? In that dramatic scene on Calvary's hill three men were crucified. We must never forget that all three were crucified for the same crime—the crime of extremism. Two were extremists for immorality, and thus fell below their environment. The other, Jesus Christ, was an extremist for love, truth, and goodness, and thereby rose above His environment. So, after all, maybe the South, the nation, and the world are in dire need of creative extremists.

I had hoped that the white moderate would see this. Maybe I was too optimistic. Maybe I expected too much. I guess I should have realized that few members of a race that has oppressed another race can understand or appreciate the deep groans and passionate yearnings of those that have been oppressed, and still fewer have the vision to see that injustice must be rooted out by strong, persistent, and determined action. I am thankful, however, that some of our white brothers have grasped the meaning of this social revolution and committed themselves to it. They are still all too small in quantity, but they are big in quality. Some like Ralph McGill, Lillian Smith, Harry Golden, and James Dabbs have written about our struggle in eloquent, prophetic, and understanding terms. Others have marched with us down nameless streets of the South. They have languished in filthy, roach-infested jails, suffering the abuse and brutality of angry policemen who look on them as "dirty nigger lovers." They, unlike so many of their moderate brothers and sisters, have recognized the urgency of the moment and sensed the need for powerful "action" antidotes to combat the disease of segregation.

Let me rush on to mention my other disappointment. I have been so greatly disappointed with the white Church and its leadership. Of course there are some notable exceptions. I am not unmindful of the fact that each of you has taken some significant stands on this issue. I commend you, Rev. Stallings, for your Christian stand on this past Sunday, in welcoming Negroes to your service on a non-segregated basis. I commend the Catholic leaders of this state for integrating Springhill College several years ago.

But despite these notable exceptions I must honestly reiterate that I have been disappointed with the Church. I do not say that as one of those negative critics who can always find something wrong with the Church. I say it as a minister of the gospel, who loves the Church; who was nurtured in its bosom; who has been sustained by its spiritual blessings and who will remain true to it as long as the cord of life shall lengthen.

I had the strange feeling when I was suddenly catapulted into the leadership of the bus protest in Montgomery several years ago that we would have the support of the white Church. I felt that the white ministers, priests, and rabbis of the South would be some of our strongest allies. Instead, some have been outright opponents, refusing to understand the freedom movement and misrepresenting its leaders; all too many others have been more cautious than courageous and have remained silent behind the anesthetizing security of stained glass windows.

In spite of my shattered dreams of the past, I came to Birmingham with the hope that the white religious leadership of this community would see the justice of our cause and, with deep moral concern, serve as the channel through which our just grievances could get to the power structure. I had hoped that each of you would understand. But again I have been disappointed.

I have heard numerous religious leaders of the South call upon their worshippers to comply with a desegregation decision because it is the law, but I have longed to hear white ministers say: "Follow this decree because integration is morally right and the Negro is your brother." In the midst of blatant injustices inflicted upon the Negro, I have watched white churches stand on the sideline and merely mouth pious irrelevancies and sanctimonious trivialities. In the midst of a mighty struggle to rid our nation of racial and economic injustice, I have heard so many ministers say, "Those are social issues with which the Gospel has no real concern." and I have watched so many churches commit themselves to a completely otherworldly religion which made a strange distinction between body and soul, the sacred and the secular.

So here we are moving toward the exit of the twentieth century with a religious community largely adjusted to the status quo, standing as a taillight behind other community agencies rather than a headlight leading men to higher levels of justice.

I have travelled the length and breadth of Alabama, Mississippi, and all the other Southern states. On sweltering summer days and crisp autumn mornings I have looked at her beautiful churches with their spires pointing heavenward. I have beheld the impressive outlay of her massive religious education buildings. Over and over again I have found myself asking: "Who worships here? Who is their God? Where were their voices when the lips of Governor Barnett dripped with words of interposition and nullification? Where were they when Governor Wallace gave the clarion call for defiance and hatred? Where were their voices of support when tired, bruised, and weary Negro men and women decided to rise from the dark dungeons of complacency to the bright hills of creative protest?"

Yes, these questions are still in my mind. In deep disappointment, I have wept over the laxity of the Church. But be assured that my tears have been tears of love. There can be no deep disappointment where there is not deep love. Yes, I love the Church; I love her sacred walls. How could I do otherwise? I am in the rather unique position of being the son, the grandson, and the great-grandson of preachers. Yes, I see the Church as the body of Christ. But, oh! How we have blemished and scarred that body through social neglect and fear of being nonconformist.

There was a time when the Church was very powerful. It was during that period when the early Christians rejoiced when they were deemed worthy to suffer for what they believed. In those days the Church was not merely a thermometer that recorded the ideas and principles of popular opinion; it was a thermostat that transformed the mores of society. Wherever the early Christians entered a town the power structure got disturbed and immediately sought to convict them for being "disturbers of the peace" and "outside agitators." But they went on with the conviction that they were a "colony of heaven" and had to obey God rather than man. They were small in number but big in commitment. They were too God-intoxicated to be "astronomically intimidated." They brought an end to such ancient evils as infanticide and gladiatorial contest.

Things are different now. The contemporary Church is so often a weak, ineffectual voice with an uncertain sound. It is so often the arch-supporter of the status quo. Far from being disturbed by the presence of the Church, the power structure of the average community is consoled by the Church's silent and often vocal sanction of things as they are.

But the judgment of God is upon the Church as never before. If the Church of today does not recapture the sacrificial spirit of the early Church, it will lose its authentic ring, forfeit the loyalty of millions, and be dismissed as an irrelevant social club with no meaning for the twentieth century. I am meeting young people every day whose disappointment with the Church has risen to outright disgust.

Maybe again I have been too optimistic. Is organized religion too inextricably bound to the status quo to save our nation and the world? Maybe I must turn my faith to the inner spiritual Church, the church within the Church, as the true *eccelesia* and the hope of the world. But again I am thankful to God that some noble souls from the ranks of organized religion have broken loose from the paralyzing chains of conformity and joined us as active partners in the struggle for freedom. They have left their secure congregations and walked the streets of Albany, Georgia, with us. They have gone through the highways of the South on torturous rides for freedom. Yes, they have gone to jail with us. Some have been kicked out of their churches and lost the support of their bishops and fellow ministers. But they have gone with the faith that right defeated is stronger than evil triumphant. These men have been the leaven in the lump of the race. Their witness has been the spiritual salt that has preserved the true meaning of the Gospel in these troubled times. They have carved a tunnel of hope through the dark mountain of disappointment.

I hope the Church as a whole will meet the challenge of this decisive hour. But even if the Church does not come to the aid of justice, I have no despair about the future. I have no fear about the outcome of our struggle in Birmingham, even if our motives are presently misunderstood. We will reach the goal of freedom in Birmingham and all over the nation, because the goal of America is freedom. Abused and scorned though we may be, our destiny is tied up with the destiny of America. Before the pilgrims landed at Plymouth, we were here. Before the pen of Jefferson etched across the pages of history the majestic words of the Declaration of Independence, we were here. For more than two centuries our foreparents labored in this country without wages; they made cotton "king"; and they built the homes of their masters in the midst of brutal injustice and shameful humiliation—and yet out of a bottomless vitality they continued to thrive and develop. If the inexpressible cruelties of slavery could not stop us, the opposition we now face will surely fail. We will win our freedom because the sacred heritage of our nation and the eternal will of God are surely embodied in our echoing demands.

I must close now. But before closing I am impelled to mention one other point in your statement that troubled me profoundly. You warmly commended the Birmingham police force for keeping "order" and "preventing violence." I don't believe you would have so warmly commended the police force if you had seen its angry violent dogs literally biting six unarmed, nonviolent Negroes. I don't believe you would so quickly commend the policemen if you would observe their ugly and inhuman treatment of Negroes here in the city jail; if you would watch them push and curse old Negro women and young Negro girls; if you would see them slap and kick old Negro men and young Negro boys; if you will observe them, as they have done on two occasions, refuse to give us food because we wanted to sing our grace together. I'm sorry that I can't join you in your praise for the police department.

It is true that they have been rather disciplined in their public handling of the demonstrators. In this sense they have been rather publicly "nonviolent." But for what purpose? To preserve the evil system of segregation. Over the last few years I have consistently preached that nonviolence demands that the means we use must be as pure as the ends we seek. So I have tried to make it clear that it is wrong to use immoral means to attain moral ends. But now I must affirm that it is just as wrong, or even more so, to use moral means to preserve immoral ends. Maybe Mr. Connor and his policemen have been publicly nonviolent, as Chief Prichett was in Albany, Georgia, but they have used the moral means of nonviolence to maintain the immoral end of flagrant racial injustice. T. S. Eliot has said that there is no greater treason than to do the right deed for the wrong reason.

I wish you had commended the Negro sit-inners and demonstrators of Birmingham for their sublime courage, their willingness to suffer, and their amazing discipline in the midst of the most inhuman provocation. One day the South will recognize its real heroes. They will be the James Merediths, courageously and with a majestic sense of purpose, facing jeering and hostile mobs and the agonizing loneliness that characterizes the life of the pioneer. They will be old, oppressed, battered Negro women, symbolized in a seventy-two year old woman of Montgomery, Alabama, who rose up with a sense of dignity and with her people decided not to ride the segregated buses, and responded to one who inquired about her tiredness with ungrammatical profundity: "My feets is tired, but my soul is rested." They will be young high school and college students, young ministers of the gospel and a host of the elders, courageously and nonviolently sitting in at lunch counters and willingly going to jail for conscience sake. One day the South will know that when these disinherited children of God sat down at lunch counters they were in reality standing up for the best in the American dream and the most sacred values in our Judeo-Christian heritage, and thus carrying our whole nation back to great wells of democracy which were dug deep by the founding fathers in the formulation of the Constitution and the Declaration of Independence.

Never before have I written a letter this long (or should I say a book?). I'm afraid that it is much too long to take your precious time. I can assure you that it would have been much shorter if I had been writing from a comfortable desk, but what else is there to do when you are alone for days in the dull monotony of a narrow jail cell other than write long letters, think strange thoughts, and pray long prayers?

If I have said anything in this letter that is an overstatement of the truth and is indicative of an unreasonable impatience, I beg you to forgive me. If I have said anything in this letter that is an understatement of the truth and is indicative of my having a patience that makes me patient with anything less than brotherhood, I beg God to forgive me.

I hope this letter finds you strong in the faith. I also hope that circumstances will soon make it possible for me to meet each of you, not as an integrationist or a civil rights leader, but as a fellow clergyman and a Christian brother. Let us all hope that the dark clouds of racial prejudice will soon pass away and the deep fog of misunderstanding will be lifted from our fear-drenched communities and in some not too distant tomorrow the radiant stars of love and brotherhood will shine over our great nation with all of their scintillating beauty.

Yours for the cause of Peace and Brotherhood

Martin Luther King Jr.

No Time to Read?

David McCullough

Once upon a time in the dead of winter in the Dakota territory, Theodore Roosevelt took off in a makeshift boat down the Little Missouri River in pursuit of a couple of thieves who had stolen his prized rowboat. After several days on the river, he caught up and got the draw on them with his trusty Winchester, at which point they surrendered. Then Roosevelt set off in a borrowed wagon to haul the thieves cross-country to justice. They headed across the snow-covered wastes of the Badlands to the railhead at Dickinson, and Roosevelt walked the whole way, the entire 40 miles. It was an astonishing feat, what might be called a defining moment in Roosevelt's eventful life. But what makes it especially memorable is that during that time, he managed to read all of *Anna Karenina.*

I often think of that when I hear people say that they haven't time to read.

Reportedly, the average American does have time to watch 28 hours of television every week, or approximately four hours a day. The average person, I'm told, reads at a rate of 250 words per minute. So, based on these statistics, were the average American to spend those four hours a day with a book instead of watching television, he or she could, in a week, read: the complete poems of T. S. Eliot two: plays, by Thornton Wilder, including *Our Town,* the complete poems of Maya Angelou; Faulkner's *The Sound and the Fury; The Great Gatsby;* and The Book of Psalms.

That's all in one week.

But a week is a long time by today's standards, when information is available at the touch of a finger. Information has become an industry, a commodity to be packaged, promoted and marketed incessantly. The tools for "accessing" data grow ever more wondrous and ubiquitous and essential if we're to keep in step, we've come to believe. All hail the web, the Internet, the Information Highway.

We're being sold the idea that information is learning, and we're being sold a bill of goods.

Information isn't learning. It isn't wisdom. It isn't common sense necessarily. It isn't kindness. Or good judgment. Or imagination. Or a sense of humor. Or courage. Information doesn't tell us right from wrong.

Knowing the area of the state of Connecticut in square miles, or the date on which the United Nations Charter was signed, or the jumping capacity of a flea may be useful, but it isn't learning of itself.

The greatest of all avenues to learning—to wisdom, adventure, pleasure, insight, to understanding human nature, understanding ourselves and our world and our place in it—is in reading books.

Read for life, all your life. Nothing ever invented provides such sustenance, such infinite reward for time spent, as a good book.

Read for pleasure. Read what you like, and all you like. Read literally to your heart's content. Let one book lead to another. They nearly always do.

Take up a great author, new or old, and read everything he or she has written. Read about places you've never been. Read biography, history. Read books that changed history: Tom Paine's *Common Sense;* the autobiography of Frederick Douglass; Rachel Carson's *Silent Spring.*

Read those books you know you're supposed to have read and imagine as dreary. A classic may be defined as a book that stays long in print, and a book stays long in print only because it is exceptional. Why exclude the exceptional from your experience?

Go back and read again the books written supposedly for children, especially if you think they are only for children. My first choice would be *The Wind in the Willows.* There's much, very much, you can learn in the company of Toad, Rat and Mole.

And when you read a book you love—a book you feel has enlarged the experience of being alive, a book that "lights the fire"—then spread the word.

To carry a book, with you wherever you go is old advice and good advice, John Adams urged his son, John Quincy, to carry a volume of poetry. "You'll never be alone," he said, "with a poet in your pocket."

The Real Generation Gap

Marianne M. Jennings

Born in 1980, today's college freshmen are part of "Generation X." They came into the world long after Vietnam, Richard Nixon, and Watergate. They never saw Senator Sam Ervin's eyebrows. Can you imagine? They were also born after *Saturday Night Fever.* They do not know John Travolta has had two movie careers. Nor do they know what it is like to live in a society in which marriage is the predominant social institution. Unfortunately, they do know about broken homes and "single-parent families." And they know what it is like to be the children of child care because 67 percent of them have mothers working outside their homes.

The members of Generation X know a lot about Madonna, Princess Diana, G. I. Jane, Michael Jackson, Michael Jordan, and Mike Tyson. They know nothing at all about Kate Smith, Mother Teresa, Rosie the Riveter, John Wayne, Babe Ruth, and Audie Murphy. Almost without exception, their favorite role models are the type of celebrities seen on MTV, ESPN, and the cover of *People.*

One disturbing poll reveals that nearly 100 percent of today's youth can name the "Three Stooges," but not even 1 percent can name three justices on the U. S. Supreme Court. Seventy-three percent want to start their own businesses, but 53 percent voted for small business foe Bill Clinton. Only 19 percent attend church regularly. Only 1 percent include a member of the clergy on their lists of most admired individuals.

What all these statistics tell us is that the gap between generations is wider than ever before. There are five areas in which the gap is most pronounced: skills, knowledge, critical thinking, work, and morality.

The Skills Gap

Iowa test scores have been a standard measurement of academic achievement for many decades. And what they have been measuring lately is frightening. Students who should be scoring at the ninetieth percentile are barely scoring at the seventieth; those who should be at the seventieth are hovering between the thirtieth and fortieth. Between 70 and 90 percent of all students entering the California State University system have to take some form of remedial course work in basic subjects like English and math. Eighty-seven percent of students entering New York community colleges flunk the placement test—they can't even pass the test that would put them into remedial courses! As New York Mayor Rudolph Giuliani observed several years ago, if skills actually determined entrance into the New York system of higher education, three of every four students would probably be denied admission. (The state has recently begun to administer such tests, and it appears that Giuliani was right.) It is also a matter of public record that national ACT and SAT college entrance test scores are steadily declining despite "adjustments" designed to boost them artificially.

Yet one-third of many high schools' students maintain 4.0 (straight A) grade point averages. Why? Because grade inflation, which occurs at every level of education, is rampant. My daughter Sarah has been in the public school system since the third grade, and she is living proof. She has consistently received good grades without the benefit of a good education.

When she enrolled in an algebra class in the eighth grade, I offered to help her with her homework. She took me up on this offer one evening when we were sitting together at the kitchen table. The first problem was: "What is 10 percent of 470?" I was stunned to discover that Sarah couldn't solve it without the aid of a calculator. Another problem involved determining 25 percent of a given figure. She not only didn't know the answer, but she didn't know that this percentage could be expressed as "one-quarter" or "one-fourth."

Here was my own flesh and blood—my straight-A student! I couldn't help asking, "Are the other kids this dumb?" Without missing a beat, Sarah replied, "Oh, they're much dumber." She may be right. On the most recent International Math and Science Survey, which tests students from forty-two countries, one-third of all American high school seniors could not compute the price of a $1,250 stereo that was discounted by 20 percent.

The Knowledge Gap

Algebra is not the only area where today's students have trouble. Hillsdale College President George Roche writes, "Tens of thousands of students do not know when Columbus sailed to the New World, who wrote the Declaration of Independence, or why the Civil War was fought." Part of the problem is that most parents don't realize that what is being taught in modern public schools is actually widening the knowledge gap between them and their children.

One of the most popular history textbooks, produced as a result of the campaign for national education standards in the late 1980s, disparages the "Father of Our Country." George Washington was not, the authors of *The United States: In the Course of Human Events* contend, really successful as a soldier, as a politician, or as a human being. Much is made of Thomas Jefferson's subjective observation that Washington was possessed of "a heart that was not warm in its affections."

How is Generation X ever going to find out that Washington the general did more than any individual to win the war that established our nation? Or that Washington the president risked his reputation and his career to ensure that we would have limited government, a sound economy, and a virtuous citizenry? Or that Washington the man constantly performed acts of kindness and charity for others, including Jefferson? It certainly isn't going to learn such important lessons from a textbook that claims Washington was not much of a man because he did not, in modern lingo, "feel our pain."

Special sections in each chapter feature biographies of people who have made a difference in history. Almost all are politically correct minorities and/or females. One, for example, is a female astronaut. The authors allege that she was unfairly excluded from Project Mercury because she had no flight experience. This, of course, is characterized as an insufficient reason to deny her the "right" to participate.

The seventeenth-century English philosopher John Locke is not mentioned—there is no room, evidently, to discuss his significant role in bringing about the Enlightenment or the American Revolution. Famous religious leaders are also ignored, although the authors do bow to the ancient gods of primitive peoples. Pre-Columbian cultures like the Toltecs are praised for their lavishly decorated temples, their calendars, their games—so what if they practiced human sacrifice?

This best-selling textbook reveals a glimpse of the version of history—or rather, non-history—Generation X is being taught. I should know. Last summer, I took Sarah, then fourteen years old, on a tour of Boston, Massachusetts. I carefully explained the historic significance of each site to her. After several hours, she said, "Now, Mom, what war was this?" While I was still in a state of shock we arrived at the Old North Church and listened to a tour guide tell the story of Paul Revere. Sarah's question this time was, "What side was he on?" I asked incredulously, "What exactly did you do in the advanced placement U. S. history class you just completed?" Her response was, "I made a great many charts, and I did a lot of little projects with painting."

I do not mean to pick on Sarah. She and her peers are victims of a pernicious system that has turned traditional liberal arts education on its head. The situation is no better in higher education. At some colleges and universities, professors deliver lectures on the "The Apostle Paul as a Homosexual" and "Jesus Acted Up: A Gay and Lesbian Manifesto." Stanford University achieved notoriety a decade ago for its course, "Black Hair as Culture and History." A current survey on American religion at another school fails to mention Catholicism. One new cutting-edge psychology course is titled, "Gender Discrepancies and Pizza Consumption."

Before long, the loss of knowledge may even make simple conversation impossible. In my classroom, I cannot say, "Never look a gift horse in the mouth," or my students will give me a blank stare. I cannot say, "Me thinks thou dost protest too much," or at least one will inevitably respond, "Excuse me, Professor Jennings, shouldn't that be, 'I thinks?'" The literary shorthand of our culture is being lost. This is no small loss either, for words are symbols of important ideas.

The Critical Thinking Gap

Indoctrination is partly to blame for the knowledge gap. This is not a new trend in education. When I was in school, I was taught about "global cooling," and my teachers predicted that the earth was going to be frozen over in a new ice age. Today, my children are told that global warming is going to bring on an ecological apocalypse. But the level of indoctrination has risen sharply. Environmentalism has become an obsession with the teachers of Generation X. They constantly bombard students with dire warnings about pollution, scarce resources, and weather-related disasters. A recent cartoon sums up the attitude the students typically develop. It shows a little girl declaring to her mother that her day in school was a bust: "We didn't do anything to save mankind or the environment. We wasted the whole day on reading and math."

Indoctrination makes students passive receivers of information. As such docile participants, most public school students are incapable of independent thought—of drawing logical inferences or exhibiting other critical thinking skills. They are also incapable of looking at a statement and determining its validity. I refer to this as the "frou-frou head" problem, because students are so lacking in skills and knowledge and are so indoctrinated by politically correct thinking that they are not able to think clearly or make sound, well-informed judgments.

High school freshman Nathan Zohmer of Idaho recently conducted an experiment in science class that reveals the serious nature of this problem. He told classmates and teachers that they should sign his petition to ban a dangerous substance, "dihydrogen monoxide," which causes excessive vomiting and sweating. He informed them that dihydrogen monoxide is a component in acid rain. In its gaseous state, it can cause serious burns. Accidental inhalation can kill. To make matters worse, it contributes to soil erosion, decreases the effectiveness of automobile brakes, and its presence has been detected in some terminal cancer tumors.

Forty-seven of the fifty students and teachers signed the petition with no questions asked. Not one thought to inquire, "Just what is dihydrogen monoxide?" If they had, they would have discovered they had signed a petition calling for a ban on H_2O—water.

The Work Ethic Gap

Then there is the work ethic gap. In a recent survey, 80 percent of Generation X respondents said they want an active social life, while only 37 percent admit success at work is important. More adult males are living at home with their parents than at any time in our country's history. Why this staggering statistic? Moms and dads provide comfortable room and board while salaries can be used for fun. The desire for independence is missing along with the drive for achieving that independence.

There is no longer a stigma attached to joining the welfare rolls or reneging on financial obligations. Personal bankruptcies are at an all-time high. What is unique about these bankruptcies is the fact that the majority are not the result of the loss of a job or health problems; they involve one or two wage earners who have simply overextended themselves. Credit card debt, which has skyrocketed in recent years, is mainly held by those whose annual income exceeds $50,000. Evidently, the willingness to save and to delay gratification, the drive for success, and the concern for reputation are fast disappearing in a culture that condones irresponsible spending.

The average time for completion of a bachelor's degree is 5.5 years, so most students are not on a fast track. And they have developed some bad habits by the time they get into college. One is whining. As long as there have been students there has been whining—about workload, about subjects, about grades. But now there is *preemptive whining.* Even before the semester begins, even before papers and tests are handed back, students come into my office at Arizona State University with a laundry list of complaints.

Last year, one-third of my students protested their grades. In my first twenty years of teaching, not a single student questioned my judgment, but I expect half of my students to do so in the next ten. They are infected with an entitlement mentality. Good grades are not earned by hard work and subject mastery but by signing up to take the class.

I once counseled a graduate student who was doing poorly by saying: "Look, the problem is that you have a lack of depth when it comes to your studies. You have no knowledge base on which you can draw. You are going to have to start reading." He said with some surprise, "What do you mean? Books?"

A recent study analyzing the habits of elementary school children revealed that the average time spent on homework is ten minutes. Worse yet, the same study found that schools are increasingly adopting a "no homework" policy. Perhaps the saddest aspect of this situation is the reason more assignments are not given: Parents complain about the work their children are given.

Following last spring's final exams, a student came to my office and said, "You made us stretch to the maximum. It wasn't a bad feeling." Unfortunately, most students do not understand the pride that comes with conquering what seems to be impossible. Generation X is filled with self-esteem but bereft of knowledge.

In the math survey mentioned earlier, students from around the world were asked how they felt they had done upon completion of the exam. While the scores proved that the United States finished in the bottom third of all countries participating, it did finish first in terms of students' perception of personal performance. Americans exhibited the highest self-esteem while students from Japan and Singapore, who finished in the top two slots, were the least arrogant about their performance.

The Morality Gap

The most grievous problem is the morality gap. Sarah is a basketball player and a devoted fan of *Sports Illustrated*. Recently, she shared with me one of the magazine's top stories, which summarized a poll of 1,000 Olympic athletes. One of the questions posed was, "If we could give you a drug that would guarantee your victory at the Olympic Games but would also guarantee your death in five years, would you take it?" Fifty-four percent said yes.

Another survey conducted by the Lutheran Brotherhood asked, "Are there absolute standards for morals and ethics or does everything depend on the situation?" Seventy-nine percent of the respondents in the eighteen to thirty-four age group said that standards did not exist and that the situation should always dictate behavior. Three percent said they were not sure.

If this poll is correct, 82 percent of all students believe that right and wrong are relative terms and that morality is a ridiculous concept. This is the den of lions into which I walk every day. It is called the modern American classroom.

When I finish teaching a course, I ask my students to fill out a written evaluation form. Many of them comment, "This business ethics class was really fascinating. I had never heard these ideas before." Mind you, I am not teaching quantum physics—I am presenting simple, basic ideas and principles that should be followed in the marketplace: Be honest. Treat other people the way that you want to be treated. Work hard. Live up to your obligations.

Comedian Jay Leno revealed during one of his street interviews on the *Tonight Show* that the same young people don't seem to know the Ten Commandments. What they do know about morality is what they have picked up in scattered, disconnected bits from parents, friends, television, and magazines. And a good deal of this is immoral rather than moral. As a result, Generation X lacks a solid moral foundation for its views on school, work, marriage, family, and community.

Closing the Generation Gap

Are there ways to close the yawning generation gap, which is really the sum of all these smaller gaps? Of course there are. We live in a miraculous age. Great changes have revolutionized the way we live. I started law school with an electric typewriter —state-of-the-art back then. Now I have a computer, a fax machine, and electronic mail. The tools of high technology allow for improved education, wider access to knowledge, more work productivity, and greater freedom to make moral decisions. But these same tools also demand greater personal responsibility.

Is Generation X ready? I don't know. Remember the 1986 disaster at the Chernobyl nuclear plant in Ukraine? The world's worst nuclear accident did not happen because nuclear power is a flawed technology. It happened because a handful of young, cocky engineers chose to disregard established safety parameters while performing a routine test of equipment. Ironically, the test was designed to provide power to operate the reactor core cooling system in the event of an emergency. The engineers' carelessness and arrogance, which caused the release of large quantities of radioactive substances into the atmosphere, has since caused the death, pain, and suffering of innocent victims in Belarus, Ukraine, and Russia.

Look at what happened to Barings Bank, the venerable institution that financed the Napoleonic wars. It went bankrupt in 1995 because one trader, twenty-eight-year-old Nick Leeson, was able to sit in front of his computer and violate the prime ethical rule of banking: You don't take other people's money and recklessly gamble with it. He made a $27 billion bet that the Japanese stock market would rally after the Kobe earthquake. The market dropped instead, and Barings' losses reached a staggering $1.3 billion.

At the end of 1997, twenty-nine-year-old Marisa Baridis entered a guilty plea when she was charged with selling inside information. For $2,000 to $10,000 a tip, she and her friends made a dramatic impact on the stock market by using nonpublic information to take advantage of others. Ms. Baridis, who profited handsomely from such cheating, was the compliance officer for the investment bank and brokerage house of Morgan Stanley. She enjoyed a great deal of technological access to confidential information and a great deal of unilateral authority. In a tape-recorded conversation, she referred to insider trading as the "illegalist [sic] thing you can do," but, lacking the basic values of fairness and honesty, she easily dismissed the law she was responsible for enforcing. She also cost shareholders and companies millions of dollars.

High technology demands *more* individual judgment and *more* moral accountability. Generation X boasts thousands of techno-wise youth. But it is missing real wisdom, informed by a strong education and a strong spiritual ethic. When I point this out to some of my students and colleagues, they say, "Hey, don't shove that Judeo-Christian stuff down our throats! We don't want that." Then I remind them that this "stuff" exists everywhere, and that it has been considered vital to civil society for centuries. I challenge them to name one country in the world where bribery and cheating are legal and approved by the populace. I tell them to examine the most basic ethical principles of Moses and Jesus and compare them to those of Aristotle, Confucius, and Mohammed. The major religions of the world are in agreement on certain universals that have stood the test of time.

One such standard of universal morality is what is referred to by Christians as the "Golden Rule": Do unto others as you would have them do unto you. The same notion of fairness can be found in the basic tenets of Buddhism, Judaism, Hinduism, and even in philosophy in the form of Kant's "categorical imperative." Throughout time, this simple test of ethics has been recognized in various cultures as a means of preserving civility, decency, and morality. Its beauty lies in its simplicity. Its profundity lies in its universal recognition and adherence.

Parents as Teachers

As parents we have to stand up and be counted. When our children come home from school, as my daughter did one day, spinning yarns about Ethan Allen and the "Green Mountain Persons," we have to set the record straight. Truth matters. It was Ethan Allen and the "Green Mountain Boys," and this fact is not a slight to women. When pre-schoolers are exposed to storybooks on "alternative" lifestyles and early sex education (endorsed by the National Education Association, by the way), we must sound our objections loudly and clearly. We must exert pressure on superintendents, principals, and teachers. We must take the initiative and run for positions on school boards and city councils.

We must also seize moments of morality with our children to teach them the difference between right and wrong and impose punishments when they stray from moral principles. Most important, we must restore the twin notions that being judgmental is not the same as being narrow-minded and that expressing moral outrage is not a form of "hate speech." What a different world we would have if choosing right and rejecting wrong were not considered fanatical!

When I graduated from law school, a speaker offered nine words I have never forgotten: "Truth is violated by falsehood but outraged by silence." The past twenty-five years have been filled with falsehoods about our history and our culture. Generation X has never lived in a time of truth. Condemning immorality has become virtually the only sin, so it has not even witnessed the courage of conviction. We have been silent as an entire generation has seen truth repeatedly violated.

There is a difference between holding beliefs and being valiant in defending beliefs. As parents, struggling to close the generation gap, we must be valiant in defending our beliefs. Indeed, this is a call to action for all who guide our youth and offer them instruction. When immorality and adultery are described as "private" and therefore "irrelevant" in the public square, with no impact on character and leadership, we must shout from the rooftops, "Personal conduct *is* character! Character does matter!" When the lessons of history, literature, science, and religion are distorted, attacked, or lost in the shuffle, we must rescue them. It is time to break our silence and confront those who have perpetrated so many myths, so much fraud, and so little substance for so long.

It is still possible to reclaim Generation X from the hopelessly flawed indoctrination it has experienced. But reclaiming our children will require the type of introspection that results in moral courage and is followed by the expression of moral outrage. One of my students commented to me at the end of a semester, "You've dispelled so many myths. Now I know morality in business is not a crime." And I responded, "It's even better, son. Neither is the moral life a sin." Breaking our silence will allow truth to emerge, and its rare and illuminating quality will attract the attention and devotion of a generation trained and raised in amoral darkness.

In Praise of the F Word

Mary Sherry

Tens of thousands of 18-year-olds will graduate this year and be handed meaningless diplomas. These diplomas won't look any different from those awarded their luckier classmates. Their validity will be questioned only when their employers discover that these graduates are semiliterate.

Eventually a fortunate few will find their way into educational-repair shops—adult-literacy programs, such as the one where I teach basic grammar and writing. There, high-school graduates and high-school dropouts pursuing graduate-equivalency certificates will learn the skills they should have learned in school. They will also discover they have been cheated by our educational system.

As I teach, I learn a lot about our schools. Early in each session I ask my students to write about an unpleasant experience they had in school. No writers' block here! "I wish someone would have had made me stop doing drugs and made me study." "I liked to party and no one seemed to care." "I was a good kid and didn't cause any trouble, so they just passed me along even though I didn't read well and couldn't write." And so on.

I am your basic do-gooder, and prior to teaching this class I blamed the poor academic skills our kids have today on drugs, divorce and other impediments to concentration necessary for doing well in school. But, as I rediscover each time I walk into the classroom, before a teacher can expect students to concentrate, he has to get their attention, no matter what distractions may be at hand. There are many ways to do this, and they have much to do with teaching style. However, if style alone won't do it, there is another way to show who holds the winning hand in the classroom. That is to reveal the trump card of failure.

I will never forget a teacher who played that card to get the attention of one of my children. Our youngest, a world-class charmer, did little to develop his intellectual talents but always got by. Until Mrs. Stifter.

Our son was a high-school senior when he had her for English. "He sits in the back of the room talking to his friends," she told me. "Why don't you move him to the front row?" I urged, believing the embarrassment would get him to settle down. Mrs. Stifter looked at me steely-eyed over her glasses. "I don't move seniors," she said. "I flunk them." I was flustered. Our son's academic life flashed before my eyes. No teacher had ever threatened him with that before. I regained my composure and managed to say that I thought she was right. By the time I got home I was feeling pretty good about this. It was a radical approach for these times, but, well, why not? "She's going to flunk you," I told my son. I did not discuss it any further. Suddenly English became a priority in his life. He finished out the semester with an A.

I know one example doesn't make a case, but at night I see a parade of students who are angry and resentful for having been passed along until they could no longer even pretend to keep up. Of average intelligence or better, they eventually quit school, concluding they were too dumb to finish. "I should have been held back," is a comment I hear frequently. Even sadder are those students who are high-school graduates who say to me after a few weeks of class, "I don't know how I ever got a high-school diploma."

Passing students who have not mastered the work cheats them and the employers who expect graduates to have basic skills. We excuse this dishonest behavior by saying kids can't learn if they come from terrible environments. No one seems to stop to think that—no matter what environments they come from—most kids don't put school first on their list unless they perceive something is at stake. They'd rather be sailing.

Many students I see at night could give expert testimony on unemployment, chemical dependency, abusive relationships. In spite of these difficulties, they have decided to make education a priority. They are motivated by the desire for a better job or the need to hang on to the one they've got. They have a healthy fear of failure.

People of all ages can rise above their problems, but they need to have a reason to do so. Young people generally don't have the maturity to value education in the same way my adult students value it. But fear of failure, whether economic or academic, can motivate both. Flunking as a regular policy has just as much merit today as it did two generations ago. We must review the threat of flunking and see it as it really is—a positive teaching tool. It is an expression of confidence by both teachers and parents that the students have the ability to learn the material presented to them. However, making it work again would take a dedicated, caring conspiracy between teachers and parents. It would mean facing the tough reality that passing kids who haven't learned the material—while it might save them grief for the short term—dooms them to long-term illiteracy. It would mean that teachers would have to follow through on their threats, and parents would have to stand behind them, knowing their children's best interests are indeed at stake. This means no more doing Scott's assignments for him because he might fail. No more passing Jodi because she's such a nice kid.

This is a policy that worked in the past and can work today. A wise teacher, with the support of his parents, gave our son the opportunity to succeed—or fail. It's time we return this choice to all students.

The *C* Word in the Hallways

Anna Quindlen

The saddest phrase I've read in a long time is this one: psychological autopsy. That's what the doctors call it when a kid kills himself, and they go back over the plowed ground of his short life, and discover all the hidden markers that led to the rope, the blade, the gun.

There's a plague on all our houses, and since it doesn't announce itself with lumps or spots or protest marches, it has gone unremarked in the quiet suburbs and busy cities where it has been laying waste. The number of suicides and homicides committed by teenagers, most often young men, has exploded in the last three decades, until it has become routine to have black-bordered photographs in yearbooks and murder suspects with acne problems. And everyone searches for reasons, and scapegoats, and solutions, most often punitive. Yet one solution continues to elude us, and that is ending the ignorance about mental health, and moving it from the margins of care and into the mainstream where it belongs. As surely as any vaccine, this would save lives.

So many have already been lost. This month Kip Kinkel was sentenced to life in prison in Oregon for the murders of his parents and a shooting rampage at his high school that killed two students. A psychiatrist who specializes in the care of adolescents testified that Kinkel, now seventeen, had been hearing voices since he was twelve. Sam Manzie is also seventeen. He is serving a seventy-year sentence for luring an eleven-year-old boy named Eddie Werner into his New Jersey home and strangling him with the cord to an alarm clock because his Sega Genesis was out of reach. Manzie had his first psychological evaluation in the first grade.

Excuses, excuses. That's what so many think of the underlying pathology in such hideous crimes. In the 1956 movie *The Bad Seed*, little Patty McCormack played what was then called a "homicidal maniac" and the film censors demanded a ludicrous mock curtain call in which the child actress was taken over the knee of her screen father and spanked. There are still some representatives of the "good spanking" school out there, although today the spanking may wind up being life in prison. And there's still plenty of that useless adult "what in the world does a sixteen-year-old have to be depressed about" mind-set to keep depressed sixteen-year-olds from getting help.

It's true that both the Kinkel and the Manzie boys had already been introduced to the mental health system before their crimes. Concerned by her son's fascination with weapons, Faith Kinkel took him for nine sessions with a psychologist in the year before the shootings. Because of his rages and his continuing relationship with a pedophile, Sam's parents had tried to have him admitted to a residential facility just days before their son invited Eddie in.

But they were threading their way through a mental health system that is marginalized by shame, ignorance, custom, the courts, even by business practice. Kip Kinkel's father made no secret of his disapproval of therapy. During its course he bought his son the Glock that Kip would later use on his killing spree, which speaks sad volumes about our peculiar standards of masculinity. Sam's father, on the other hand, spent days trying to figure out how much of the cost of a home for troubled-kids his insurance would cover. In the meantime, a psychiatrist who examined his son for less time than it takes to eat a Happy Meal concluded that he was no danger to himself or others, and a judge lectured Sam from the bench: "You know the difference between right and wrong, don't you?"

The federal Center for Mental Health Services estimates that at least six million children in this country have some serious emotional disturbance and, for some of them, right and wrong take second seat to the voices in their heads. Fifty years ago their parents might have surrendered them to life in an institution, or a doctor flying blind with an ice pick might have performed a lobotomy, leaving them to loll away their days. Now lots of them wind up in jail. Warm fuzzies aside, consider this from a utilitarian point of view: Psychological intervention is cheaper than incarceration.

The most optimistic estimate is that two thirds of these emotionally disturbed children are not getting any treatment. Imagine how we would respond if two thirds of America's babies were not being immunized.

Many health insurance plans do not provide coverage for necessary treatment, or financially penalize those who need a psychiatrist instead of an oncologist. Teachers are not trained to recognize mental illness, and some dismiss it, "Bad Seed" fashion, as bad behavior. Parents are afraid, and ashamed, creating a home environment, and national atmosphere, too, that tells teenagers their demons are a disgrace.

And then there are the teenagers themselves, slouching toward adulthood in a world that loves conformity. Add to the horror of creeping depression or delusions that of peer derision, the sound of the C word in the hallways: crazy, man, he's crazy, haven't you seen him, didn't you hear? Boys, especially, still suspect that talk therapy, or even heartfelt talk, is somehow sissified, weak. Sometimes even their own fathers think so, at least until they have to identify the body.

Another sad little phrase is "If only," and there are always plenty of them littering the valleys of tragedy. If only there had been long-term intervention and medication, Kip Kinkel might be out of jail, off the taxpayers' tab, and perhaps leading a productive life. If only Sam Manzie had been treated aggressively earlier, new psychotropic drugs might have slowed or stilled his downward slide. And if only those things had happened, Faith Kinkel, William Kinkel, Mikael Nickolauson, Ben Walker, and Eddie Werner might all be alive today. Mental health care is health care, too, and mental illness is an illness, not a character flaw. Insurance providers should act like it. Hospitals and schools should act like it. Above all, we parents should act like it. Then maybe the kids will believe it.

A Crime of Compassion

Barbara Huttmann

"Murderer," a man shouted. "God help patients who get *you* for a nurse.

"What gives you the right to play God?" another one asked.

It was the Phil Donahue show where the guest is a fatted calf and the audience a 200-strong flock of vultures hungering to pick at the bones. I had told them about Mac, one of my favorite cancer patients. "We resuscitated him 52 times in just one month. I refused to resuscitate him again. I simply sat there and held his hand while he died."

There wasn't time to explain that Mac was a young, witty, macho cop who walked into the hospital with 32 pounds of attack equipment, looking as if he could single-handedly protect the whole city, if not the entire state. "Can't get rid of this cough," he said. Otherwise, he felt great.

Before the day was over, tests confirmed that he had lung cancer. And before the year was over, I loved him, his wife, Maura, and their three kids as if they were my own. All the nurses loved him. And we all battled his disease for six months without ever giving death a thought. Six months isn't such a long time in the whole scheme of things, but it was long enough to see him lose his youth, his wit, his macho, his hair, his bowel and bladder control, his sense of taste and smell, and his ability to do the slightest thing for himself. It was also long enough to watch Maura's transformation from a young woman into a haggard, beaten old lady.

When Mac had wasted away to a 60-pound skeleton kept alive by liquid food we poured down a tube, i.v. solutions we dripped into his veins, and oxygen we piped to a mask on his face, he begged us: "Mercy . . . for God's sake, please just let me go."

The first time he stopped breathing, the nurse pushed the button that calls a "code blue" throughout the hospital and sends a team rushing to resuscitate the patient. Each time he stopped breathing, sometimes two or three times in one day, the code team came again. The doctors and technicians worked their miracles and walked away. The nurses stayed to wipe the saliva that drooled from his mouth, irrigate the big craters of bedsores that covered his hips, suction the lung fluids that threatened to drown him, clean the feces that burned his skin like lye, pour the liquid food down the tube attached to his stomach, put pillows between his knees to ease the bone-on-bone pain, turn him every hour to keep the bedsores from getting worse, and change his gown and linen every two hours to keep him from being soaked in perspiration.

At night I went home and tried to scrub away the smell of decaying flesh that seemed woven into the fabric of my uniform. It was in my hair, the upholstery of my car—there was no washing it away. And every night I prayed that Mac would die, that his agonized eyes would never again plead with me to let him die.

Every morning I asked his doctor for a "no-code" order. Without that order, we had to resuscitate every patient who stopped breathing. His doctor was one of several who believe we must extend life as long as we have the means and knowledge to do it. To not do it is to be liable for negligence, at least in the eyes of many people, including some nurses. I thought about what it would be like to stand before a judge, accused of murder, if Mac stopped breathing and I didn't call a code.

And after the fifty-second code, when Mac was still lucid enough to beg for death again, and Maura was crumbled in my arms again, and when no amount of pain medication stilled his moaning and agony, I wondered about a spiritual judge. Was all this misery and suffering supposed to be building character or infusing us all with the sense of humility that comes from impotence?

Had we, the whole medical community, become so arrogant that we believed in the illusion of salvation through science? Had we become so self-righteous that we thought meddling in God's work was our duty, our moral imperative and our legal obligation? Did we really believe that we had the right to force "life" on a suffering man who had begged for the right to die?

Such questions haunted me more than ever early one morning when Maura went home to change her clothes and I was bathing Mac. He had been still for so long, I thought he at last had the blessed relief of coma.

Then he opened his eyes and moaned, "Pain . . . no more . . . Barbara . . . do something . . . God, let me go."

The desperation in his eyes and voice riddled me with guilt. "I'll stop," I told him as I injected the pain medication.

I sat on the bed and held Mac's hands in mine. He pressed his bony fingers against my hand and muttered, "Thanks." Then there was one soft sigh and I felt his hands go cold in mine. "Mac?" I whispered, as I waited for his chest to rise and fall again.

A clutch of panic banded my chest, drew my finger to the code button, urged me to do something, anything . . . but sit there alone with death. I kept one finger on the button, without pressing it, as a waxen pallor slowly transformed his face from person to empty shell. Nothing I've ever done in my 47 years has taken so much effort as it took not to press that code button.

Eventually, when I was as sure as I could be that the code team would fail to bring him back, I entered the legal twilight zone and pushed the button. The team tried. And while they were trying, Maura walked into the room and shrieked, "No . . . don't let them do this to him . . . for God's sake . . . please, no more."

Cradling her in my arms was like cradling myself, Mac, and all those patients and nurses who had been in this place before, who do the best they can in a death-denying society.

So a TV audience accused me of murder. Perhaps I am guilty. If a doctor had written a no-code order, which is the only *legal* alternative, would he have felt any less guilty? Until there is legislation making it a criminal act to code a patient who has requested the right to die, we will all of us risk the same fate as Mac. For whatever reason, we developed the means to prolong life, and now we are forced to use it. We do not have the right to die.

Our Vanishing Night

Most city skies have become virtually empty of stars.

Verlyn Klinkenborg

If humans were truly at home under the light of the moon and stars, we would go in darkness happily, the midnight world as visible to us as it is to the vast number of nocturnal species on this planet. Instead, we are diurnal creatures, with eyes adapted to living in the sun's light. This is a basic evolutionary fact, even though most of us don't think of ourselves as diurnal beings any more than we think of ourselves as primates or mammals or Earthlings. Yet it's the only way to explain what we've done to the night: We've engineered it to receive us by filling it with light.

This kind of engineering is no different than damming a river. Its benefits come with consequences—called light pollution—whose effects scientists are only now beginning to study. Light pollution is largely the result of bad lighting design, which allows artificial light to shine outward and upward into the sky, where it's not wanted, instead of focusing it downward, where it is. Ill-designed lighting washes out the darkness of night and radically alters the light levels—and light rhythms—to which many forms of life, including ourselves, have adapted. Wherever human light spills into the natural world, some aspect of life—migration, reproduction, feeding—is affected.

For most of human history, the phrase "light pollution" would have made no sense. Imagine walking toward London on a moonlit night around 1800, when it was Earth's most populous city. Nearly a million people lived there, making do, as they always had, with candles and rushlights and torches and lanterns. Only a few houses were lit by gas, and there would be no public gaslights in the streets or squares for another seven years. From a few miles away, you would have been as likely to *smell* London as to see its dim collective glow.

Now most of humanity lives under intersecting domes of reflected, refracted light, of scattering rays from overlit cities and suburbs, from light-flooded highways and factories. Nearly all of nighttime Europe is a nebula of light, as is most of the United States and all of Japan. In the south Atlantic the glow from a single fishing fleet—squid fishermen luring their prey with metal halide lamps—can be seen from space, burning brighter, in fact, than Buenos Aires or Rio de Janeiro.

In most cities the sky looks as though it has been emptied of stars, leaving behind a vacant haze that mirrors our fear of the dark and resembles the urban glow of dystopian science fiction. We've grown so used to this pervasive orange haze that the original glory of an unlit night—dark enough for the planet Venus to throw shadows on Earth—is wholly beyond our experience, beyond memory almost. And yet above the city's pale ceiling lies the rest of the universe, utterly undiminished by the light we waste—a bright shoal of stars and planets and galaxies, shining in seemingly infinite darkness.

We've lit up the night as if it were an unoccupied country, when nothing could be further from the truth. Among mammals alone, the number of nocturnal species is astonishing. Light is a powerful biological force, and on many species it acts as a magnet, a process being studied by researchers such as Travis Longcore and Catherine Rich, co-founders of the Los Angeles-based Urban Wildlands Group. The effect is so powerful that scientists speak of songbirds and seabirds being "captured" by searchlights on land or by the light from gas flares on marine oil platforms, circling and circling in the thousands until they drop. Migrating at night, birds are apt to collide with brightly lit tall buildings; immature birds on their first journey suffer disproportionately.

Insects, of course, cluster around streetlights, and feeding at those insect clusters is now ingrained in the lives of many bat species. In some Swiss valleys the European lesser horseshoe bat began to vanish after streetlights were installed, perhaps because those valleys were suddenly filled with light-feeding pipistrelle bats. Other nocturnal mammals—including desert rodents, fruit bats, opossums, and badgers—forage more cautiously under the permanent full moon of light pollution because they've become easier targets for predators.

Some birds—blackbirds and nightingales, among others—sing at unnatural hours in the presence of artificial light. Scientists have determined that long artificial days—and artificially short nights—induce early breeding in a wide range of birds. And because a longer day allows for longer feeding, it can also affect migration schedules. One population of Bewick's swans wintering in England put on fat more rapidly than usual, priming them to begin their Siberian migration early. The problem, of course, is that migration, like most other aspects of bird behavior, is a precisely timed biological behavior. Leaving early may mean arriving too soon for nesting conditions to be right.

Nesting sea turtles, which show a natural predisposition for dark beaches, find fewer and fewer of them to nest on. Their hatchlings, which gravitate toward the brighter, more reflective sea horizon, find themselves confused by artificial lighting behind the beach. In Florida alone, hatchling losses number in the hundreds of thousands every year. Frogs and toads living near brightly lit highways suffer nocturnal light levels that are as much as a million times brighter than normal, throwing nearly every aspect of their behavior out of joint, including their nighttime breeding choruses.

Of all the pollutions we face, light pollution is perhaps the most easily remedied. Simple changes in lighting design and installation yield immediate changes in the amount of light spilled into the atmosphere and, often, immediate energy savings.

It was once thought that light pollution only affected astronomers, who need to see the night sky in all its glorious clarity. And, in fact, some of the earliest civic efforts to control light pollution—in Flagstaff, Arizona, half a century ago—were made to protect the view from Lowell Observatory, which sits high above that city. Flagstaff has tightened its regulations since then, and in 2001 it was declared the first International Dark Sky City. By now the effort to control light pollution has spread around the globe. More and more cities and even entire countries, such as the Czech Republic, have committed themselves to reducing unwanted glare.

Unlike astronomers, most of us may not need an undiminished view of the night sky for our work, but like most other creatures we do need darkness. Darkness is as essential to our biological welfare, to our internal clockwork, as light itself. The regular oscillation of waking and sleep in our lives—one of our circadian rhythms—is nothing less than a biological expression of the regular oscillation of light on Earth. So fundamental are these rhythms to our being that altering them is like altering gravity.

For the past century or so, we've been performing an open-ended experiment on ourselves, extending the day, shortening the night, and short-circuiting the human body's sensitive response to light. The consequences of our bright new world are more readily perceptible in less adaptable creatures living in the peripheral glow of our prosperity. But for humans, too, light pollution may take a biological toll. At least one new study has suggested a direct correlation between higher rates of breast cancer in women and the nighttime brightness of their neighborhoods.

In the end, humans are no less trapped by light pollution than the frogs in a pond near a brightly lit highway. Living in a glare of our own making, we have cut ourselves off from our evolutionary and cultural patrimony—the light of the stars and the rhythms of day and night. In a very real sense, light pollution causes us to lose sight of our true place in the universe, to forget the scale of our being, which is best measured against the dimensions of a deep night with the Milky Way—the edge of our galaxy—arching overhead.

In Defense of Prejudice

Jonathan Rauch

The war on prejudice is now, in all likelihood, the most uncontroversial social movement in America. Opposition to "hate speech," formerly identified with the liberal left, has become a bipartisan piety. In the past year, groups and factions that agree on nothing else have agreed that the public expression of any and all prejudices must be forbidden. On the left, protesters and editorialists have insisted that Francis L. Lawrence resign as president of Rutgers University for describing blacks as "a disadvantaged population that doesn't have that genetic, hereditary background to have a higher average." On the other side of the ideological divide, Ralph Reed, the executive director of the Christian Coalition, responded to criticism of the religious right by calling a press conference to denounce a supposed outbreak of "name-calling, scapegoating, and religious bigotry." Craig Rogers, an evangelical Christian student at California State University, recently filed a $2.5 million sexual-harassment suit against a lesbian professor of psychology, claiming that anti-male bias in one of her lectures violated campus rules and left him feeling "raped and trapped."

In universities and on Capitol Hill, in workplaces and newsrooms, authorities are declaring that there is no place for racism, sexism, homophobia, Christian-bashing, and other forms of prejudice in public debate or even in private thought. "Only when racism and other forms of prejudice are expunged," say the crusaders for sweetness and light, "can minorities be safe and society be fair." So sweet, this dream of a world, without prejudice. But the very last thing society should do is seek to utterly eradicate racism and other forms of prejudice.

I suppose I should say, in the customary I-hope-I-don't-sound-too-defensive tone, that I am not a racist and that this is not an article favoring racism or any other particular prejudice. It is an article favoring intellectual pluralism, which permits the expression of various forms of bigotry and always will. Although we like to hope that a time will come when no one will believe that people come in types and that each type belongs with its own kind, I doubt such a day will ever arrive. By all indications, *Homo sapiens* is a tribal species for whom "us versus them" comes naturally and must be continually pushed back. Where there is genuine freedom of expression, there will be racist expression. There will also be people who believe that homosexuals are sick or threaten children or—especially among teenagers—are rightful targets of manly savagery. Homosexuality will always be incomprehensible to most people, and what is incomprehensible is feared. As for anti-Semitism, it appears to be a hardier virus than influenza. If you want pluralism, then you get racism and sexism and homophobia, and communism and fascism and xenophobia and tribalism, and that is just for a start. If you want to believe in intellectual freedom and the progress of knowledge and the advancement of science and all those other good things, then you must swallow hard and accept this: for as thickheaded and wayward an animal as us, the realistic question is how to make the best of prejudice, not how to eradicate it.

Indeed, "eradicating prejudice" is so vague a proposition as to be meaningless. Distinguishing prejudice reliably and nonpolitically from nonprejudice, or even defining it crisply, is quite hopeless. We all feel we know prejudice when we see it. But do we? At the University of Michigan, a student said in a classroom discussion that he considered homosexuality a disease treatable with therapy. He was summoned to a formal disciplinary hearing for violating the school's policy against speech that "victimizes" people based on "sexual orientation." Now, the evidence is abundant that this particular hypothesis is wrong, and any American homosexual can attest to the harm that the student's hypothesis has inflicted on many real people. But was it a statement of prejudice or of misguided belief? Hate speech or hypothesis? Many Americans who do not regard themselves as bigots or haters believe that homosexuality is a treatable disease. They may be wrong, but are they all bigots? I am unwilling to say so, and if you are willing, beware. The line between a prejudiced belief and a merely controversial one is elusive, and the harder you look the more elusive it becomes. "God hates homosexuals" is a statement of fact, not of bias, to those who believe it; "American criminals are disproportionately black" is a statement of bias, not of fact, to those who disbelieve it.

Who is right? You may decide, and so may others, and there is no need to agree. That is the great innovation of intellectual pluralism (which is to say, of post-Enlightenment science, broadly defined). We cannot know in advance or for sure which belief is prejudice and which is truth, but to advance knowledge we don't need to know. The genius of intellectual pluralism lies not in doing away with prejudices and dogmas but in channeling them—making them socially productive by pitting prejudice against prejudice and dogma against dogma, exposing all to withering public criticism. What survives at the end of the day is our base of knowledge.

What they told us in high school about this process is very largely a lie. The Enlightenment tradition taught us that science is orderly, antiseptic, rational, the province of detached experimenters and high-minded logicians. In the popular view, science stands for reason against prejudice, openmindedness against dogma, calm consideration against passionate attachment—all personified by pop-science icons like the magisterially deductive Sherlock Holmes, the coolly analytic Mr. Spock, the genially authoritative Mr. Science (from our junior-high science films). Yet one of science's dirty secrets is that although science as a whole is as unbiased as anything human can be, scientists are just as biased as anyone else, sometimes more so. "One of the strengths of science," writes the philosopher of science David L. Hull, "is that it does not require that scientists be unbiased, only that different scientists have different biases." Another dirty secret is that, no less than the rest of us, scientists can be dogmatic and pigheaded. "Although this pigheadedness often damages the careers of individual scientists," says Hull, "it is beneficial for the manifest goal of science," which relies on people to invest years in their ideas and defend them passionately. And the dirtiest secret of all, if you believe in the antiseptic popular view of science, is that this most ostensibly rational of enterprises depends on the most irrational of motives—ambition, narcissism, animus, even revenge. "Scientists acknowledge that among their motivations are natural curiosity, the love of truth, and the desire to help humanity, but other inducements exist as well, and one of them is to 'get that son of a bitch,'" says Hull. "Time and again, scientists whom I interviewed described the powerful spur that 'showing that son of a bitch' supplied to their own research."

Many people, I think, are bewildered by this unvarnished and all too human view of science. They believe that for a system to be unprejudiced, the people in it must also be unprejudiced. In fact, the opposite is true. Far from eradicating ugly or stupid ideas and coarse or unpleasant motives, intellectual pluralism relies upon them to excite intellectual passion and redouble scientific effort. I know of no modern idea more ugly and stupid than that the Holocaust never happened, nor any idea more viciously motivated. Yet the deniers' claims that the Auschwitz gas chambers could not have worked led to closer study and, in 1993, research showing, at last, how they actually did work. Thanks to prejudice and stupidity, another opening for doubt has been shut.

An enlightened and efficient intellectual regime lets a million prejudices bloom, including many that you or I may regard as hateful or grotesque. It avoids any attempt to stamp out prejudice, because stamping out prejudice really means forcing everyone to share the same prejudice, namely that of whoever is in authority. The great American philosopher Charles Sanders Peirce wrote in 1877: "When complete agreement could not otherwise be reached, a general massacre of all who have not thought in a certain way has proved a very effective means of settling opinion in a country." In speaking of "settling opinion," Peirce was writing about one of the two or three most fundamental problems that any human society must confront and solve. For most societies down through the centuries, this problem was dealt with in the manner he described: errors were identified by the authorities—priests, politburos, dictators—or by mass opinion, and then the error-makers were eliminated along with their putative mistakes. "Let all men who reject the established belief be terrified into silence," wrote Peirce, describing this system. "This method has, from the earliest times, been one of the chief means of upholding correct theological and political doctrines."

Intellectual pluralism substitutes a radically different doctrine: we kill our mistakes rather than each other. Here I draw on another great philosopher, the late Karl Popper, who pointed out that the critical method of science "consists in letting our hypotheses die in our stead." Those who are in error are not (or are not supposed to be) banished or excommunicated or forced to sign a renunciation or required to submit to "rehabilitation" or sent for psychological counseling. It is the error we punish, not the errant. By letting people make errors—even mischievous, spiteful errors (as, for instance, Galileo's insistence on Copernicanism was taken to be in 1633)—pluralism creates room to challenge orthodoxy, think imaginatively, experiment boldly. Brilliance and bigotry are empowered in the same stroke.

Pluralism is the principle that protects and makes a place in human company for that loneliest and most vulnerable of all minorities, the minority who is hounded and despised among blacks and whites, gays and straights, who is suspect or criminal among every tribe and in every nation of the world, and yet on whom progress depends: the dissident. I am not saying that dissent is always or even usually enlightened. Most of the time it is foolish and self-serving. No dissident has the right to be taken seriously, and the fact that Aryan Nation racists or Nation of Islam anti-Semites are unorthodox does not entitle them to respect. But what goes around comes around. As a supporter of gay marriage, for example, I reject the majority's view of family, and as a Jew I reject its view of God. I try to be civil, but the fact is that most Americans regard my views on marriage as a reckless assault on the most fundamental of all institutions, and many people are more than a little discomfited by the statement, "Jesus Christ was no more divine than anybody else" (which is why so few people ever say it). Trap the racists and anti-Semites, and you lay a trap for me too. Hunt for them with eradication in your mind, and you have brought dissent itself within your sights.

The new crusade against prejudice waves aside such warnings. Like earlier crusades against antisocial ideas, the mission is fueled by good (if cocksure) intentions and a genuine sense of urgency. Some kinds of error are held to be intolerable, like pollutants that even in small traces poison the water for a whole town. Some errors are so pernicious as to damage real people's lives, so wrong-headed that no person of right mind or goodwill could support them. Like their forebears of other stripe—the Church in its campaigns against heretics, the McCarthyites in their campaigns against Communists—the modern anti-racist and anti-sexist and anti-homophobic campaigners are totalists, demanding not that misguided ideas and ugly expressions be corrected or criticized but that they be eradicated. They make war not on errors but on error, and like other totalists they act in the name of public safety—the safety, especially, of minorities.

The sweeping implications of this challenge to pluralism are not, I think, well enough understood by the public at large. Indeed, the new brand of totalism has yet even to be properly named. "Multiculturalism," for instance, is much too broad. "Political correctness" comes closer but is too trendy and snide. For lack of anything else, I will call the new anti-pluralism "purism," since its major tenet is that society cannot be just until the last traces of invidious prejudice have been scrubbed away. Whatever you call it, the purists' way of seeing things has spread through American intellectual life with remarkable speed, so much so that many people will blink at you uncomprehendingly or even call you a racist (or sexist or homophobe, etc.) if you suggest that expressions of racism should be tolerated or that prejudice has its part to play.

The new purism sets out, to begin with, on a campaign against words, for words are the currency of prejudice, and if prejudice is hurtful then so must be prejudiced words. "We are not safe when these violent words are among us," wrote Mari Matsuda, then a UCLA law professor.

Here one imagines gangs of racist words swinging chains and smashing heads in back alleys. To suppress bigoted language seems, at first blush, reasonable, but it quickly leads to a curious result. A peculiar kind of verbal shamanism takes root, as though certain expressions, like curses or magical incantations, carry in themselves the power to hurt or heal—as though words were bigoted rather than people. "Context is everything," people have always said. The use of the word "nigger" in *Huckleberry Finn* does not make the book an "act" of hate speech—or does it? In the new view, this is no longer so clear. The very utterance of the word "nigger" (at least by a non-black) is a racist act. When a *Sacramento Bee* cartoonist put the word "nigger" mockingly in the mouth of a white supremacist, there were howls of protest and 1,400 canceled subscriptions and an editorial apology, even though the word was plainly being invoked against racists, not against blacks.

Faced with escalating demands of verbal absolutism, newspapers issue lists of forbidden words. The expressions "gyp" (derived from "Gypsy") and "Dutch treat" were among the dozens of terms stricken as "offensive" in a much-ridiculed (and later withdrawn) *Los Angeles Times* speech code. The University of Missouri journalism school issued a *Dictionary of Cautionary Words and Phrases,* which included "*Buxom:* Offensive reference to a woman's chest. Do not use. See 'Woman.' *Codger:* Offensive reference to a senior citizen."

As was bound to happen, purists soon discovered that chasing around after words like "gyp" or "buxom" hardly goes to the roots of the problem. As long as they remain bigoted, bigots will simply find other words. If they can't call you a kike then they will say Jewboy, Judas, or Hebe, and when all those are banned they will press words like "oven" and "lampshade" into their service. The vocabulary of hate is potentially as rich as your dictionary, and all you do by banning language used by cretins is to let them decide what the rest of us may say. The problem, some purists have concluded, must therefore go much deeper than laws: it must go to the deeper level of ideas. Racism, sexism, homophobia, and the rest must be built into the very structure of American society and American patterns of thought, so pervasive yet so insidious that, like water to a fish, they are both omnipresent and unseen. The mere existence of prejudice constructs a society whose very nature is prejudiced.

This line of thinking was pioneered by feminists, who argued that pornography, more than just being expressive, is an act by which men construct an oppressive society. Racial activists quickly picked up the argument. Racist expressions are themselves acts of oppression, they said. "All racist speech constructs the social reality that constrains the liberty of nonwhites because of their race," wrote Charles R. Lawrence III, then a law professor at Stanford. From the purist point of view, a society with even one racist is a racist society, because the idea itself threatens and demeans its targets. They cannot feel wholly safe or wholly welcome as long as racism is present. Pluralism says: There will always be some racists. Marginalize them, ignore them, exploit them, ridicule them, take pains to make their policies illegal, but otherwise leave them alone. Purists say: That's not enough. Society cannot be just until these pervasive and oppressive ideas are searched out and eradicated.

And so what is now under way is a growing drive to eliminate prejudice from every corner of society. I doubt that many people have noticed how far-reaching this anti-pluralist movement is becoming.

In universities: Dozens of universities have adopted codes proscribing speech or other expression that (this is from Stanford's policy, which is more or less representative) "is intended to insult or stigmatize an individual or a small number of individuals on the basis of their sex, race, color, handicap, religion, sexual orientation or national and ethnic origin." Some codes punish only persistent harassment of a targeted individual, but many, following the purist doctrine that even one racist is too many, go much further. At Penn, an administrator declared: "We at the University of Pennsylvania have guaranteed students and the community that they can live in a community free of sexism, racism, and homophobia." Here is the purism that gives "political correctness" its distinctive combination of puffy high-mindedness and authoritarian zeal.

In school curricula: "More fundamental than eliminating racial segregation has to be the removal of racist thinking, assumptions, symbols, and materials in the curriculum," writes theorist Molefi Kete Asante. In practice, the effort to "remove racist thinking" goes well beyond striking egregious references from textbooks. In many cases it becomes a kind of mental engineering in which students are encouraged to see prejudice.

Ah, but the task of scouring minds clean is Augean. "Nobody escapes," said a Rutgers University report on campus prejudice. Bias and prejudice, it found, cross every conceivable line, from sex to race to politics: "No matter who you are, no matter what the color of your skin, no matter what your gender or sexual orientation, no matter what you believe, no matter how you behave, there is somebody out there who doesn't like people of your kind." Charles Lawrence writes: "Racism is ubiquitous. We are all racists." If he means that most of us think racist thoughts of some sort at one time or another, he is right. If we are going to "eliminate prejudices and biases from our society," then the work of the prejudice police is unending. They are doomed to hunt and hunt, scour and scour and scour.

What is especially dismaying is that the purists pursue prejudice in the name of protecting minorities. In order to protect people like me (homosexual), they must pursue people like me (dissident). In order to bolster minority self-esteem, they suppress minority opinion. There are, of course, all kinds of practical and legal problems with the purists' campaign: the incursions against the First Amendment; the inevitable abuses by prosecutors and activists who define as "hateful" or "violent" whatever speech they dislike or can score points off of; the lack of any evidence that repressing prejudice eliminates rather than inflames it. But minorities, of all people, ought to remember that by definition we cannot prevail by numbers, and we generally cannot prevail by force. Against the power of ignorant mass opinion and group prejudice and superstition, we have only our voices. If you doubt that minorities' voices are powerful weapons, think of the lengths to which Southern officials went to silence the Reverend Martin Luther King Jr. (recall that the city commissioner of Montgomery, Alabama, won a $500,000 libel suit, later overturned in *New York Times* v. Sullivan [1964], regarding an advertisement in the *Times* placed by civil-rights leaders who denounced the Montgomery police). Think of how much gay people have improved their lot over twenty-five years simply by refusing to remain silent. Recall the Michigan student who was prosecuted for saying that homosexuality is a treatable disease, and notice that he was black. Under that Michigan speech code, more than twenty blacks were charged with racist speech, while no instance of racist speech by whites was punished. In Florida, the hate-speech law was invoked against a black man who called a policeman a "white cracker"; not so surprisingly, in the first hate-crimes case to reach the Supreme Court, the victim was white and the defendant black.

In the escalating war against "prejudice," the right is already learning to play by the rules that were pioneered by the purist activists of the left. Last year leading Democrats, including the President, criticized the Republican Party for being increasingly in the thrall of the Christian right. Some of the rhetoric was harsh ("fire-breathing Christian radical right"), but it wasn't vicious or even clearly wrong. Never mind: when Democratic Representative Vic Fazio said Republicans were "being forced to the fringes by the aggressive political tactics of the religious right," the chairman of the Republican National Committee, Haley Barbour, said, "Christian-bashing" was "the left's preferred form of religious bigotry." Bigotry! Prejudice! "Christians active in politics are now on the receiving end of an extraordinary campaign of bias and prejudice," said the conservative leader William J. Bennett. One discerns, here, where the new purism leads. Eventually, any criticism of any group will be "prejudice."

Here is the ultimate irony of the new purism: words, which pluralists hope can be substituted for violence, are redefined by purists *as* violence. "The experience of being called 'nigger,' 'spic,' 'Jap,' or 'kike' is like receiving a slap in the face," Charles Lawrence wrote in 1990. "Psychic injury is no less an injury than being struck in the face, and it often is far more severe." This kind of talk is commonplace today. Epithets, insults, often even polite expressions of what's taken to be prejudice are called by purists "assaultive speech," "words that wound," "verbal violence." "To me, racial epithets are not speech," one University of Michigan law professor said. "They are bullets." In her speech accepting the 1993 Nobel Prize for Literature in Stockholm, Sweden, the author Toni Morrison said this: "Oppressive language does more than represent violence; it is violence."

It is not violence. I am thinking back to a moment on the subway in Washington, a little thing. I was riding home late one night and a squad of noisy kids, maybe seventeen or eighteen years old, noisily piled into the car. They yelled across the car and a girl said, "Where do we get off?"

A boy said, "Farragut North."

The girl: "*Faggot* North!"

The boy: "Yeah! Faggot North!"

General hilarity.

First, before the intellect resumes control, there is a moment of fear, an animal moment. Who are they? How many of them? How dangerous! Where is the way out? All of these things are noted preverbally and assessed by the gut. Then the brain begins an assessment: they are sober, this is probably too public a place for them to do it, there are more girls than boys, they were just talking, it is probably nothing.

They didn't notice me and there was no incident. The teenage babble flowed on, leaving me to think. I became interested in my own reaction: the jump of fear out of nowhere like an alert animal, the sense for a brief time that one is naked and alone and should hide or run away. For a time, one ceases to be a human being and becomes instead a faggot.

The fear engendered by these words is real. The remedy is as clear and as imperfect as ever: protect citizens against violence. This, I grant, is something that American society has never done very well and now does quite poorly. It is no solution to define words as violence or prejudice as oppression, and then by cracking down on words or thoughts pretend that we are doing something about violence and oppression. No doubt it is easier to pass a speech code or hate-crimes law and proclaim the streets safer than actually to make the streets safer, but the one must never be confused with the other. Every cop or prosecutor chasing words is one fewer chasing criminals. In a world rife with real violence and oppression, full of Rwandas and Bosnias and eleven-year-olds spraying bullets at children in Chicago and in turn being executed by gang lords, it is odious of Toni Morrison to say that words are violence.

Indeed, equating "verbal violence" with physical violence is a treacherous, mischievous business. Not long ago a writer was charged with viciously and gratuitously wounding the feelings and dignity of millions of people. He was charged, in effect, with exhibiting flagrant prejudice against Muslims and outrageously slandering their beliefs. "What is freedom of expression?" mused Salman Rushdie a year after the ayatollahs sentenced him to death and put a price on his head. "Without the freedom to offend, it ceases to exist." I can think of nothing sadder than that minority activists, in their haste to make the world better, should be the ones to forget the lesson of Rushdie's plight: for minorities, pluralism, not purism, is the answer. The campaigns to eradicate prejudice—all of them, the speech codes and workplace restrictions and mandatory therapy for accused bigots and all the rest—should stop, now. The whole objective of eradicating prejudice, as opposed to correcting and criticizing it, should be repudiated as a fool's errand. Salman Rushdie is right, Toni Morrison wrong, and minorities belong at his side, not hers.